Chase THE Light

The Gruesome Art of
Becoming Unbreakable

CESAR A. PEREZ

HOUNDSTOOTH
PRESS

Chase the Light

The Gruesome Art of Becoming Unbreakable

ISBN 978-1-5445-2886-1 Paperback

　　　978-1-5445-2887-8 Hardcover

　　　978-1-5445-2885-4 Ebook

To my mother

this book is affectionately dedicated...

Thank you for always being there and never giving up on me.

Everything I am is because of you.

Contents

Introduction

THE FIRST RESPONDERS HAD TO USE SPECIALIZED equipment to remove me from the wreckage. That's how bad the accident was. Bones were broken, my brain was hemorrhaging, but the will to fight never left. The will to survive. I wasn't going to let those breaks *break me*.

Almost everything I know about that night I have pieced together from other people's accounts. It's a blessing I don't remember anything about the accident because when I was finally healed enough, I was able to get behind the wheel again without harrowing flashbacks. That isn't to say it was without trauma; I became acquainted with trauma and pain on a whole new level. God blessed me in countless ways leading up to and on that night, but for a long time, I didn't want to acknowledge that. It's truly a miracle I survived. By all accounts, I shouldn't still be walking this earth. By most accounts, I shouldn't even be walking. I coded several times that night, which means my heart stopped and the paramedics had to revive me. You'll understand when you see pictures of my car after the accident, which I'll share with you later.

It was January of 2018, the start of a new year that brought so many promises but left them unfulfilled. Instead of my life taking the path I thought it would, it veered completely off track when a drunk driver and a big rig hit me. It's crazy to think I could ever put down in words the emotions I've felt these past years. An agonizing pain pulses in my hand as I type the first few pages of my book, and this endless loop of pain and anger still isn't over.

For a split second, I had everything I ever wanted and worked so hard to achieve. I was destined for greatness... but now I was destined to endure this pain and somehow accept what happened and move on. That's part of what makes my story unique. Whereas most inspirational stories involve the requisite upward trajectory, they usually start from a level place or the bottom and work their way up. My story, on the other hand, starts at the top, walks you through my drastic fall, and then shares my rebound up, where I had to trust the process again and endure.

As I sit here and write my story two years after the accident, my mother's question keeps replaying in my head: "Mí hijo, por qué no has empezado a escribir tu historia?" Translation: "My son, why haven't you started writing your story?" It's a question she asks me frequently because she knows how important it is to me. If the story of my suffering could help others, I knew I had to write it eventually. But first, I needed to learn my own lessons.

I believe everyone has a story to tell. There are countless stories that have yet to be written but nonetheless need to be told—just like this one. I have learned so much from the trials and tribulations of my journey. I want to share what I've learned with you. But, more than that, I want you to know that if I can go through what I have and come back stronger—*unbreakable*, even—then you can go through your own trial by fire and prove to yourself that you're also unbreakable.

You'll encounter several themes in this book: love, strength, perseverance, and others. You'll see the roller coaster of emotions, from anger and despair to joy and peace. You'll walk with me on my journey to acceptance.

What you *won't* find in this book is a formulaic "how to" or "Five life hacks to come back stronger," because as I'm sure you know by now, everyone has different trials in life.

Acceptance was definitely the hardest part for me. Acceptance is not something many people know how to deal with. I used to think it was so simple. Accepting is coming to terms with what has happened and realizing you can't change it. So there's no point dwelling on the past. Instead, focus all that anger, pain, and sorrow into changing what happens from here on out. You didn't get the job of your dreams you just applied for? Accept it. Accept that something was missing in your experience, your resume, or your interview that didn't let you stand out from the other applicants. However, don't just accept it and do nothing about it, telling yourself, "Well, that sucks. I gave it my best shot, but I'm not what they're looking for."

No! If it's something you truly want, accept the failures, but use what you learned. Take responsibility, and make changes that'll propel you forward. This is something I had always practiced growing up. Now, it proved to be valuable in a whole new way as getting where I wanted to be took on an entirely new meaning.

I'm not saying this book will instantly change your life for the better. That would be a lie. We must find it within ourselves to make a difference and make that change. It's a long road you must take to find the thing that motivates you. But hopefully this book serves as a guide to finding it. Perhaps seeing my transformation and how I came to my driving force will help you. Many people have told me my story is inspirational, and I hope it serves you in that way as well. Our bodies are strong, and if anyone knows about strong bodies, it is me. I worked for years, transforming my body into a well-oiled machine that was athletic, strong, and agile. You can be in the best physical shape of your life, but your mind is the driving force behind everything. It's a precious gift that is both strong and fragile.

All your hopes and fears lie within your mind. The real challenge is exercising your mind to be resilient and conquer your fears or doubts. Take this moment to really ask yourself: *What do I want? What have I been dying to do/become/create?* It might be a change in your career. Maybe you want to get a degree, or maybe just get a job in general. Analyze what you are doing to move toward that goal. You might say, "There are obstacles in the way of achieving my goal." Well, then MOVE THEM! Just get rid of them. You shouldn't hold on to anything that prohibits you from achieving your goals or dreams. This isn't to say throw responsibility out the window. If you have responsibilities, assume them and just make sacrifices where you're able to. It's easy to *think* about doing something or to *say* you'll do it. It's another thing entirely to put those thoughts into action.

What wouldn't I, or anyone for that matter, give to go back to a time when we had no worries? If I could talk to my younger self today, I would tell him to make the most of every moment because tomorrow is never promised. I would hug him and ask him to forgive me for all the pain I would put him through in the years to come. I would share with him the knowledge and wisdom I've gained from life so he could prepare himself for the bruises, the pain, and the scars. Unfortunately, I am not able to do this. Life is a one-way street, and there is no going back. Hopefully, I can help you prepare for life that, although unexpected, can still be beautiful. I'm a strong believer that you don't have to be broken to understand brokenness. In sharing my story with you, I hope you can find that driving force without needing to experience what brokenness is. This is my story. Let's become unbreakable—together.

CHAPTER 1

Meant for More

WITH HOPE FOR A BETTER FUTURE, MY PARENTS emigrated from El Salvador to the United States in 1996 with my two sisters and me. They came to the US with nothing but a dream and the will to turn it into reality, so they made sure they taught us to take responsibility for where we wanted to be. They demonstrated it with their actions. I'm sure it was one of the most valuable lessons they taught us regardless, but in my life, taking ownership of where I wanted to be would take on a whole new meaning.

For my sisters and me, it was easier adapting to the new culture. It was a lot harder for my parents to adapt, not only due to the language barrier but also because they had left family and half of their lives back home. To this day, I consider my parents the bravest and most courageous people I know. They are the driving force behind everything I do and who I am today. Our journey to the US was eventful and contains enough stories to fill multiple books, but they aren't my stories to tell. They belong to my parents.

My mother made us a promise when we came to the US. She said she would never let us forget our Spanish and she would make sure we knew how to read and write it. This, of course, came at a price. My parents were never able to work on their accent or perfect their English. Nowadays their English has improved substantially, and my sisters and I make sure they practice it with us.

The reason I'm sharing this with you is so you can better understand where I come from, so you can comprehend the magnitude of the events that happened years in the future. My family and I came to a new country with nothing but dreams. We didn't have the money or the material things everyone around us had, but we knew we had each other, and that was all we needed to keep going. My mother focused heavily on our education. She is a smart woman who never had the opportunity to further her own education back home, so she made it her mission to ensure that her children did. Every day after we came home from school, she would ask us how our day went and what we had learned. Then she would give us our writing journals and make us do more work, all in Spanish. I remember one time I got in trouble at school for talking too much, and she proceeded to make me write six full pages in cursive, repeating the phrase "Los niños buenos no hablan en clase cuando está hablando la maestra." This literally translates to "Good kids do not talk in class when the teacher is talking." At the time, like any other kid my age, I was angry and did not understand her reasoning for making us do extra work.

Math lessons followed our Spanish lessons. Keep in mind this all happened after school at around 3:30 every afternoon, all while my mom was cooking and making our dinner. To this day, I don't know where she found the energy to do everything. My favorite subject was math because it came easy to me, and I've always liked working with numbers. I would quickly finish my work and then proceed to our last subject, which was grammar and speaking. My sisters and I would take turns reading from a book my mother brought with her from El Salvador that contained several poems in Spanish. I can't tell you how many times I stood in front of my mom and read those poems, but it will suffice to say I still remember them now.

All throughout kindergarten, my days would be like this, and the lessons only concluded when my father came home. When Dad was home, it was playtime for me, and I knew it. I would rush toward him when he stepped through the door and ask him to play with me because my mom had been overworking us. My dad would tire me out so I could go to sleep and begin another day of pretty much the same stuff. The interesting thing is . . . at that moment in time, I had no worries. I only had the responsibility of going to school, coming home, doing homework, and going to bed on time.

I grew up in Richmond Hill, Georgia (a mostly-white community in the suburbs of Savannah). When we first moved there, we were just one of a handful of Latino families. My mother made sure we always behaved when we were out because it reflected our upbringing and our family. She would drive us to school every day, even in high school. At the time, it bothered us to be driven to high school by our parent(s) because our friends were driving to school in their own cars. But the reality was we weren't like everybody else. We were living day to day with my mom's and dad's paychecks, and it was a blessing to even have one car to get from place to place.

My mother was petrified about driving at first, but she knew she had to get us to school one way or another. She only asked that we get good grades in return. I have never met a more selfless person in my life. Her number one priority was her kids, and she made sure we knew this. After school, she would pick me up or wait until I finished with soccer practice, and then it was off to classical bass lessons. If it wasn't bass one day, it was French or trumpet lessons the next. Either way, each day had an activity scheduled as soon as she picked me up from school. Sometimes my friends would ask me to come over for a party or to "just chill" and play video games. As much as it hurts to admit it, I'd lie to them. "I can't. I have to go to another friend's house," I'd say.

It wasn't only *my* lessons though. Sometimes it would be piano, cello, violin, or art lessons for my sisters. Still, my mother would pick me up, and we would all have to go. That's the thing about my family. We did everything together. My father always said, "We will rejoice together if something good happens to one of us, but we will also suffer together if one of us is hurting." This was true. As I look back at all our moments together, all the joy and pain we experienced, I wouldn't want to experience it with anyone else. From perfect recitals to broken hearts, we felt everything as a unit and helped each other get through everything.

I am the youngest of three, and my sisters always protected me. Oftentimes they had to be the ones paving the way. By the time I came around to some obstacle in life, I knew how to overcome it, having learned from my sisters' experiences. My oldest sister, Alicia, was the first one to go to college, and at the time, none of us had any idea of the process of applying and getting accepted. She paved the way for my sister and me. After Alicia got accepted and started attending Armstrong University, my other sister, Carolina, had a better idea of the system. Things weren't easy for her, but she figured out she could apply to several schools to try and see which college provided her the best education and scholarships. Despite her being older than me and having a different personality, Carolina was always my partner in crime.

Everywhere she or I went, you could always find the other one right behind. Carolina received a big scholarship offer from Agnes Scott College, and my mom asked her if she was going to take it or just go to Armstrong like Alicia. At that point I had already started the process of applying and looking at schools/scholarships. I had received a lot of attention for my academics and my musical talent, so Carolina told my mom she would go to Armstrong and wait to see where I got accepted so she could then apply there. Carolina helped me apply for scholarships I didn't even know about. I got an email one day from Georgia Southern University (GSU) in nearby Statesboro, Georgia. They wanted to interview me for the 1906 scholarship. To me, it all sounded great. In my head, a scholarship meant money, and I knew we needed it.

I didn't fully understand that the 1906 Scholarship at GSU fully covered all tuition and was renewable every year, as long as I met the requirements. It never occurred to me to look it up online or check to see what the requirements were before going to the interview. At the time of the interview, GSU had already offered me a music scholarship, which I hadn't accepted yet. I still didn't know where I wanted to go. Interview day came around, and I got in the car with my mom and sister, and drove all the way to Statesboro. The entire ride there I was relaxed, but my mom was anxious. I had always thrived when speaking in public, so I wasn't nervous about being in a close group with other smart and talented individuals.

They put us into small groups and then took us to the first part of the interview. There, they analyzed how we interacted with the group but also how we addressed the questions they asked. I left the first portion of the interview feeling pleased and proceeded to the individual portion. By the end of the entire interview, I felt good about my performance and the answers. Then, as people often do when competing with others, I started critiquing my answers and thinking I could've said something better, but it was too late—the interview process was over.

My mom and Carolina had been walking around campus during the interview, so I called as soon as it was over, and they picked me up. The entire ride home was basically a second interview, with both of them asking me how it went, who I met, if I thought I got it, or if there would be a second interview. I was honest when I told them, "I think I got it. I feel good about it, and I made a few of the interviewers laugh, which is always a plus." As I said this, I laughed a bit, which might be why my mom and my sister were a little skeptical about how my interview actually went, but I was stating the truth. I had always been a confident speaker and good at standardized tests, which is why my sister would sometimes get mad when I never studied and still got a good grade on something when she had been studying for several nights. My brain was just wired that way. I stored information well and could quickly think on my toes. It must have been a combination of all these things that came together the day I interviewed because a few weeks later, I received another email stating I was one of the finalists who would receive the 1906 Scholarship if I chose to attend Georgia Southern.

To say my family was happy would be putting it mildly. They were ecstatic. When I received that email, it took me a second to process the information. My sister had actually done her research and knew this was a full-ride scholarship and told my mom she would go to GSU with me. Only then did it hit me that I would go to GSU with fully paid tuition and money to spare since I had also received the Hope Scholarship, a Pell Grant, and my String Performance scholarship. The 1906 Scholarship was a prestigious award, and only ten to fifteen students received it each year. My parents were very proud of me, and I became the first person in our entire family to go to college on a full ride.

I felt honored to receive the 1906 Scholarship and to be part of the Honors program at Georgia Southern. I had to maintain a good GPA and meet the other requirements to keep my scholarship. Luckily, by working hard and always striving to make my family proud, I maintained my scholarship each year. I entered GSU in 2011, and in May of 2015, I graduated with honors and presented my capstone project. I was the final Pérez in the family to graduate college, and it meant the world to my parents. It was the reason my mother had brought us here. She wanted to give us a better future and knew there was nothing we couldn't do if given the opportunity. I know most graduates are happy to just finish school and go on with their lives, but to me, what meant the most was seeing my parents' smiles that day as I walked onstage for my diploma.

Cesar Perez with his parents after graduation at Georgia Southern

Cesar Perez reporting for the Sun Belt Conference as Georgia Southern's first digital media correspondent

As I left campus with my family the following day, I said goodbye to many professors, and every single one of them said they expected great things from me. It was a bittersweet feeling saying goodbye to a place that had been home for four years, but I was excited to start my life and new career. I had chosen Multimedia Communications as my field of study at Georgia Southern. After college, I was hired at WTOC-11 (a local news TV station in Savannah), which was owned by Raycom Media. I started off as a news content specialist, and the hours were rough. My commute alone was tiring. I had to leave an hour in advance to make it to the station by 6:00 a.m., meaning I would normally wake up at 4:00 a.m. I knew things would be hard at first; every recent graduate must endure these first steps to gain experience and beef up their resume. My duties and coworkers weren't the problem.

I enjoyed my time at the TV station and developed friendships with the meteorologists, hosts, and guests on the show. The issue was time. After leaving work, I had roughly four hours left in the day to get everything else done. My goal was to be in bed by 8:30 p.m., just to start it all over the next morning. I stayed at WTOC for half a year and in the meantime got another job working for a radio company as part of their promotions/marketing team. During my time there, I kept searching for other opportunities and eventually landed the lead graphic designer position at Savannah's Candy Kitchen (SCK).

I worked at SCK for almost a year, and during my time with them, I honed my skills but always knew I was meant to do more. I thoroughly enjoyed my time there, and a twelve-year-old me would've been in heaven with all the candy that surrounded me every day. But at the time, I was very cautious about what I ate since I was striving to have the most athletic and agile body. I took great pride in how I had transformed my body since college. There was almost nothing I couldn't physically do, and I knew I helped motivate a lot of people, including my family and friends. While employed at SCK, I still searched for answers. I wondered where I could make the most difference and have the biggest impact. I had heard of a new movie studio being built in Savannah. Due to the tax incentives, Georgia was rapidly becoming the second Hollywood as productions kept coming to shoot on the East Coast. I didn't know when the new studio would be built, but I figured I could submit my information in case they needed a graphic designer, an animator, audio mixes, or help in any post-production. I got a call a few months later saying the production designer for a new film shooting in Savannah wanted to meet with me.

She introduced herself as Nava. I met with her and the team, and we hit it off instantly. And that film became one of many we would work on together. It was the beginning of a blossoming friendship as Nava knew I would always put forth my best effort. That first movie was called *Dear Dictator*, starring Michael Caine, Odeya Rush, and Katie Holmes. It felt so good to be part of a production and to help bring a story to life. I stayed in touch with some of the art department and even some of the crew for what became the beginning of my career in the movie industry. I also kept in touch with one of the casting directors, Chad Darnell. He was always trying to promote local talent, and I was able to get on board several productions as an extra or background actor working with him. He helped me learn what it felt like being in front of the camera rather than just behind the scenes. Because of him, I received the opportunity of a lifetime. A new production was about to start filming in Savannah, and they needed some local talent. He threw my name in because he believed in me, and I will be forever grateful to Chad for that. He asked me if I was willing to record a video with some sides—which is what they call a small sample of the script used for casting purposes. I immediately said yes and sent him the video, wishing for the best but not sure what to expect.

Several weeks passed, and I was heading to lunch one day at SCK when I received the call that changed my career path. The call was from Chad. "Are you sitting down?" he asked. "I have some news." He told me I had blown everyone away with my self-taped audition. He said the part of "Pablo" was officially mine and that I had beaten out everyone who auditioned for the part in LA. He finished by saying he would send over the paperwork for me to sign.

I remember exactly where I was that day because I felt so ecstatic and full of life. The following week, Nava called to ask me if I would work with her again on a production filming in Savannah. Of course, I said yes. Turns out the film was *Beast of Burden*, starring Daniel Radcliffe, and I had just been cast to star opposite him as "Pablo." It was a crazy turn of events because not only would I be part of the cast but also part of the art department, helping to create graphics and props. To put it into perspective, I rehearsed lines for my scenes one night, while another night, I created a fake passport for Daniel Radcliffe. Today, if you see the movie *Beast of Burden* and roll the credits you'll see my name appear twice.

That is what jump-started my career path in the film industry, and I knew it was just the beginning. Soon after I finished filming *Beast of Burden*, Chad reached out to ask if I'd audition for a role in the movie *Blind Trust* filming in Atlanta. "Just tell me what you need from me," I said. And a few weeks later, he called to notify me that the director and producers wanted to meet with me to offer me the part of "Javier." My character would star opposite the main protagonist, "John O'Donnell," which was meant to be played by the famous Mexican actor, Eugenio Siller. I got the call, and that same week I put in my two weeks' notice at SCK.

Even though it was scary leaving my job to chase my passion, I knew I was doing the right thing, and I went for it. I'd never been one to just sit and hope for things to fall into my lap. I'd always been proactive and done everything in my power to steer toward my goal. That's why, even while filming the movie, I applied for several positions in Atlanta. My mom always said I needed to have insurance should anything happen, which is why I was adamant about finding a full-time position with benefits. Several companies called me for interviews, and they all went great. Some of them even offered me a position by the end of the interview, but I was not pleased with the pay or benefits, so I kept searching.

My dream job was working for COX in Atlanta. I knew someone who worked there who I had met through the GAB Radio Talent Institute in May of 2015. The Institute was held in Athens at the University of Georgia, and there I met Kim Guthrie. At the time, she was working for COX and spoke to us about how to prepare in order to excel in entry-level positions upon graduating. She also discussed how to get started in a successful career in broadcasting. She was full of life and personality, which intrigued me. At the end, she asked the room if we had any questions. I raised my hand and introduced myself. "Oh, so you're Cesar, like the dog whisperer," she said. I laughed and knew she would at least remember my name. After she answered my question, I waited until everyone was heading out and went over to speak with her one-on-one. I wanted a successful career in broadcasting, and she gave me one of her business cards.

I took great care of that card and figured now would be the time to reach out to her regarding the open position I had applied for. I hoped she could at least forward or move along my resume to the hiring manager. Turns out she had moved up in position and was now the president of COX Media Group. It didn't take long before I received an email and call stating they would like to interview me for the position. Just like the day Chad called to tell me I had landed the role of Pablo in *Beast of Burden*, I remember exactly where I was that day and what I was doing. It's one of those moments in life you never forget because the joy is so real and authentic. I had heard nothing but good things about them, and the pay was competitive. With no hesitation, I told them I was free whenever they were available. I met with several of the managers and explained how I could bring all my skills to meet their needs and be part of the team. The position I applied for was video producer/editor for the sports verticals, which were relatively new. I spoke with Michael Carvell, who oversaw the hiring, and explained to him how I could help them reach their goals and get more sponsors through branded programming. The interview could not have gone better, and as I met all my future coworkers, I felt at peace and like I belonged. I spoke with the senior content strategy manager, Christopher Smith, and he filled me in on their needs and goals. After I answered his questions fully and presented my portfolio, I could sense a new friendship forming. The interview ended, and I felt very optimistic about my future.

After filming *Blind Trust*, I went back to Richmond Hill. Thankfully I had saved enough money to get me through several months. It wasn't long before I was freaking out since I was technically unemployed. I was running out of time. It was already summer, and although I worked on a few productions, I still didn't have a stable income to rely on. Knowing the breaking point was approaching, I sat down at a coffee shop in Pooler and just prayed. I remember praying for a sign that everything would be alright and that I had made the right choice in leaving my old job. So many feature films and productions were coming to Atlanta that year, so I knew I needed to find a job there. If nothing happened, I would go back to Savannah and take whatever job was available. Forty-five minutes later, I received the phone call I was waiting for. It was COX offering me the position in Atlanta. I immediately called my family to share the good news with them. Finishing my coffee and staring out the window, I couldn't help but smile. My life had taken a monumental turn, and I knew I wasn't alone on this journey.

CHAPTER 2

Prepared for Anything

I F YOU HAD MET ME IN COLLEGE OR SHORTLY AFTER, you would have known how much I was into fitness. I made sure to always go to the gym after work. Everyone always asked me, "Cesar, why do you work out so much?" The truth is I initially started working out just to look good, but over time, it evolved into something more: a foundation of discipline and hard work. I saw that working out not only kept me out of trouble but also helped me stay more goal-oriented and focused on things I wanted to accomplish.

Once I achieved the physical body I wanted, I didn't stop there. I continued my routine and kept striving toward new goals. They had just placed a rope at the gym from ceiling to floor, and people used it for exercises to shimmy up and down. I sometimes imagined crazy scenarios where I'm stuck in an elevator with a bunch of people and the only way out is to shimmy my way out through the elevator shaft. That became my new goal. I knew that if the lives of others somehow depended on me in a stuck elevator, I would be able to save them. I'd be ready. As crazy and improbable as it sounds, I made sure I was prepared for anything. I took pride in being ready, and I always seemed to be two or three steps ahead, whether it was work, interviews, research, or relationships. I walked into every situation with a plan and a solution should problem A, B, or C arise. I felt I was ready for anything life could throw my way.

Cesar after a workout, before the car accident

The discipline I developed from working out and striving to reach new goals permeated every aspect of my life. I applied that same motivation and persistence in my acting and professional career. And it's what drove me to actively seek out and learn new skills so I could become more marketable.

I've never liked asking for help. I'm not sure if it's a cultural thing, but I've always considered myself independent, and I thought there was nothing I couldn't do. When I graduated college, most of the positions I wanted to apply for required knowledge of Adobe Creative Suite (ACS), which contained video-editing software. I was well versed in ACS but knew there was a lot more to learn, so rather than complain, I decided to learn more on my own through textbooks and YouTube videos. As I searched for more ways to beef up my skills, I realized we live in a very privileged day and age. Everything I needed to learn was at my fingertips; all I had to do was look for it and dedicate time to learning it. Today, we have even more technology within reach and fewer excuses as to why we are not where we want to be. If you want it, you'll find a way to get it done. People often ask me where I learned all this, and they're surprised when I tell them I learned it on my own. Though college prepared me with some of the tools I would need in my career, I had to find more ways to stand out from the crowd.

When I left Richmond Hill in the summer of 2017, I told my parents I would take care of everything in Atlanta and that they wouldn't have to help me financially. I was as independent as could be and felt very blessed that COX hired me and helped pay for my relocation to Atlanta. All my life, I had lived under my parents' roof and had to follow their rules. I was never allowed to bring anyone home or have gatherings at their house. I don't even think many of my friends knew where I lived because I never had them over. This feeling of being fully independent and on my own was new to me. Despite missing my family, I was excited to start this new chapter in my life. I rented a nice one-bedroom apartment in Dunwoody, only five minutes from my job. The location was perfect: not too much city but just enough for a young professional like me.

I loved my position at COX and the people I got to work with. The first few days consisted of signing paperwork and trying to determine what benefits to sign up for. I called my mom one night to ask her opinion. Without hesitation, she told me to get the best health insurance they offered, no matter how expensive it was. I grumbled. I didn't think I would need it or use it because I was so healthy. Reluctantly, I did what she suggested and signed up for the best insurance they offered for healthcare, vision, and dental.

Throughout my time at COX, I felt like all my advice and recommendations were taken seriously, and it made me want to work even harder. I felt right at home when I was at work and felt I was making a difference. We were a well-oiled machine, where everyone worked together and felt comfortable producing their best work. Just like I did at WTOC-11, I made many friends—not just with my coworkers but also with guests we had on our shows, and to this day, we still keep in touch.

I can say with all honesty that I was living and enjoying life the way I wanted. Then one day in November, I sat outside on my porch just thinking about how much work I had put in to get to where I was. People would message me through text and social media and say things like "You're living the life, man!" This, to me, was more motivation to continue working hard. People could see where I was, but not the road it took to get there. Oftentimes friends would invite me out to grab a drink, but I'd choose to stay home instead and learn something new online that would help me do my job even better. If I wasn't at home working, I was either working out or writing down some songs. There were weekends I would spend hours just playing my guitar, trying to find the perfect melody for songs I was creating. I had always considered myself a storyteller, someone who could use visuals and audio to tell a story. Therefore, acting came naturally to me, and I enjoyed my time in front of the camera as well as my time behind it, creating all the visuals to help portray the story. I would often write songs about my personal experiences or sometimes use stories I heard from other people. Either way, it was a way of letting my creative persona run wild and free.

My love life has always been a big roller coaster. There have definitely been highs and lows, but somehow, I've managed to survive every experience and learn from it. Finding a girl was never an issue for me in college, and I was living my best life when I moved to Atlanta. Love was never missing in my life, and by that, I mean my family always gave me the best example of what true love was; I knew someday I wanted to find that in someone and start a family, but I was happy at the time with just being single after my previous relationship ended. My parents would call to ask how I was doing in Atlanta and if I had met anyone, hoping one day I would say, "Yeah I met a nice girl, and we are dating." Meeting new people wasn't the problem; opening up to the possibility of spending more than one night with someone was.

One day it hit me. I saw my parents' marriage and realized I wanted something like it, and if not the same, at least similar. Yeah, it was fun being single and having no one to answer to, but I knew I wanted someone to share my life with, and for that to happen, I needed to be open to the possibility of dating someone. That very day, I made some changes in my life and tried coming to terms with dating again.

I had been talking to a girl in early fall of 2017. From here on out, I will call her "Heather," though this is not her actual name. She was about three years younger than me and attending Georgia Southern University. What first attracted me to her was that she would always ask me how my day was going. It may not have meant much in the grand scheme of things, but back then, I at least felt she cared. Combine that with the fact that she wanted a career as a physical therapist, and I felt I had found a caring and goal-oriented person like myself with the same culture and values... or so I thought. In my whole life, I can count on one hand the number of people from El Salvador I've met and kept in touch with. Living in South Georgia, I never really met many Salvadorans. As it turned out, Heather was the daughter of two Salvadoran immigrants, too. One particular week she came down to visit me, when I had been invited to the movie premier and first screening of *Blind Trust*. I didn't hesitate to ask her if she wanted to be my plus-one, and I told her I was also taking my two sisters. She immediately kissed me and said, "Yes! Can I take and post any pictures?!"

We weren't dating at the time, but I thought maybe I should be open to the possibility. It had been a while since I had dated someone, and something about Heather kept drawing me closer. I just remember being happy and content around her. The feeling was mutual. When she went back to school or I had to go work, I couldn't wait for the days to go by faster so I could see her again. The way she carried herself as a lover and a rebel is one of the many things that captivated me. She was feisty but caring, at least in those moments I knew her. Only later did I realize I didn't know her at all, not the real Heather at least. In life many of us are just acting out the roles we want the world to see... not who we really are. It took me some time to come to that glaring realization because I, too, was fooled by her performance.

At the movie premiere, she met my sisters, and they were upset from the very beginning that I had brought Heather with me. They played their roles well though and treated her nicely. My sisters even took pictures of us, despite their feelings that it should have just been us three. I presented everyone to each other, and when it came time to present Heather, I panicked and said she was my girlfriend. It wasn't until we left the premiere that she and I were able to talk about what had transpired. I told her I was sorry if I gave her a title she didn't want but that I would be honored if she would be my girlfriend, and then I formally asked her out. She had said she loved me a few nights before, so I wasn't freaking out about what her answer might be. My father always reminded me to never assume things. We had been talking for a while, but we had not been dating, so this was a huge step for me in trying to start something real with someone.

One day, early in our relationship, she told me she had seen my face on the honors magazine at campus. The magazine showcased pictures of me on movie sets, and Heather said that's when she knew she wanted to be with me. I didn't think this superficial at the time, but it would all come back full circle years later. When I went to see my family in Savannah, I would always stop by GSU to see Heather and several friends who were still there. I would wait for her to close the shoe store she worked at and then take her out to dinner. Being in a relationship again, I knew I had to give more of myself, and I focused on doing so. I wanted her to know I didn't mind waiting in the car for her after driving hours, just to take her to dinner. In my mind, this is what a relationship was all about—being there for one another.

All in all, everything was going great for me at the start of 2018. We had just finished an incredible sports season at work, and I had several movie/ show auditions lined up. About two months prior, I had auditioned for *America's Got Talent* in Savannah, and I played a song I wrote for Heather. Everyone auditioning actually gave me a standing ovation. Several of them asked to take pictures with me, saying, "You are definitely going places." I finished 2017 in spectacular fashion. And on New Year's Day, I hugged my sisters and Heather and told them 2018 would be an amazing year. "Everything I have worked so hard for is coming to fruition," I told them, and I thanked them for sharing that moment with me. It's funny (some would say cruel) how life plays out sometimes. My hopes and expectations for 2018 were sky-high, and it promised so much...yet 2018 is a year I barely remember and wish had never happened.

CHAPTER 3

Life Isn't Fair

JANUARY 12, 2018, WILL FOREVER MARK MY LIFE. IT started out like any other day. I finished work early, and since college sports were ending, I started working on a proposal for the next season. My plan was to present it to my bosses the following week. We had accomplished a lot since I came on board, so I was excited about the next season and what could be done to improve our shows. Every year, someone got nominated for the President's Award, and we were nominating someone from our sales team, but I was the one in charge of creating the video and making it look good. I already had a substantial amount of the video made and a proposal for the next season, so I left work feeling good about everything I had accomplished that day. I messaged one of my coworkers, Nate, and asked him if he wanted to grab some food before I hit the road. It was Martin Luther King Jr. weekend, and rush hour traffic was horrible in Dunwoody. Nate knew I was driving down to Statesboro to see Heather and my family in Savannah that weekend, so he told me to beat rush hour and get out of the city before traffic got worse. He didn't have to tell me twice, but I first stopped at Chick-fil-A. I remember the cashier gave me her number with hearts on the receipt, and I laughed about it as I called Heather to tell her what had happened. But she was livid. She asked me for the cashier's name and who she was. I told her not to worry about it because I had thrown away the receipt before I left, and I was on my way.

My mom had told me not to come down. It was a long weekend and there were bound to be drunk people on the road, she'd said. I told her not to worry. I had driven up and down I-16 at least a hundred times. There wasn't too much traffic as I got on the highway, which meant I would get to Statesboro before Heather got off work. I had already been driving for a while on the interstate when I received a text from Bryan, an old college friend. He had graduated and gone into the military, so while he was in training, we hadn't stayed in touch. He texted me, wanting to catch up, and I texted him back: "Yo, what's happening man?! How's life?" I answered because traffic was fine, and I never lost sight of the road or my surroundings. Once I sent the text, I drove for maybe a minute, then suddenly, I saw the car in front of me drastically veer right. Lights flickered, and then complete darkness followed.

The darkness for me lasted moments, though in reality it was more like days, followed by weeks of secondary darkness. I was in a coma, and even when I regained consciousness, I don't remember anything about that time. For my family, that fog of darkness lasted years and still hasn't lifted. Even as I write this today, waiting for my last surgeries, I know life still isn't normal for my family, and it may never be again. Every time I made a long trip, my mom would ask me to call her to tell her I made it safely. I never got the chance to make that call this time. My mom called me, but I didn't answer. She called multiple times and told my sisters to call as well because she hadn't heard from me. All they got was my voicemail. My mom and dad had gone grocery shopping for the weekend and were driving home while trying to get in touch with me.

Alicia called my girlfriend, but Heather could only tell her that I'd been an hour away at the time she last spoke with me. When the information got back to my mom, her heart sank. My dad kept trying to calm her down, saying I was fine, but even he started to feel that something was wrong. They were stopped at the Kroger in Richmond Hill, about to take the road home, but my dad asked my mom what she wanted to do. "We can go home and wait for him to call," he said, "or we can start driving toward I-16." My mom told him to just start driving, and they did. The groceries in the car were of no importance to my mom at that point. She didn't care if everything they bought was spoiled; she just needed to know where I was and that I was okay.

The calls never stopped the entire drive. My dad deduced I had been around Dublin when I'd called Heather. Alicia told Carolina to start calling hospitals and police departments around there. Minutes felt like an eternity as my parents drove toward I-16 and still heard nothing regarding my whereabouts. My mother started thinking the worst had happened and that I was either in an accident or had been arrested. I was a good kid and had no reason as to why I would've been arrested, but my mother was grasping at straws at that point, trying to somehow survive the anxiety of not knowing.

It's important to note that my parents don't drink. They never have, and they say they never will. This was something they were always adamant about: no drinking. I was very into fitness and seldom drank, but since my college days, I wasn't opposed to drinking. I would, every now and again, go out with friends for a drink. The feeling of losing control was never appealing to me, so I always knew when to stop. I never drank at home by myself, and I didn't actually like it; it was more of a way to blend in with everyone else. This of course caused a small rift between my family and me. We all knew I didn't need to drink to fit in because everyone flocked to me regardless. My dad and I had not spoken since our last argument when he got upset and asked me what benefits drinking brought me. I didn't know how to respond, so I just hadn't spoken to him since.

My dad knew I hadn't done anything stupid and hadn't been arrested. He started to shake a little as they finally got on I-16. He gravely told my mom, "I'm sorry to break it to you, but he did not get arrested. If he had, he would have been allowed to make one call, and I know he would have called you." This was obvious to my mom, but hearing it out loud made her heart sink further as she frantically called Carolina to ask if she had heard anything. Carolina was living in Peachtree City and had been calling hospitals and police stations around Dublin. Every time she got through to someone at the hospital, they wouldn't give her much information. She had called several hospitals and found out I wasn't in any of those. There was one hospital left on her list, and she made the call. The hospital she called was Fairview Park. She got through to someone and asked if there had been a car accident and if her brother was there. After a few minutes, they told her I was there. "The only information we can give you at the moment is yes, he is here, and he is stable . . . for now."

My sister's world crumbled, and as I write this, I can almost feel the despair she felt hearing those words: "he is stable . . . for now" Carolina managed to pull herself together and relay the news to my other sister. Alicia freaked out and started calling the hospital to try and get more information, demanding to know more. She was able to get some additional information from the doctors. They told her I had been in a terrible accident and that I was stable for now, seeing as most of the injuries were on my face. Hearing this made Alicia break down because she knew the movies I was involved in, the projects that were forthcoming, and how much I had worked to get where I was. In tears, she called Carolina, and they braced for what the next days would bring.

As my sisters spoke, my parents were still driving. They hadn't heard the news of my accident nor that I was in a hospital. Together my sisters changed their tone to address the issue of how to inform my mom. After calming down a bit, Alicia called my parents. She addressed my mom first. "Mom, I need you to stay with me and stay strong despite what I'm about to tell you," she said. "Cesar was in a very bad accident. Keep driving toward Dublin. He is currently at Fairview Park Hospital and is stable for now. I need you to be prepared because the Cesar you knew before might not be the same person you see at the hospital. Most of the injuries were on his face."

My mother tells me about that day and says her life came burning down when she heard those words, the words that broke every one of my family members: he is stable . . . for now. All my mom recalls about the rest of that ride to the hospital is how much the car was shaking and rattling. She soon realized it was my dad who was trembling and making the whole car shake. Alicia had already started driving toward Statesboro. She'd called Heather and told her she'd pick her up. The entire drive, she kept calling the hospital to try and get more information. But the only news they told her was that I would be airlifted to Navicent Health Hospital in Macon. She called my parents to tell them.

My dad was still shaking but kept driving toward Macon. Carolina was on her way as well, driving from Peachtree City. The calls never stopped. My sisters called my closest friends and asked them to pray for me and the family because they had no idea what to expect upon reaching the hospital. My mother called her sister. Everyone in the family was notified, on the way to Macon, of what had happened. I can only imagine what my parents and sisters were going through. They knew I was stable, but no one knew for how long. What would they see when they reached the hospital? What if I didn't make it through the night? All these questions were only magnified for my parents as they reached the hospital parking lot. At least the first thing they saw at the hospital was a familiar face; Carolina had arrived ten minutes before them.

Together they went inside, and Alicia and Heather were there a few minutes later. I hadn't arrived yet. But just moments later, they heard a helicopter landing atop the medical center. It's truly unbelievable that my parents and sisters made it to the hospital before I was even there.

My mother begged the hospital staff to let her see me. Unfortunately, the whole family would have to wait a while since they had to clean me up and make me presentable. The next couple of hours felt like days for family and, nothing could console them. All the while, nobody knew why or how the accident had occurred, and they didn't care. What kept them together was knowing I was still alive.

It was way past midnight when my family was escorted to where I was being held. I can't imagine the pain they must've felt when they finally got to see me. I was in an induced coma and covered from head to toe in white sheets. My nostrils were the only things not covered, and the first thing my mom noticed was a big metal weight strapped and dangling from my left leg. Turns out my femur was broken and protruding out of my leg. As gruesome as that may sound, it was only the tip of the iceberg. My mom asked the doctor why there was a weight on my leg, and he explained that it was part of the procedure in preparing my leg for surgery. After Heather and my family got a chance to see me, to hold my hand and cry, the medical team asked everyone to step out. The doctors had to operate on my leg as soon as possible.

Today, if you do an X-ray on my left leg, you'll see a huge titanium rod going from hip to knee. Fortunately, the surgery was a success, and if you see me walking now, it's as if nothing happened. I have to thank the doctors at Navicent because not only were they all amazing at their job, but they were also understanding of my family's pain. My family didn't leave the hospital for the next two weeks. After the leg surgery was done and I could have someone in the room, my mother wasted no time getting to my bedside and holding my hand. From that moment, she never left my side. No one could trade places with her; she was where she needed and wanted to be. She focused all her energy on me.

So far, nobody had seen my face. It was completely wrapped, and my sisters wondered if I had gashes on my face or if the accident had caused some permanent deformation. Alicia was especially concerned about my teeth and feared I had lost them. She knew how expensive dental treatment was and decided to start a GoFundMe page on my behalf, asking family, friends, and colleagues to donate to help the entire family deal with the medical bills that would undoubtedly be astronomical.

My sisters came up with a game plan. I had been diagnosed with a brain injury, so Alicia told the whole family to take pictures and videos so that someday it could help me regain my memory. The pictures would also help keep the people who were donating up to date on my situation. Carolina just had one condition to add. Every picture shared on social media or anywhere online had to go through her first. She wanted to make sure the pictures didn't show my face. Carolina didn't know how I looked, but she didn't want me to feel self-conscious about any of the images they shared.

I wish I could remember everyone who came to see me at Navicent, but unfortunately, that period is a dark void in my memory, and no matter how hard I try to remember, I still can't. If it weren't for the pictures and videos my sisters took of everyone that came to see me, I wouldn't know how many people cared enough to come to the hospital and show their support for me and my family. I was on a ventilator from day one due to every bone in my face being broken and preventing me from breathing. There was also a tube going through the front of my scalp, monitoring the internal hemorrhaging of my brain. The doctors told my mom I had a severe brain injury and most of the impact was on my frontal lobe. The frontal lobe is the part of the brain that controls emotions, language, and memory, to name a few of its functions.

That Saturday, one of the troopers who had been at the scene of the accident got in contact with my sister. She thanked him for the call and told him they were at the hospital before I had even arrived. He was taken by surprise. It was uncommon, he said. It was normally a lengthy process getting in touch with relatives after an accident of that magnitude.

The trooper shed some light on what had happened. He said I'd been hit head-on by a drunk driver on I-16 and then hit a second time by a tractor trailer. I wouldn't know any of this until months later. After getting hit by the drunk driver, I was spun 180 degrees toward oncoming traffic. That's when the big rig hit me and dragged me for a bit, leaving me in nothing but a heap of twisted metal, as it ran across the median into the other lanes. If the rig had been in proper operating condition with correctly functioning brakes, there would've been enough time to avoid the second impact. A year later, I learned that it should have never been on the road due to several service violations. Maybe my injuries wouldn't have been as severe, or maybe I wouldn't have coded on the paramedics had it only been one impact. We saw later on the news that both westbound and eastbound lanes had been shut down since the tractor trailer had crossed the median into the other lanes.

The officer also told my sister that the drunk driver was currently at the same hospital I was. She hurried to tell my parents the news. The tears kept coming. They were tears of sorrow, pain, and anger. My father tells me today, when they told him the drunk driver was there, he felt so much anger he could have easily gone into his room and killed him. He decided instead to stay by my mother's side because the love he felt for her and me was greater than any anger boiling inside him. He tried not to think about the other guy and instead focused all his energy on me and my mother, who at the time he thought might not make it out. It still amazes me to think she kept it together despite her rage and anger. That day of my accident, a lot of things broke in each one of us, but they broke in my mother the most. Today she and I talk, and she recounts the events in which I was unconscious, and I realize that she is still fighting her own demons from that night. There is an art to becoming unbreakable, and unfortunately, it's not pretty or fast. I realize she is still on that journey but closing in on that finish line as she sees me waiting on the other side for her—unbroken.

My mother has had an internal fight with all her beliefs since my accident. Every day she asked God to protect her children. My sisters and I were her greatest treasure. We were the reason she and my dad had sacrificed so much. To see your greatest treasure nearly destroyed would make anyone angry at whoever was entrusted with guarding said treasure. My mother was a religious woman and had always read us the Bible so we would grow up to be good Christians. When we were little, we would kneel and pray together before bed, and my mother always prayed out loud. I can remember it so vividly because she would ask for the same thing every time: for God to watch over the family and take care of her children. The thing is, she never just went through the motions of saying it again and again. She actually believed it in her heart. The one entrusted with guarding her biggest treasure was God, and she felt He had drastically failed her. To go into a hospital and see your only son on his potential deathbed is not something any mother should experience.

It was a holiday that following Monday, and my father didn't have to go to work. He instead sat down and typed an email for his boss, stating he would not be able to work for an unknown amount of time due to a severe accident involving his son. At that point, nobody knew how long I would be in a coma or if I would even survive, so at the end of his email, my dad offered his resignation. He was willing to resign if management wouldn't allow him to be where he needed to be: by my mother's side, next to me. Thankfully, the company was understanding and allowed him to take leave for as long as he needed, and the owner said she would help find me a personal injury lawyer. That same day, my dad and Carolina had an appointment with the state trooper to go where the remainder of the vehicles were being held. No one was allowed anywhere near the vehicles without an officer present, and my sister wanted to retrieve my belongings from my car.

My family had a vague idea of how the accident had occurred, but no one had seen the wreckage yet. Nothing could've prepared my dad and sister for what they were about to see. When they arrived, they both burst into tears when they saw what remained of my vehicle. The officer told them it was truly a miracle I survived such an impact. My car was unrecognizable and utterly destroyed from front to back. I had just bought that car, a 2017 Toyota Camry, brand new during the winter of 2016, so I'd had it for just over a year the day of the accident. As my sister and dad approached the car, my headshot was lying on the driver's seat, pristine and untouched. That was enough to make my sister an emotional mess. It was my face on the driver's seat—or at least who I was before that night. My sister asked the officer to retrieve the picture and asked if they could keep it. He said they could and proceeded to get my other belongings, including my work equipment. My dad was at a loss for words, seeing the damage on my vehicle, not knowing how long I had been trapped and bleeding with no one to help. I believe this was the hardest part for my parents: knowing I'd been in a desperate situation and they hadn't been able to help.

Cesar's vehicle after the accident, 2017 Toyota Camry

Big rig post-accident, after hitting Cesar's car

Remains of the vehicle driven by the drunk driver, Alexander Lopez-Vazquez.

No one could've predicted any of this, so I try to help them let go of that burden because it wasn't their fault. The officer told Carolina I had coded several times. I had no idea what this meant previously, but it meant I went into cardiac arrest and they had to revive me. He said it was due to the first responders and EMS personnel, who never gave up on me, that I survived. My dad and sister thanked the officer for letting them retrieve my belongings and giving them more information, and they headed back to Macon. But my dad had to stop the car. Carolina couldn't keep it together. "Why?" she kept asking. She held my headshot in her lap but turned it face down. She would never again look at pictures of me before the accident.

My dad held her in his arms, and they both cried. They decided they couldn't show my mother pictures of the car or let her know I had coded several times. "That would destroy her," my dad said, so they made a pact not to tell anyone other than Alicia. When they returned, it was getting late, and several of my friends who had come to see me were still there. My parents rented two hotel rooms in Macon so nobody would have to drive back home with emotions high. Seeing what an accident had done to our family, my parents didn't want to risk anyone else going through something similar by driving late. How many nights passed I'm not sure, but my mom wrote everything in her calendar, which is how we know that on the eighth day after my leg surgery, they were ready to operate on my face.

My father stayed by my mom's side as she signed paperwork giving doctors consent to begin. She hadn't left my side since day one, but she entrusted one of my friends to hold my hand while she stepped outside. The doctors explained what procedures they would perform and what she could expect.

All the while, the days were merging for everyone. Carolina would go to work every day at East Coweta High School, and when the school day ended, she would drive back to the hospital. This continued for the first two weeks I was there. She would drive three hours every day just to be there with me and my parents, wishfully thinking I'd wake up any minute, and she didn't want to miss that. Alicia did the same thing. She would drive over six hours every day from Savannah to be there with me. Alicia told my mom she would stop by Statesboro every day on her way to the hospital to pick up Heather and make sure she was present in case I woke up.

As my life unraveled in the hospital, my sisters knew what was important to me. Heather was important to me. I didn't want to include her in my story, but in the end, she was an integral part of my journey. You'll hear my side of the story, but for obvious reasons, you won't hear hers. When I regained consciousness, I had no recollection of the events except that I had been on my way to see her. It was all my brain kept replaying. She took up every thought in my mind. She was a raft in the middle of the ocean in which I found myself. My intentions were pure and born of love, and my mind did not register the obvious red flags apparent to my family. You'll see her true colors as I discovered them along my journey. Perhaps you'll see them sooner than I did, and you'll wonder why I let her get away with so much. I desperately wanted that part of my life to stay intact, so Heather could do no wrong in my eyes. I thought if we could make it out of this, there was nothing we couldn't accomplish together. It seemed like a reasonable expectation at the time because love was involved, but it was only flowing in one direction.

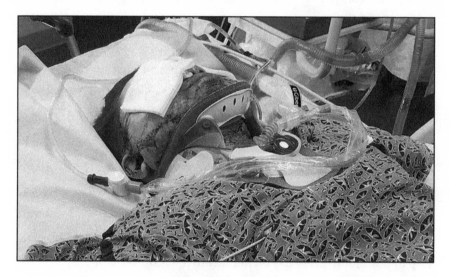

Cesar recovering at Navicent after initial facial reconstruction

My severe brain injury heightened everything I felt. If I loved her before, that feeling grew exponentially. There were a few moments in the beginning, as you'll see, where I could still see the person I fell in love with. I wished those moments would never end, but inevitably they did. I was in an ocean of pain but I kept pushing that raft, perhaps in the wrong direction and hanging on to the wrong person... but... in the end, I made it to shore. It's true that love is often blind. Therefore, the lesson I learned and my advice for others is to be with the person you know will walk with you, even in the darkest of times. Everything I did was for Heather, and she was the reason I wanted to get better. Though my motivation was erroneously placed and she isn't a part of my life anymore, it still kept me moving forward. For that I'm thankful. If my body was a machine, Heather was the engine that kept me going.

Amidst the long and confusing days, everyone did their best to be supportive. The outpouring of love and affection I received was nothing short of epic. People came and went, said their words of encouragement, and continued with their lives. Only those who truly loved and cared for me put their life on hold. Not because I asked them, not because they owed me, or because I wanted them to, but simply because they loved me.

I've stopped to think about this many times. How do you keep living when the reason to live has been exterminated? I was that reason for my family, just as they are for me. Their reason to continue was on the edge of fading out, which is why they hadn't given up just yet. There was still *hope*—a word that brings joy and torment. I'll touch more on that later. Their life was on pause, but for how long? No one knew, but they waited. Heather waited with them in the beginning. But then she started finding excuses not to come. You know how it is when you're blinded by love? Being blinded to another person's faults happens even in normal conditions, but on top of it all, I had a traumatic brain injury that made the circumstances even worse.

I don't think the conditions Heather and I were placed in were the most fertile soil on which to grow a great relationship. We were thrown into an unknown environment, and I understand it must have been difficult for her. All I knew was if there was love, there was nothing to fear. We would make it out. Most importantly, my family still managed to put everything aside and be there for me, so I know that true, selfless love does exist.

When Heather began to make excuses as to why she couldn't make it, my mom says Alicia would literally wait until Heather finished whatever she was doing and drive with her to see me. She was, after all, my girlfriend and the reason I had been driving down the day of the accident. Alicia felt it was her responsibility to make sure Heather made it to the hospital to see me. They would then drive back each night and do it again the following day. All this was going on while I was still in a coma, unaware of what had happened. I wish I could remember if I saw my life flash before my eyes, or what I saw when life left me in the moments when I coded, but I can't. I'd be lying if I said I had a great revelation or had visions. It's all just darkness. My family, on the other hand, remembers the events in great detail. My mom still has trouble sleeping as dreams turn to nightmares and she relives the whole thing.

Each week when my sisters came to the hospital, my mom would give Carolina and Alicia one hundred dollars each. This was to help with gas, food, and expenses. From the first week she started doing this for my sisters, she took Heather aside too. My mom told her she would give her one hundred dollars every week to help with any expenses of coming to see me. To be fair, Heather never asked for the money. For my mom, it was her way of helping, knowing I would never have wanted to feel like a burden on my girlfriend. "I have three children, and I would do the same for any one of them," she said to Heather. "I give Carolina and Alicia the same amount, and it's what I would give my son if he were awake. But you are a part of him, so I want you to have it." Still, despite getting a hundred dollars each week from my mother, Heather was still getting picked up by my sister. When I asked my sister today why she didn't just let my girlfriend drive herself instead of waiting hours for her, Alicia said she wasn't sure Heather would show up.

My family stared down the barrel of a loaded gun as the days in the hospital continued to drain them emotionally, spiritually, physically, and economically. Despite all this, they never faltered. They were there every single day, sending all their love, prayers, and positive energy toward me.

My father used up his 401(k) to pay for hotels (for visitors), food, gas, and other expenses that occurred along the way. Since my family and I had emigrated to the US, we hadn't been back to El Salvador, not even to visit. We had set aside the year 2018 to return for the first time after twenty-two years. The only reason this was even feasible was because my sisters and I were financially independent, and my parents had saved up enough money to make the trip. All those dreams went up in flames January 12, but it didn't matter to my mom. She was right where she wanted and needed to be, by my side.

As she signed the papers giving consent to proceed with my facial surgery, she feared what the future held for all of us. She went back in and thanked my friend Charles for holding my hand and staying with me while she had stepped outside. I still had tubes and wires coming out of my entire body. Some of them were to regulate, others to drain, and some administered antibiotics and painkillers.

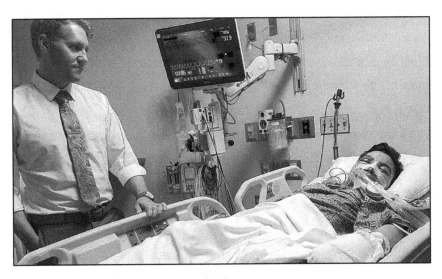

Charles Elvington watching over Cesar while his mother stepped away to give doctors consent for the next surgery

As my mom and dad watched the tube in my mouth continue to drain blood, the doctors asked them to leave so they could prepare me for surgery. During the previous few days, Carolina had been desperately trying to get in touch with some of my coworkers to let them know what happened. Despite already having a full-time job as a teacher, she got in touch with my boss and told him that whatever my responsibilities were, she would do them. Carolina didn't have the slightest idea of all the duties I had at work, but these were desperate times and called for desperate measures. She just wanted to make sure I was taken care of and that my health benefits would not terminate when I needed them most.

Thankfully, COX stuck by me and gave me their support by keeping me on and letting me apply for Long-Term Disability once I was discharged from the hospital. It was a long process but one that was worth it as it allowed me to recover. Several of my coworkers came to Navicent to see me and also to retrieve my computer containing all my work. Remember, I had been tasked to create a video package highlighting one of our sales team member's accomplishments. He was our nomination for that year's President's Award, which is why the video was essential to showcase his sponsorships. I had been working on it the day of my accident and had already created most of the 3D animation, graphics, and transitions the video needed. It was almost complete. Thankfully, my coworkers were able to retrieve the work and complete what was not finished. From what I learned afterward, the video was a great success and the award was given to him. They spoke for a while with my family, and again my sister offered to do my work, seeing as bills were beginning to pile up.

Once they left, Carolina told my mom she would get another job to pay my bills and my rent. Between the four of them, they split the bills and tried to cover everything on my behalf. Carolina got another job online with Georgia Southern all while maintaining her full-time position at East

Coweta. My mom says both my sisters looked like they would pass out at any moment from the exhaustion of everything they were doing and how much they were driving.

My family was demonstrating true, sacrificial love every day as they put their own needs and lives aside to be there for me when I needed them most. They never thought twice before hitting the road and coming to see me at the hospital.

CHAPTER 4

A Crushed Mango and a Scratched Disc

EVEN MY EXTENDED FAMILY SHOWED US HOW MUCH they cared. My aunt and uncle, from my mother's side, were living in Arkansas and made the long road trip to be with us during that difficult time. I was falling in and out of consciousness during my last days at Navicent but not enough for me to really remember. Several friends stopped by to see me, and one of my good friends from college, Nick Flott, brought his ukulele. My sisters thought it would be a great way to awaken my brain if they played and sang a few songs for me. I have no recollection of any of this, but there's a video where Nick is playing a song and I am slowly moving my left hand to the beat as if conducting him. Everyone was so happy to see me respond to sounds. I don't know if it was an automatic response of my body, due to how well-trained that area in my brain was, but I don't remember any of it. My family decided to set some rules that day: my parents would only talk to me in Spanish, and my sisters would only speak to me in English. They didn't know if I would lose my ability to communicate in either language due to my brain injury. Carolina even tried speaking French around me at times since we both knew some. Alicia bought a little speaker to place close to my head and play classical music. She thought maybe certain frequencies and sounds could help stimulate different parts of my brain. I'm not sure what helped the most, but the fact that I'm here today is all the proof I need to know that a combination of everything my family did worked.

None of my family were in the medical field, but they tried everything they could to help me recover. If they discovered something that could potentially help any part of my body, they would buy it and bring it to the hospital. Carolina and my mom had been reading about how to heal the body after a traumatic event. They found literature on energy healing, indicating that we're all made up of energy. With this energy, the literature said, humans are able to heal themselves from within. I'm not here to tell you to believe in energy healing or to shun modern medicine; I'm only recounting the events. Even now, I don't know if it worked or if it was a combination of everything. Carolina and my mother would rub their hands together and make them hot with friction. Then they would hover their palms over my head, my leg, my face, and my hands. My mom would do this every night and then continue to hold my left hand.

She held my left hand because the right arm had all the tubes, wires, and medications going through it. She was scared to go near it; she didn't want to touch any of the cables. Ironically, my left hand was the one that was visibly injured, but I could still move it. For the longest time, no one had seen me move anything other than my left hand. But when my aunt came into my hospital room the week she first visited, she held my right hand. There I was with my mom holding my left hand and my aunt holding my right, telling me everything would be alright and that better days would come. And suddenly, I moved my right thumb. No one had seen me move my right arm or hand before that. The tears in everyone's eyes turned into tears of joy as a little glimmer of hope shone down on my family, letting them know that recovery was possible.

Leading up to my first facial reconstruction, a lady at the hospital saw how distraught my mother was and approached her. She asked my mom if she wanted to send me to the best place possible, where I would have the best chance at a full recovery. Without hesitation, my mother told her yes, that she would do whatever was necessary for me to go to the best place. That place, it turns out, was called Shepherd Center.

After meeting with a representative from Shepherd Center later that week and answering several questions, they told my family I had been accepted. They were happy, but none of them knew what to expect. One of my childhood friends, Sean, told my parents Shepherd Center was the best place I could go. He eased their minds and told them it was the best place for a traumatic brain injury like the one I had. It made my parents feel optimistic. I'd go to the best place, the place that could give me a fighting chance.

When they brought me back from facial reconstruction, my mom held my hand again and didn't leave. My face was all wrapped, and I had gel packs on my eyes to help the swelling go down. The doctors told my parents the swelling would get worse before it got better. The first day was fine, but the swelling increased the following day.

It wasn't until later that my family fully understood the magnitude of my injuries. When they did my first facial reconstruction at Navicent, the surgeon had to go in beneath the eye sockets to repair the broken bones around my eyes. My nose was broken, and they did their best to properly reset it. My mouth and jaw were the worst. I had lost a lot of bone in my upper jaw, and my palate was split in half. My teeth were crushed and pushed together, but miraculously, I only lost one tooth that had broken across the middle. Because my jaw and teeth were so badly damaged, the surgeons tried putting me back together the best they could, and to do so, they wired my mouth shut. It was one of the hardest things my mom had to see. She knew how much I liked to talk, so seeing me with my mouth wired shut was painful for her. But even that was nothing compared to what awaited her on the ambulance ride to Shepherd Center.

I was moved from the ICU room into a smaller room overlooking the parking lot where the ambulance would arrive to take us. My mom never let go of my hand as minutes felt like hours and she didn't see the ambulance appear. As we waited, the parents of my friend Peter stopped by to check on the family and me. The moment Peter was notified about my accident, he dropped everything he was doing and immediately drove up to see me at the hospital. I had met Peter in college and formed a great friendship with him and his brother. The day he saw me in the hospital, he told my parents I would make it. "Cesar's a fighter," he said. His parents both echoed the sentiment as they walked into the waiting room.

My mom hugged Peter's parents and thanked them for coming. She says that seeing me in that hospital bed, unrecognizable, hit them both pretty hard. The entire time she talked with them, amidst tears, my mom worried I might soil my sheets. She and my dad did their best to ensure I remained clean. Regardless of the fact that I wasn't mentally stable, my parents treated me as if I was, and they made sure I was never dirty. They did everything according to how I'd have liked to be treated if none of this had happened. I received daily nutrition through the feeding tube in my stomach and therefore still had to relieve my bowels. Despite how embarrassed I feel as I type this, my dad tells me sometimes I would soil myself. Again, my brain was in a jungle of confusion and I don't remember. Just know this: everything that's written here is the truth. I would love to tell you it was a lot simpler and that the worst part was over, but it was just beginning. Thankfully, I didn't soil myself as we waited for the ambulance, which finally arrived.

My mom said goodbye to Peter's parents and got into the back of the ambulance with me and one of the paramedics. My dad followed close behind in their car. The hour it took to transport us to Shepherd felt like a lifetime for my mom. She later told me everything that happened on the trip.

She said I went crazy in the back of the ambulance. I started hitting it with my fist and kept trying to get up. My mom was worried that if the paramedic or anyone saw me acting this way, they would send me somewhere else where she couldn't go, so she tried to calm me down. When I relaxed a little, she reached out to hold my left hand, but I grabbed her hand and twisted it hard. She says the pain she felt was agonizing, but all she did was whimper and hide her hand with mine latched onto hers. She didn't want the paramedic to notice I was hurting her because then he would try to help and I could get hurt more than I already was.

It's sad hearing what I put her through. If I had been in control, I would've never acted that way. Unfortunately, the trauma on my brain was so severe that I wasn't aware of what I was doing or that I was hurting her. My mom and I rode the rest of the way to Shepherd just like that, me with a death grip on her wrist. The most disturbing thing for my mom, she said, was seeing my eyes as I twisted her hand. I couldn't talk or move anything else, but when I twisted her wrist, she said I smirked as if it brought me pleasure, as if I derived satisfaction in seeing someone else feel even a portion of the pain I experienced.

When we finally arrived at Shepherd, my mom felt a huge relief being reunited with my dad after such a horrible ride. Despite the pain in her wrist, my mom never left my side and continued to hold my hand day and night. My dad was there to help, and he made sure I didn't hurt my mom's hand again, even though I would do it to anyone who touched my left hand.

I wish I could put down in words what went through my brain at the time, but I can't because I don't know. Only now can I fully understand how serious and grave my brain injury was. I would never want to hurt my family or anyone. I just know I was angry and in pain.

My leg began to wake up, and with it came more pain. Physically, I was going through a lot, but the biggest battle raged inside my brain. My dad would sometimes switch out with my mom and take turns holding my hand. His hands are big and firm from all the hard labor he's done in life. As soon as he held my hand, I tried twisting it as well, and despite my extensive injuries and the muscle loss, my dad said my grip was still strong. His hands could withhold my grip, and he would sometimes just let me do it. He hoped it would make me feel better somehow, getting it out of my system.

The day we arrived at Shepherd Center, my face was so swollen you could barely see my eyes. They took me to a room on the third floor, and when we arrived, two of my friends were there. They hadn't been able to visit me while I was at Navicent. The new room was bigger and more comfortable for my parents. I tried to interact with my friends, but I have no recollection of it. Thankfully, the pictures and videos my sisters took of everyone who visited helped me put some of the pieces together.

A bunch of family and friends stopped by in the following days since I wasn't in the ICU anymore. At night, all hell broke loose, and there was nothing much my parents could do but just be there with me. The pain in my leg was unbearable, and at night I would frequently wake up to try and cough, or because the pain was too much. My dad spent many nights holding my leg at an elevated angle so I could get some rest, disregarding his own. My mom...well, she rarely slept. She was always analyzing me while I slept and kept rubbing my right hand, hoping it would one day move again.

Within the first few nights, my mom was given several documents to sign, informing her what to expect with my recovery. Shepherd Center became an oasis for my family, and they slowly began to see why it is such a revered trauma rehabilitation hospital. One of the documents contained a summary of the accident and all the injuries I had. Now is as good a time as any to describe them:

- ▸ Every bone structure in my face had been broken.

- ▸ My left femur was broken and had been protruding out of my leg.

- ▸ My right arm was paralyzed due to a brachial plexus injury.

- ▸ I had a tracheal tube to help me breathe.

- ▸ I was diagnosed with a severe brain injury.

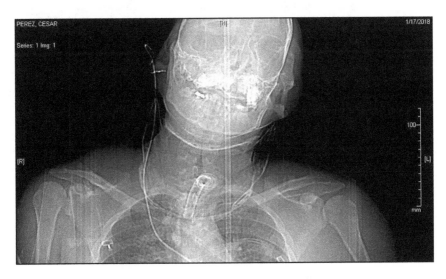

One of the first X-rays, taken after the accident,
of Cesar's head and shoulders

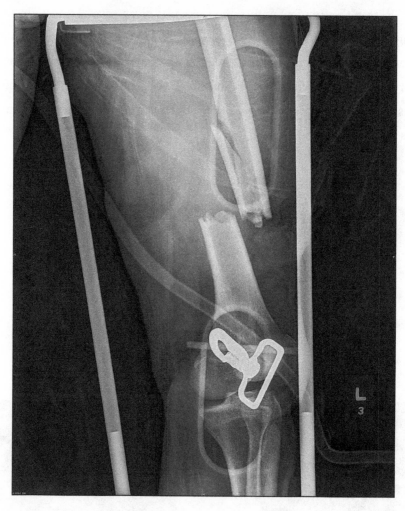

X-ray of Cesar's broken left femur

My medical team discovered even more injuries after I started physical therapy (PT) a week later. My family was given an apartment in the housing complex next to the hospital. That's one of the amazing things about Shepherd Center; they value family and know the importance of having them nearby. They want to ensure families are close and provide support without

CHASE THE LIGHT

the added financial burden of hotel costs. In the two and a half months we were there, my mother only went once to the apartment to shower. My father and sisters would just go there to shower as well or offer it to some of the visitors who came to see me.

One of the nurses gave my mom a pamphlet explaining what a brain injury is and what level I was categorized as. They used the Rancho Los Amigos Scale with level 1 being the worst (no response) to level 8 being the best (purposeful, appropriate response). I was categorized at a level 4 (confused and agitated response) which states, "Patient exhibits bizarre, non-purposeful, incoherent or inappropriate behaviors, has no short-term recall, attention is short and nonselective." Before I started PT, I was tested several times to monitor my brain injury. I acted in a frantic manner and had spasms at night.

In the following days, several of my friends continued to visit me and show their support. One of the people who kept coming back was Sean. Each time, he brought something useful for my parents that could either help me or them pass the time better. My entire family and I are forever grateful to him because it was his idea to bring a small dry-erase board. Because I couldn't talk, he thought it'd be best to see if I could communicate with my left hand. I should clarify that I am, and always have been, right-handed. I have no idea how I managed to learn to write so quickly with my left hand. My parents say within a week I was writing full sentences and with good penmanship.

There's a Bob Marley quote I read awhile back that says, "You never know how strong you are until being strong is the only choice you have." That couldn't be more true, and it defines my time in the hospital. I had no idea I could ever write legibly with my left hand, but when the need to communicate surpasses every other need, and you've lost your ability to do so, you somehow find a way. That is what I did. Despite my brain injury and pain, I was determined to communicate. The first thing I wrote was "How did I get here?"

Friends gathered together waiting to see Cesar at Navicent

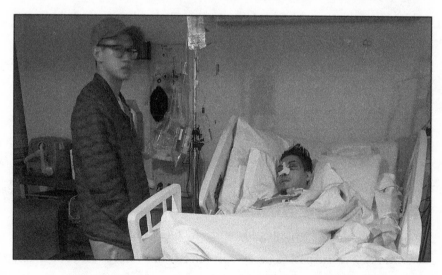

Sean Hsu watching over Cesar after initial facial reconstruction

I didn't understand how heavily impaired my brain was at the time. My right leg and my internal organs were the only things that had not been affected. Thanks to the physical state I had accomplished with my body, the muscles guarded my internal organs from damage. My dedication to transforming my body into the best version of myself paid off and helped keep me alive. All the hours of training and hard work had been worth it, but the work awaiting me at Shepherd Center and the following years would be the hardest thing I'd have to do by far. I can't tell you when I started physical therapy because it's all a blur. To be honest, I didn't understand where I was or that I was even in Atlanta. None of it mattered to me. My parents say I started PT the following week after arriving at the hospital. In the meantime, I had been evaluated by several doctors and nurses to determine what therapy treatment I would begin.

My dad tells me the best way to describe the physical state of my face is that it was like a crushed mango. Mangos, once ripe and sweet, tend to get soft and sometimes fall from the trees. If you were to come across one on the floor, it would be wide and smooshed with light orange liquid oozing from the torn peel. When I see the pictures of me in the hospital, I understand what he means. My face was so swollen and oozing orange liquid mixed with blood from the incisions. I'm sure even some of the nurses were shocked when I first arrived, despite seeing traumatic cases constantly. Anyone who saw me the first week would've been dubious about my ability to recover. And how could I blame them? When I see the pictures, I can't help but marvel at the strength God gave me to make it out of the darkest time in my life. But that's why they transferred me to the best place, where I had a fighting chance to recover. The therapy I required had to be aggressive if I was ever to make it out. And Shepherd provided it. Not only were all the doctors, nurses, and therapists under-standing of my pain but also the turmoil brewing inside my parents and sisters. I can't thank them enough for giving me the opportunity to take my life back, but what means the most to me is how kind and understanding they were with my family.

Some of the most excruciating pain I felt was due to the trach tube. I'm not sure if the brain injury had something to do with this, but anytime somebody touched the tube, I felt the worst pain and felt like I was suffocating. My parents dreaded nightfall, because every night someone from respiratory would clean my trach tube. They would come into my room and clean around the insertion point in my throat. They did it to prevent bacteria from entering my body and causing an infection. They cleaned it with the utmost care, but no matter how gentle they were, it still felt like I was dying. The worst part of the process was the suctioning part and clearing the mucus from the tubes and cannula. To get the mucus out, I had to cough it up. Sometimes I was able to do it, and other nights, because of the pain, I was unable to cough. If I couldn't clear the mucus, they would spray saline inside, which made me feel like I was drowning and caused me to cough nonstop. Out of everything, that's the part my mom couldn't bear to watch. Every time they sprayed the saline, she says, she could see the suffering in my eyes. Those were the only times my mother stepped out of the room because she couldn't stand it.

Eventually my parents learned to clean my trach tube on their own and switch out the inner cannula.

I still felt the pain when my dad tried to clean it, but he did it in such a manner that the gauze removal didn't hurt as much. The entire time my dad cleaned and switched out the gauze, my mom would hold my hand and tell me to look at her. She would talk to me to help deviate my thoughts from what was happening. My dad became my personal respiratory nurse while at Shepherd. I didn't want anyone but him going near my trach tube. Whenever I felt mucus in my cannula, I would snap my fingers and point to my throat. My dad would open a new cannula and replace the old one with a clean one. Sometimes respiratory therapists would still have to clean it, but most nights they would come and notice my trach tube was fine and continue to the next patient. My parents knew what time they usually came and always tried to do it before they got there.

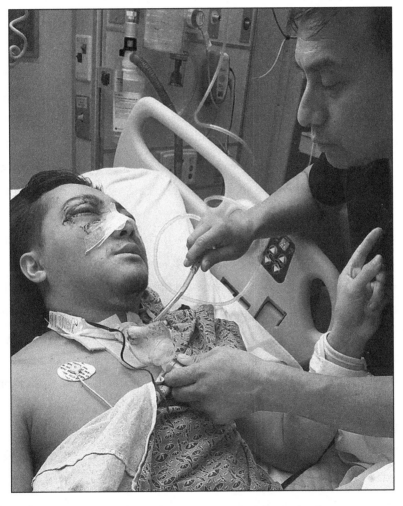

Cesar's dad cleaning the area around the trach tube

When I started PT, something clicked—something from the old me. It was the drive and determination I had used in my life to get to where I had been. The first therapy I underwent was for my leg, to try and get me to stand. I remember asking Heather to be there and join me at therapy, not so much for me but rather to network and meet other amazing therapists. She was finishing her undergrad, but she wanted to continue her education and become a physical therapist. My mind wasn't always working coherently, but when it came to Heather, things just clicked, and even in my wild mental state, I kept thinking of ways I could help her. I felt practically useless trying to help her because physically I couldn't do much. So my only option was to use my circumstances to get her into the PT world, where she could meet therapists from a well-known and respected hospital like Shepherd Center. I knew she had shadowed other therapists before, but I figured this would mean more. She'd get to see the huge impact her future profession had on someone close to her. To me, that felt like the best thing I could do at the time.

Heather agreed to go to therapy with me a few times. My mom and dad would come too, and always offered to help the therapist in any way they could. They kept taking pictures and videos of my exercises to help me do the movements in my room. My personal injury lawyer, Jeremy McKenzie, mentioned to my family that pictures and videos could not only help my memory but my future lawsuit as well, when the discussion of damages was brought up. That was never their priority, but they saw it as an added benefit and kept putting my recovery on record. Heather would sit there, but she only volunteered to help when pictures or videos were being taken. Whenever she was at one of my therapies, I gave each exercise 110 percent effort. She was the driving force, the motive behind everything I did. I needed her to know I wasn't giving up on myself, on her, or on us. Heather became the unexpected catalyst that ignited my recovery. My family was motivating me in every way they knew how, but they simply weren't *Heather*.

She was still the light of my life, and in my altered state of mind, the only thing that mattered. I just wanted to get better for her and give her the life we had envisioned together.

It's tough to explain to someone how a brain injury works unless they've gone through it, especially one as severe as mine. The best way I can describe it is that it's like a scratched disc. My mind retained certain information and kept replaying it over and over. I was there in the hospital but not actually living the moment. The moments I lived were the moments my brain kept replaying. I had been driving down to see Heather on January 12, and I had been so excited to get there and take her to dinner. That's what kept replaying in my head, not the accident or the fact that I was in the hospital trying to recover.

So much had changed for me in real life, but I couldn't see it at first. To me, the one thing that remained constant in my life was Heather. I remember telling her several times that once she graduated, she could move in with me and continue with graduate school. That's the only thing that was on my mind at first. Today I realize how unfair it was for me to not even ask about my mom, dad, or sisters, seeing as they were the ones by my side day and night. Unfortunately, I didn't have room in my mind for them because of my brain injury. Heather was my world at the time, and she took all the space in my head and heart. There were many days when all I would write was her name and draw a heart around it. My mom would always talk to me (treating me like the old Cesar, as if I understood the situation) and ask me what I wanted to do when I got out of the hospital. My only answer was "I want to hug Heather."

Everything came back to Heather. My mother spent nights on end analyzing me as I lay there with a lifeless expression and would sometimes ask me what I was thinking about. Her concern, and I believe everyone else's too, was trying to decipher what was going through my head, and in doing so, push away any negative thoughts that might build momentum. There were no negative thoughts at first but rather just Heather. When she came with my sister to visit on weekends, my world lit up. As cliché as it sounds, the pain was still present when she was there, but it didn't matter to me because I was content just seeing her.

Today, I can look back at my time in the hospital (the parts I remember) and try to understand how my brain was functioning. Everything revolved around Heather. The magnitude of my brain injury was so severe that if she had told me to jump off a bridge, I would have done it without hesitation, even many months later. All I wanted to do was please her and make her happy. I was surrounded by crying family and friends, so my mission was to save Heather from that emotional distress. Whenever she showed up, I would mask my pain. Those moments she was with me are the few times I recall being calm and at peace.

As the facade began to crumble, I realized Heather's true colors weren't nearly as beautiful as I had hoped. "Forever and a day," we said back on brighter days. How quickly things change. Suddenly forever seemed not so long at all. My intentions hadn't changed. We had discussed getting married, and I had planned to propose. I had every intention of honoring that plan, but I feared something was changing on Heather's end—her mind, her heart, or both.

Heather could do no wrong in my eyes, and she knew it. After the first several times she visited me, my fear came true, and I could sense that all the events had begun to weigh down on her. Something inside my convoluted brain told me things were changing, and I got scared. My family could see it. They understood how the brain injury had magnified everything Heather meant to me.

She was on my mind almost every second of every day. My family treated Heather with the utmost care and made sure she was always happy because seeing her smile kept me at peace. Alicia also started noticing a change in Heather's demeanor. She asked my parents and Carolina what they would do if Heather decided she couldn't continue with the relationship and my situation. Alicia recommended they stop bringing up Heather's name as often, to gradually taper me off "my drug." My family just wanted what was best for me, to give me a fighting chance at a full recovery. "I'll pay her if I have to," Alicia said. "If that's what it takes to help Cesar recover, I'll pay her to keep showing up."

I wasn't aware of any of this at the time. All I knew was that on weekends, Heather was coming. So when Fridays came around, I was ecstatic. I got to see my better half. She would show up on Saturdays, and I would already have scooted to the edge of my bed so she could lay there and sleep. Despite everything that had happened, having her there made me feel normal again. She wouldn't say much, but I didn't need her to. I did most of the talking by writing on my board. I told her she made me the happiest person in the world, even though I couldn't smile. I told her she was all I'd ever wanted.

My parents were always close by, observing me. They didn't care about their own comfort; their goal was to make sure I never needed anything. It snowed one day in Atlanta while we were still at the hospital, and my parents knew how much I enjoyed seeing the snow fall. They looked out my hospital window and sat beside me as the flurries kept coming down. My dad says it was ironic seeing something so beautiful when they were going through hell. I think it was one of the few nights I didn't wake up with nightmares and my parents actually slept a little.

In the morning, my dad complained of pain in his foot. When my dad took his shoes off, his feet were cracked and bloody. In shock, my mom took off her shoes as well, only to find she was in a similar situation. The hospital rooms were kept dry to avoid the propagation of bacteria since patients could be there for months at a time. The lack of moisture in the room had caused their skin to dry up and crack. My mom told my dad to buy some lotion at the nearest store. She wasn't leaving my side, she told him, and they would both remain in the room with me.

The days continued to drag, but regardless, time never stopped. When Valentine's Day came around that year, I remember staying up crying with my mother holding me in her arms. She tried calming me down as I wrote down, "I had big plans with Heather, and I can't even hug her today. This isn't fair. I didn't ask for this," I wrote. My mom held me in her arms and said Heather knew I wanted to be with her, but right now, it was important for me to get better so I could spend future Valentine's Days with her. That somehow did the trick. She always knew what to say to calm me down and refocus my energy into recovery. My mother knew what string to pull to make me do something, and it was Heather. She said if Heather was who I wanted to be with forever, then the best way to prove my love for her was to heal and walk out of that hospital. "When you walk out of this hospital, she will know you love her because you never gave up," my mother said. "You wanted to be with her, so you pushed forward every day. This will prove to her that you're not a quitter. No matter what tough moments you go through as a couple, you will never give up on either of you."

I didn't write anything then, but she knew I understood. Once I was calm, she told me Alicia had gone out and bought Heather presents and flowers on my behalf. She had them shipped to Heather's place in Statesboro and also bought her a necklace. The necklace was half a heart that said "moon of my life," and there was a second necklace in black, the other half, which said "my sun and stars." Alicia gave that one to me. When you combined Heather's necklace with mine, it made a whole heart. I didn't feel complete without Heather, and Alicia thought it'd be a good way to let her know I was always thinking about her. Heather and I had been binge-watching *Game of Thrones* before my accident, and she was obsessed with it. In the show, Khal

Drogo calls his wife, Khaleesi, "Moon of my life." In return, she says, "My sun and stars." I know the necklaces sound a little cheesy, but it made me happy at the time since I couldn't give her much. Since the first few days I learned to write complete sentences with my left hand, I would write what I loved about Heather. Alicia would take pictures and write down what I wrote, and she used it to write Heather a nice Valentine's Day card on my behalf.

Heather was so happy with her present; she came up that weekend with my sister to give me mine. She was obsessed with sloths. Sure, I think they're cute, but her love for sloths was on another level. Heather would say she was the embodiment of a sloth because all she did was sleep. She brought me a card and a little stuffed baby sloth. I started tearing up, and for the first time, they were tears of joy. It wasn't the sloth that made me happy but rather seeing she had taken the time to think of me and get a gift too. In my mind, it was as if nothing had happened and my being at the hospital hadn't changed how she felt, or at least that's what I hoped.

That baby sloth became the most important thing to me when Heather wasn't around. There wasn't a night I didn't sleep with it and hold it close to my chest. I asked her to name it with me and we decided to call him Diego. When Heather was gone, Diego was my companion, helping the days go by quicker. To me, that baby sloth embodied her because she had given it to me as a present. Whenever I went to PT, I would ask my mom to bring it for me. I felt Heather was watching me if the sloth was at my therapy session, and it made me try harder. That baby sloth proved to be my lifesaver many nights when I couldn't sleep. In hugging it, I felt I was with her and that kept me calm. Heather continued to be my inspiration, even when she wasn't around. I know I would've made it out of that hospital one way or another, because my family wouldn't let me give up. But Heather provided me with the fastest route possible. I guess in the end, I am grateful for that. Motivation is what I needed, a reason to continue the fight, and that's what she gave me at the time. *Gracias*. My mom always wanted me calm, so she told my dad and sisters the baby sloth could never be removed from the room. She also told them not to get it dirty because I slept with it close to the trach tube opening. I had no idea what Diego would turn into years later. He was my companion then and is my companion now.

The following days went smoother as my brain started waking up a little more. They started me on other forms of therapy, including music therapy (MT) and occupational therapy (OT). Although there wasn't any external physical damage on my arm, it never moved, and there was a slight subluxation (partial or incomplete dislocation) that kept increasing as the days progressed. They started me on OT to see if they could trigger some movement in my arm. Everything from my right shoulder down to my wrist was completely paralyzed. The first few OT sessions aimed to try and wake up any muscle in my right arm, but it was futile. One night, something in my arm woke me. I snapped my left fingers—it was the only way I could get anyone's attention—so my mom could get me the board. I wrote that I felt a huge bolt of electricity under my right arm. My tricep was having spasms. For the next three days, my tricep would randomly jump, and it allowed me to progress a little in OT. My doctor said I might have a brachial plexus injury. That meant the nerves, ordering functions to my arm, could have been jeopardized or damaged. He ordered an electromyography (EMG) test to see if the nerves had any signal and to determine which nerves had been compromised. I had no idea what the brachial plexus was before any of this, but it turns out it's the power grid that sends signals from the spinal cord to the shoulder, arm, and hand.

The EMG consisted of sticking fine needles into my shoulder and bicep. Every time the needles would go into my body, the doctor would ask me to contract a certain muscle to see if the device would pick up a signal. I don't know if it was normal to feel a lot of pain during the exam or if my brain injury again played a role, but I felt a horrible pain when contracting some of the muscles in which the needles had been inserted. When the test was finished, I was so relieved and just hoped whatever damage my nerves had could be repaired. The results came later that week, and the doctor sat down with us to explain the magnitude of my brachial plexus injury. My tricep was finally working, but my bicep and shoulder still weren't responding. Turns out several nerves had been badly affected, but there were options to fix the damage. He recommended continuing OT to give the nerves time to heal and reconnect on their own, and then we could talk about surgery and other potential alternatives. He concluded by saying that nerves take the longest to heal and repair on their own, so it was going to be a long process. I continued going to OT with the hope that the functionality in my arm would return. They said the nerves might've been stretched, pinched, or severed.

I kept going to PT, which consisted of weight-bearing and trying to integrate some coordination in my left leg. One day at therapy, I was sitting in my wheelchair and dragged my left foot back. As I moved it, my therapist Carolyn, noticed a shift in my tibia that caused it to sag as I slid my foot back. She brought the other therapist to double-check what she saw, and they asked me to do it again. I did it again and they both saw the same movement that caused her original concern. She told me it appeared my tibia was sagging backward past my femur, which was an indication of a PCL tear. These types of injuries are very common in motor vehicle accidents as the knee hits the dashboard, causing the ligament to tear. She proceeded to write it in her notes and ordered an MRI for my left leg to see if I indeed had a torn PCL.

My therapist explained to me the important thing was to continue PT and strengthen my leg since people sometimes don't even get their PCL repaired and can live fine without it. But I knew, even then, that would never be me. My biggest concern was that I wasn't the type of person that liked to live a sedentary life. My hope was to someday return to the soccer field and play without being concerned that I had a torn ligament. She told me only the MRI would tell if it was torn and then it would be my decision on what I wanted to do. To say it was overwhelming—for everyone involved—would be an understatement. But in those times, you can only do what you have control over. At that point, all I could do was persevere and keep taking things one day at a time. So that's what I did.

CHAPTER 5

My Broken Reflection

THE NURSES AT SHEPHERD BECAME VERY FOND OF MY family. Eventually, those who cared for me at Shepherd became like an extended family to my own. Everyone could feel the love my family exuded when they came into my room. It wasn't an act, a facade, or mere passing phase. It was a genuine and constant devotion. The nurses saw my family's longing for past days when none of this had happened, and they tried helping in any way they could. They told my parents it helps patients recover quicker if they feel they are in a familiar place rather than a hospital, so if they wanted to bring stuff to decorate the room to resemble my apartment, they could do so. My mom asked Carolina to bring anything I had on the walls of my apartment, hoping it would help me feel more at home. She quickly went and grabbed some picture frames and two big movie canvas posters I had hanging on the walls. They were movies in which I had played a role. Alicia bought a sign that said, "A cord of three strands is not easily broken" (a verse from Ecclesiastes 4:12) and another one that read, "We may not have it all together, but together we have it all." Heather brought me two wooden puzzle pieces that said, "I love you to pieces." I wished to remain in those rare flickering moments in which she showed some care and affection. Maybe they weren't real, but it was the reality I wanted to live. Perhaps she cared in the beginning, but my accident had immediately put the brakes on our relationship. Like a train rolling to a stop, it takes time, but eventually it does come to a halt. How much longer before we came to a stop, unable to proceed on this journey together? No one knew for sure, but it was evident we were slowing down. I didn't know, though. I was just enjoying our relationship, unaware of the deceleration. The brakes had been slammed on January 12, literally by me in my car and figuratively by Heather in how she felt.

Thanks to the new decor, when nurses came into my room, it was like they were stepping into my apartment, just with a little more medical equipment. A few of them asked about the movie posters, and my family explained to them that I was an actor. That same week, Super Bowl LII was airing, and several nurses came running into my room. "You're in a Super Bowl commercial!" they said.

It took me a minute to remember what they were referring to, and I didn't personally get to see it until months later. I was in a halftime commercial for Pepsi, with Kyrie Irving as "Uncle Drew." Everyone kept talking about it and sending my family messages saying they had seen me on TV during the Super Bowl. The sad thing is I didn't even watch the Super Bowl. I didn't care about anything I did pre-accident because it just reminded me of what I could no longer do. My world was broken, and I didn't even fully comprehend it. All I wanted to do was sleep so the pain would go away. But even when I closed my eyes, I never rested peacefully unless Heather was next to me. That following Friday, another movie I was in was released in theaters. Again, people who went out to see the movie *The 15:17 to Paris* messaged my parents to say they enjoyed seeing me on the big screen. My sisters were proud but also distraught at everything I had accomplished and wasn't getting to enjoy.

Carolina bought me a new cell phone, thinking that interacting with a new phone could help my brain heal quicker since I worked with a lot of media. It was the newest Android Samsung Galaxy Note 8. She thought it would be easier for me to see and interact on a bigger screen using the stylus. Along with the phone, Carolina also bought a PopSocket so it would be easier to hold since only one of my arms was working. I owe my sister so much, not monetarily but rather for everything she did to try and make things easier for me so I wouldn't feel useless. The moment I got the phone, I set it aside. I wanted nothing to do with it and didn't even open it. My mom told her to bring me my laptop and see if I remembered any of the work I used to do before. She brought it and the same thing happened. I didn't even open it. I'm not sure what was going through my head at that moment, but seeing my computer took me back to my life before the accident. That life was gone, taken from me, and I didn't want anything that reminded me of what I didn't have anymore. My mother says a few days passed before I would even look at the phone. When I finally opened it, it didn't take me long to get used to all the functionalities.

Heather came to see me the following weekend and started joking that only girls used PopSockets. I'm sure she was joking, and I might've taken it as such had I not had a brain injury, but it hurt me deeply. I had only started messing with the phone to keep in touch with her while she was at school. I didn't know what she did during the week since she only came on weekends when my sister picked her up. I somehow managed to download all the social media apps on the new phone in hopes of being more in touch with Heather since that's where she spent most of her time. Miraculously, I remembered my username and passwords. I found this fascinating. Although I had a brain injury, it hadn't affected my long-term memory. I wrote it down on my board to let my mom know I was able to remember. She quickly notified everyone in the family that at least some of my memory was returning.

I finally decided it was time to face my demons and see if I remembered the work I used to do. My mom passed me the laptop, and I realized it wasn't my personal laptop but rather my work-issued computer. On my personal laptop, I could just log in with my fingerprint, but this computer required a username and password. After trying several times to remember the password, I grew frustrated and gave up. I cried myself to sleep that night, knowing there were still some things I couldn't locate in my brain. But the username and password came to me in the middle of the night. In the morning I asked for my computer so I could try again, and thankfully, what I entered successfully logged me in. I couldn't do much on the laptop because I needed to be connected to our work network. But it didn't matter. I remembered my login.

Now that I had my phone and could use it, I asked for it every chance I got. I was on my phone all the time when I wasn't in therapy or had visitors. One day I decided to check my email. There were so many unread emails, I just started deleting most of them. Some I would stop and read. One caught my eye because it was from *America's Got Talent*. It was congratulating me for making it to the next round of auditions. I then realized nothing I had done before mattered because I couldn't do it anymore. Was I about to go to the next audition barely able to walk, my right arm paralyzed, and with my mouth shut? I deleted the email. Everything from my past just reminded me how much I had lost. I kept opening emails and deleting them. My parents didn't find out about my *America's Got*

Talent audition until much later, when I was talking to my lawyer about damages. I never told anyone I had auditioned because if I didn't make it to the next round, I wouldn't have to explain anything. Memories started coming back to me, and they made me distraught, realizing how much had been taken from me.

After clearing my inbox, I started looking at pictures of Heather to help me calm down. It was the only thing that worked to stabilize my emotions. The one thing I still had (or so I thought) was Heather, and that prevented my anger and depression from raging out of control. Looking back, I could've easily seen my face with the front-facing camera, but despite always asking my mom for a mirror, it never occurred to me. The phone was just for talking with Heather. I would text her every chance I got and tell her about my therapy sessions. Video calls helped my days go quicker, and even though she wasn't with me, I felt like she was when we video chatted.

One day I started having horrible pain, and the nurses gave me medication to help deal with it. That night, as I slept, I had another nightmare. I'd been having nightmares about my accident, but that night they were about Heather. I dreamt she had started seeing someone else and only kept coming to see me because it would look awful on her part if she didn't. Even before the accident, I knew Heather cared a lot about what people thought of her. She had always sought validation from her friends, and I remembered this in spite of my brain injury. I wouldn't allow my injuries to affect my memories of Heather. I woke up angry and crying. My mom asked me what was wrong, and I wrote down my nightmare. She told me not to worry and to let those negative thoughts go. Heather loved me, she said, even though she never truly believed it.

My mother stepped aside to speak with my dad about why I had been crying. She said it was because of the medication, that it was making my thoughts and emotions go crazy. Thankfully the pain was starting to sub-side, so now I just had to let the medication run its course and leave my body. I calmed down a bit, but the feeling of betrayal still weighed heavily on my mind. I grabbed my phone and texted Heather, asking her if she was cheating on me or if she didn't want to be together anymore. No one knew what Heather had been doing in college on days she wasn't visiting me. When I spoke with her, she would usually tell me she'd been studying, and I believed her. To this day, I don't know if she was lying, but I like to think she wasn't. I like to think that for a moment she at least cared enough to respect my love for her. Had I been in the right state of mind, I'd have never asked if she was cheating, but I didn't know how else to deal with my emotions. Heather angrily replied that she wasn't going to put up with that. She then texted Alicia and told her not to pick her up that weekend because she wasn't coming.

I get it. I should have never asked her, and I spent the following days apologizing for it so she would reconsider and come see me. Only my parents truly understood what I was going through. The doctors had given them an orientation explaining the severity of my brain injury and what to expect. I had received two massive impacts to the frontal lobe of my brain. My mother even spoke with Heather, telling her I didn't know what I was asking because I was under the influence of a lot of medication. She begged her to come see me that weekend. I spent days calling and texting her but with no response. She was angry at me and only communicated with my sisters. I asked Alicia to take a picture of my board and send it to her. I wrote down, "You are my everything. Let me love you." I then wrote why I was in love with her and I was going to get better because I wanted to grow old with her. She eventually reconsidered and came to see me.

Heather still wasn't happy and didn't talk to me much. My mom and sisters kept trying to explain to her that the way I was acting was due to the medication and brain injury. They expected her to understand at least a little since she was studying to be a therapist herself. But she remained upset with me for several days. At the end of my journey, I've often stopped to think about those moments and how Heather responded. Perhaps her age played a role in it. Maybe she just wasn't mature enough to handle the gravity of the whole situation. I don't know. I realize the situation wasn't easy, but I was trying my best to keep the life we had envisioned together from imploding. I thought that would be enough since it was all I could do.

Messages Cesar wrote to Heather

The frontal lobe of the brain is considered the emotional control center. It helps form our personality. I'm not excusing my actions, but I really had no idea how to deal with the flow of emotions. The dam that held certain emotions at bay had broken, and they were running rampant inside me. Once all the pain medication left my body, I began to think a little clearer and never questioned her again. Every now and again when they gave me more medication to ease the pain, my mother would hide my phone so I couldn't text Heather or post anything online. I can't thank her enough for always being there trying to protect me, even from myself. It didn't matter to me if Heather understood or not; I just wanted her to be happy. And because my family knew how important Heather was to me, they did their best to ensure she was happy and had everything she needed.

I knew she was graduating on May 5 that year because she had told me several times she needed to buy a new outfit for graduation. May 5 seemed so far away, but I set that date as my goal to get better and be able to walk during her graduation. The next time I saw her, I promised to be at her graduation without a wheelchair. There was still some fight left in me, and I used that energy to give it my all during therapy. Yet again, even though she was unaware of it, she provided me with a lofty goal and the motivation to strive for it.

That same week, I received invitations from two of my closest friends, to their weddings on May 5. I didn't even think about it. I knew what my choice was. I messaged saying I wouldn't make it because although I was still in the hospital at the time, I had plans to be at Heather's graduation. My mission was May 5, and the doctors had said I could be discharged on March 27. This was a tentative date though, and no one knew if I would leave in a wheelchair, or with the feeding tube or trach tube. I told my mom I was leaving before May 5 no matter what because it was my promise to Heather. My friends understood where my heart was and were okay with me going to Heather's graduation instead of their weddings. I apologized to them years later because although my heart was fine at the time, my mind was not. Had I known everything I do now, brought on by hard life lessons, I would've chosen differently. These are friends you don't find often, and they would stick by me to the end. I wish my brain had healed more quickly because I couldn't see a lot of the things that were evident to everyone else. I continued going to therapy, but once PT ended, I asked my dad to help me do more exercises. If I didn't make it to Heather's graduation, it damn sure wouldn't be because I didn't try.

As the days progressed, a reconstructive plastic surgeon was assigned to my case and stopped by on certain days to check my jaw and teeth. Each time he looked at my mouth (still wired shut), he said it needed more time to heal before he could remove the wires. The day finally came, and he told us I'd be ready to have the wires removed the following week.

I had been waiting with anticipation for this day. It would be the first time I opened my mouth in over a month, so everyone in my family anxiously waited for the doctor to finish. We were painfully wrong in thinking I'd be able to open my mouth to talk. He removed two metal plates that had been holding some of my upper and lower jaws together, but then he placed stiff rubber bands on each tooth. He said the bands were to keep the mouth shut but also to help my jaw muscles ease back into mobility. I was so angry when he left, because due to the thick bands, my mouth still wouldn't move. My family would have to go a bit longer without hearing my voice.

A few days later, when I was on a call with Heather, sadness turned to joy. Normally I would call just to hear about her day because I couldn't say anything. I wanted her to know that despite everything I was going through, I still made time for her. She was finishing up the conversation and was about to get off the phone, when suddenly, I tried to say something. My mouth was shut, and the trach tube opening was the only opening close to my vocal cords. I don't know how I managed to get the sound out, but with all my strength I said, "I love you so much." My mother, in shock, started crying. I had been on mute for over a month, but this proved to everyone, including me, that I would be able to talk. Heather, on the other end of the call, was also able to hear it. She asked if that had been me, doubtful at what she had just heard. It took everyone a moment to grasp the fact I had spoken. I wheezed out a "yes," and she started cheering in excitement. Hearing her happy and saying she was proud was payment enough for me for all the hard work I had put in. I couldn't move my mouth, but I was definitely smiling, if only on the inside. Despite not opening my mouth, the diction in what I said was not bad and was understandable. The only issue with speaking was the amount of effort it took on my end, and it would make me feel slightly dizzy afterwards. The sound was coming from the trach tube opening as well as from inside my mouth. I'm not exactly sure how it worked or how it affected my vocal cords, but it didn't matter. I had finally spoken.

After that, I kept trying to talk more. Everything I said had to be short and concise because it would leave me exhausted or with little air. My mom noticed and told me to stop talking and just wait until they removed the bands. The rubber bands started giving in to the stretch I would cause every time I tried opening my mouth. I decided to save my energy and not talk as much until Heather visited because I wanted to keep impressing her. Her opinion was the only one that mattered to me. Now I could tell her "I love you" and "I want to be with you forever." Her parents visited me on weekends if they could. I waited that specific weekend until they showed up and said, "Hola." They couldn't believe it. It wasn't loud, but it was audible.

One night, after PT and OT, I continued to feel tired, like I couldn't catch my breath even after lying still. I wrote on my board, "I don't feel like I'm getting enough air." The interpreter and my mom told the doctor, and he made a note for the ENT doctor to come see me. Someone from respiratory came to check if the trach tube needed cleaning or if there was too much mucus preventing the proper flow of oxygen. But after they cleaned and replaced the cannula, I still felt I wasn't getting enough oxygen. The ENT, Dr. Dockery, came to see me the following day. He sprayed lidocaine in my nostrils to help numb them, and then used an endoscope with a little camera to look inside my throat. It was the only option available since I couldn't open my mouth.

Once he finished, he explained what he found and why it was cause for concern. The reason I wasn't getting enough oxygen was because I had tracheal stenosis, scar tissue that had formed due to how the trach tube had been inserted. He said the next step would be surgery but that ideally, to remove the scar tissue, it was best to go through an open mouth. Dr. Dockery said he would take the rubber bands off during surgery and see if he could go through my mouth, but if he couldn't, he'd have to make incisions where the trach tube was inserted. He finished by saying surgery had to be done soon because scar tissue would continue to grow while the trach tube was still there. I had no idea what was in store for me with this surgery. The doctor said I would feel a huge difference in my oxygen intake once it was done. That made me excited for the procedure.

Surgery day came, and as they moved me into another bed, I gave my mom a thumbs-up to let her know everything would be okay. The next few moments I can't recall. I just know the surgeon started to lift my upper lip to remove the bands and then my world went dark as the anesthesia kicked in. When I woke up, I had already been transferred into an ICU room where the nurses monitored me closely. The anesthesia was still leaving my body, but they had already started me on pain medication in case it wore off completely. My mom held my hand and told me everything would be alright. I didn't see my dry-erase board in the room, so I tried to speak. I wanted to ask her the time and also how long I had been in surgery. I had been hoping my mouth would be without bands since the surgeon had taken them off, but when I tried to open my mouth, it didn't budge. Before, the rubber bands had stretched enough that I could at least open my mouth enough to get some sound through. This time, as I tried to say something, it felt like someone had locked my jaw together once again. I frantically waved at my mom with my left hand, and pointed to my mouth, wanting to know why I couldn't open it. She understood the puzzled look on my face and what I was asking. My mom lifted my upper lip, and she told me the rubber bands were still there, but they were new.

Dr. Dockery came to see me later and said he had to enter through the trach tube incision. Despite removing the bands, my mouth could barely open and he wasn't going to jeopardize all the surgical procedures that had been done on my mouth already. Surgery was successful, and he asked me if I could feel a difference in my oxygen intake. I told him I couldn't because my whole throat was numb, and I couldn't even swallow. But he said I'd feel a difference once the numbness went away. My only other concern was that I couldn't cough because it was super painful, but I had a lot of mucus building up. He said respiratory could come in and suction it out so I would feel better, but my mom quickly intervened. "Please, no," she said. "I think once the numbness goes away, he will be able to cough it up on his own."

Fortunately, once the anesthesia and numbness started leaving my body, it felt easier to breathe. Nobody told me the pain I would feel the next couple of days would be the most agonizing of my life. I do believe my brain injury magnified certain pains, but this one was excruciating. There are experiences too traumatic for the memory to retain, so the brain decides to erase them in order to give the body the optimal chance for survival. That's what my brain did for me, and not just with the accident but also with this surgery. I don't remember the accident or the pain I was in when they pulled me out of the wreckage, and I don't remember the pain of this surgery either. All I remember is that I spent days and nights in agony. Despite the pain medication they gave me, it was still unbearable. My mom says I wrote down that it felt like someone was slowly cutting into my throat. The one thing the nurses could give me to help take the edge off the pain was morphine, and before administering it, they asked me, "On a scale from 1–10 with 10 being the worst, how bad is the pain you are feeling right now?" I wrote down 9. They proceeded to inject the morphine into my IV.

Now I hope you've never needed, and never will need, morphine, but this is how I remember it. I could immediately tell as it entered my bloodstream. It felt warm, as it moved from my arm to the rest of my body. It spread quickly. Sometimes it made some of my functioning muscles twitch as it dispersed throughout my body. The nurses said I could only receive the morphine every four hours. At first, the pain subsided enough for me to calm down and interact with Sean, who came to see me in the ICU. He brought with him ointments and balms he had purchased to give my mom should I ever start feeling localized physical pain. My parents and I thanked him, but just as I was about to write something else, I felt the pain start up again. Only three hours had gone by, so it was way too early to receive another morphine dose. They told me to hold off until three hours and forty-five minutes had passed. I did my best to hold it together, but once the time had passed, I asked for the nurse because I couldn't stand it any longer.

The next couple of days went the same, but they moved me into my old room after three days in the ICU. I had therapy scheduled for most of the days, but I told the doctors and therapists I couldn't do it. The pain was too much, so I didn't go to therapy at all that week. My days started and ended the same, with me lying in bed for a week. I didn't even get up to use the restroom. If I needed to urinate, I used a plastic container the hospital provided so I didn't have to get up. The only time I would get up was when I felt a bowel movement coming on. Regardless, I didn't have bowel movements often, perhaps only twice a week. The morphine also made bowel movements more difficult, but I didn't care, so long as the pain was kept in check. That entire week, the doctors and I agreed to start tapering me off the morphine and extend the hours I went without it. Fortunately, by the end of the week, I was able to get off of it and use less intense painkillers. The morphine helped me immensely, and I was able to sleep on the nights they gave it to me. But as the days wore on, my parents grew concerned that I would become addicted to it. Thankfully I never did. I didn't ask for it again, and the trach tube incisions continued to heal.

The following week, I was eager to get out of bed and continue therapy. Heather stopped by, and I was reminded why I needed to get better. She unknowingly helped me continue to keep my eye on the prize of not only getting out of there and going to her graduation, but walking and advancing even further in my recovery. Beyond just wanting to be there for her, I *needed* to walk so I could attend her graduation. My therapists happily welcomed me back as I started on more PT. There was a little garden area outside with a trail. The therapists sometimes walked it with patients to escape the monotony of being stuck inside. Every time I tried to walk, one of my therapists was beside me, making sure I didn't fall. They used what they called a "gait belt" to try and assist me when I needed help. They told my parents if they wanted to walk with me, they would have to hold the gait belt. I have so many pictures of me walking with my dad and my mom right beside me. My dad would hold the belt. Despite me being smaller and skinnier than before, it was too much weight for my mom's fragile frame, but she still walked with us. She was scared she would hurt me more if she wasn't holding it correctly, so she let my dad hold it.

The nurses told my family they could take me to the garden area if someone was with me that knew how to use the suctioning equipment. To do this, they had to pass a "training course" on how to use the equipment, beyond the cleaning they had already been trained on, and the procedures to follow. I took that machine with me everywhere I went. It was mandatory to ensure I didn't have an emergency in which I wasn't getting enough oxygen through my trach tube. My parents and Carolina agreed to take the training so they could take me, in my wheelchair, to the garden area. They wanted to break up the monotony of the days for me, which again were all blurring together. Training day came, and the nurses explained that each person getting certified had to practice the steps on me. All this time, my mom had thought they'd practice on a dummy or body double. The last thing she wanted to do was spray the saline solution and watch me gasp for air. She threw her hands up and just said, "I can't." She walked out of the room and my sister went after her. My mom was crying out of anger at not having the strength to do it. Carolina told her she didn't have to. If she and my dad did it, they could still take me out of the room, as long as one of them was certified. She remained outside while I coughed up a storm, as my dad and Carolina proceeded with the training course. They passed the certification, which is all my mom needed to know. I was finally able to leave the room with them.

Several of my friends came to see me after the stenosis removal. One of them who showed up several times was my friend Mo. He was at Georgia Southern at the time as well, finishing his undergrad. We met in college, playing intramural sports, and had been friends ever since. Heather knew Mo, and I asked him to be there for her while I was at the hospital. He told me I was his brother and that anything I needed, he would do. Mo would visit, even during the week, and spend time with me. He talked and joked with me like old times, making me feel like everything could maybe go back to normal. The days he came, he would spend playing games and even going to OT with me. He would participate so I wouldn't feel like the only one having difficulty with certain activities. I genuinely enjoyed the moments he was there, and I felt optimistic about the future. Mo kept asking if he could walk with me or help me in OT, even when no one was taking pictures. Those are the moments when true friendship is revealed. Mo was there so often that my parents felt he was another one of their children. They were always happy to see him because he was one of the few people who could make me laugh. It was more like a chuckle, not really a laugh, but it was more than my parents had heard from me for so long.

We all went outside to show Mo the garden area, and I tried walking with him while he held onto the gait belt. He sat me down in my wheelchair when I got tired and then wheeled me inside the building. My parents talked with Mo for a while, telling him about the pending surgeries and updating him on how my brain was healing. Mo said everyone in Statesboro had been asking about me. Up until that point, I knew I had been in a car accident involving a drunk driver, but I didn't understand the magnitude of the events. Carolina must've sent him the pictures because he asked if I wanted to see them. I nodded. Despite me asking several times, my parents had prevented me from seeing the pictures. They didn't want me getting emotional or distressed. But Mo pulled out his phone and showed me the pictures of the drunk driver's vehicle, the big rig, and then my car.

For the first time since the accident, I realized I was a living miracle. My eyes filled with tears, and Mo quickly put his phone away as my mom came to see what was wrong. I was happy he had shown me because now I fully understood the magnitude of the events. This was not going to be a short and easy journey. Mo told my mom he showed me pictures of the vehicles because I had wanted to see them. We both still laugh about it today because I know he felt bad for showing me the pictures as tears rolled down my cheeks, but it somehow helped me get a stronger hold on the reality I was living. I started asking my parents for more details about my accident in the following days. All they said was that a drunk driver and a big rig had hit me on I-16, so I received two huge impacts that resulted in the pictures Mo had shown me. I asked, "Who hit me?" but my parents didn't know much except that he was of Latino descent. It all sounded so crazy to me. My parents tried changing the subject quickly so I wouldn't go down a dark path of emotions.

My world was blurry. I had pretty bad eyesight even before the accident, and I normally wore contact lenses. The contacts I was wearing the day of the accident were removed at one of the first two hospitals. This left me with blurry vision for the next couple of weeks. My mom had kept my glasses from middle school and asked my dad to bring them one day when he had to go back to Richmond Hill. When he brought the glasses, my mom asked the doctor if I could wear them. She hoped that despite the change in my prescription, I'd be able to see a little better. But the doctor said I couldn't wear them because my face was still healing, and my nose could be damaged by the glasses resting on my septum. I figured I could just hold them with my left hand whenever I wanted to see. I did this for several days and it worked, but Sean said there had to be a better way.

The next day he came to see me, he brought several tools with him. He gave them to my dad and pulled out two hats. One of the hats had glasses on them. Sean had spent all night tinkering with some glasses, trying to connect them to the hat. He figured the hat would keep the glasses at the level of my eyes without ever touching my nose. It helped, and I was able to wear my glasses for longer periods of time. Carolina bought me new glasses with my correct prescription and had them shipped to the hospital. I tried to wear the hat with glasses every time I went to therapy. They helped me regain my balance; I could focus my eyes on something as I did my exercises. I could see my surroundings clearer. But I could also see the extent of my injuries.

Up to that point, I still hadn't seen my reflection. There was a mirror in the bathroom where I could've seen my reflection had I had my glasses. I was able to walk to the bathroom now whenever I felt a bowel movement coming on. For the first time, I stopped in front of the mirror with my glasses on. I stood there dumbfounded, not recognizing the person looking back at me. My mom always followed me to the bathroom in case I needed help sitting or assistance in cleaning myself. She stopped behind me, and I leaned forward and tried touching my face. I refused to believe it was actually me. After a few minutes of touching my face—especially the right side where most of the damage was—I started crying and turned to my mom. She didn't cry, even though the tears were there. My mom took my hand and made me stop poking at my face for fear I could cause more damage, seeing as my face was still swollen.

She would later ask the medical team what doctors they recommended for the issues with my facial bones, and I would spend the next few months meeting with each one of them to see what they could do for me. So far, I hadn't seen my teeth. I'd never had braces before, but there's a first time for everything, and deep down I knew I'd have to get my teeth fixed and realigned. The extent of the damages in my mouth was severe, but none of us knew to what extent. We wouldn't get to see the full scope of the damage until I could open my mouth.

My mother walked me from the restroom to my bed and sat me down to talk. As she held me in her arms, she wiped my tears away and told me how much she loved me. I felt depressed and angry. Why did I have to go through all this when I had lived life the best I could? Everyone who visited said I was a miracle and that God had a bigger plan for me. I knew they meant well, but nobody understood the pain I was going through or the immense anger I had toward life now. After seeing myself in the mirror, I knew nothing would be the same inside me. I had heard people talk about my injuries, but what I saw in my reflection broke me further.

My mother kept consoling me. "You are the strongest person I know, and we all love you so much. Life would not be worth living if you weren't here with us," she said. "Don't worry about your face…they can fix the bones. You are the biggest gift in my life. That's why I'm not leaving your side until we can finally close this horrible chapter." I stayed in her arms for a while longer because at least there I felt safe. I knew my family were the only ones who would love me for who I was and not care about how

I looked. Heather cared a lot about appearances, so despite me clinging to the fantasy that she would see past the exterior, I knew deep down it'd be hard for her. Hell, it was hard for me to accept it, and IT WAS ME. If I couldn't come to accept it, how could I expect Heather to? I'll touch more on this later, but I had to learn how to love and accept myself again. I was still the same guy but with a convoluted brain, and for that, I couldn't see past the face in the mirror. I wanted to stay in my mother's arms forever. But life is not always fair. I knew I would have to interact with other people eventually, and that kept the tears coming. I couldn't sleep that night. My mind kept racing back to the person I saw in the mirror. I couldn't turn my brain off, and the negative thoughts started creeping in. It's the only time I can honestly say I ever contemplated suicide.

In my head, I had lost everything, even my identity because I looked completely different. I didn't want life if this was how it would be from here on out. It had taken me twenty-four years to get where I was before the accident, and I wasn't about to spend another twenty-four years trying to get there again. *Life shouldn't be like this,* I thought. I even started questioning my faith and questioning God. *God can't have a bigger plan for me,* I thought. *My God would have never allowed this to happen. I didn't deserve this.* That night, I decided God didn't exist, and I thought more about suicide because if God didn't exist, then what was the purpose of living?

The next night, I brainstormed how I would go about ending it. I had been through enough pain already, so I wanted it to be quick and painless. After I thought about it for some time, I started crying again, but this time out of despair. Even if I wanted to end it, I couldn't. I could barely walk, my arm was paralyzed, and my mom was always holding my hand, so the dream of ending my misery died that night. I couldn't even kill myself without needing to ask for someone's help in doing it. My mom (sleeping in the chair she placed beside me) woke up and asked me if I wanted to talk.

I motioned for my board and wrote, "This is not fair." She brushed the hair from my face. "It really isn't," she said. "You didn't deserve this, but trust me . . . someone will pay for this. Someone must. I refuse to believe God let this happen to you for a purpose. No purpose would justify any of this. I can never again stand tall and tell someone to pray because . . . what good did it do me . . . or you?" Tears rolled down my mother's cheeks, and in the midst of my breakdown I realized we both had been broken. I received all the physical damage, but something had truly shattered in my mom. Was it repairable? Only time would tell, just like it did with my broken bones, except this break went much deeper. We all saw my mom survive what we thought would kill her, seeing her only son on what appeared to be his deathbed. Like me and the rest of the family, she endured. Through all the pain and suffering, we made it out. We were put to the test of how much each of us could stand, and though parts of us may have broken, we never gave up on each other. If our faith broke, there was always someone to pick up the slack. I'm reminded of the sign Alicia bought for me that said, "A cord of three strands is not easily broken." We were a cord of five, so even if one of us broke down, we would remain as we always were—unbreakable. My mom was hurting, and I knew I wasn't the only one having a difficult time accepting what had happened. She understood how I was feeling that night.

As my mom wiped the tears from her cheeks, I decided to keep fighting and continue pushing forward with my recovery. There was no bigger reason for me to do so than my mother. She and my dad had shown me what true love was and had never left my side, so I would do it for them. If God loved me, He hadn't shown it to me. This went through my head as I wrote, "We will make it out of this." It was my turn to be strong for my mom who'd been my rock since the beginning. My mom managed a half-smile. "I don't doubt you are going to get through this," she said. "You will get everything back that was taken from you, and then you can enjoy your life with Heather like you planned . . . before all this."

My mom was right. *We* would make it out of this. All of those lessons they taught us when we were kids were coming to fruition, when my dad would say, "We will rejoice together if something good happens to one of us, but we will also suffer together if one of us is hurting." We were suffering, yes, but we were doing it together. And we would certainly rejoice together when I made it to the other side.

CHAPTER 6

Why Me?

A NEW EMOTION OVERTOOK ME AS I CONTINUED MY therapy. Determination took the wheel. Anger, though still present and prominent, sat in the passenger's seat. I knew I couldn't break down again because my mom and family were sacrificing so much to see me get better. Walking got easier, and I was able to spend more time in the garden with my parents. Tears formed in my eyes as the cool breeze hit my face. So much had changed, and I wondered if something in me had changed too. We walked a little farther and my dad asked, "Que pasa, viejo?" He had called me viejo ever since I could remember. It literally translates to "old," but he used it as a term of endearment, and it made me fondly remember my dad playing with me as a kid. For a second, when he called me "viejo," I felt like the little kid from twenty-two years prior. But what came next was the realization that that little kid had died on January 12, 2018. Something had definitely changed in me. Whether for better or worse, I still didn't know.

The movie *Beast of Burden*, in which I starred opposite Daniel Radcliffe, was released that same weekend, and several people messaged my family to say how proud they were of me. It was ironic. These things were happening while I was still at Shepherd, unable to enjoy the fruits of all my hard work. The year 2018 bore many promises . . . but left them all unfulfilled. I didn't get to see any of the productions in which I was involved until months later, and it made me feel even more bitter.

Cesar Perez as Pablo in the film **Beast of Burden**

Another week passed, and Alicia decided to tell our parents about her boyfriend in California. I was always drifting in and out of sleep but always listening. She was about to be on spring break at Armstrong, and the plan was to come be with my mom and me at the hospital. Because of work and Heather's school, they would always leave on Sunday. My mom was excited Alicia would be able to spend all week in the hospital with us, which would allow my dad to go back home and check on the house, the chickens, and the dogs. When Alicia told them she was planning to go to California during spring break, my parents didn't know what to say. I know my mom was hurt that she would decide to leave, for whatever reason, during such a crucial time. My dad was upset too but was not about to stop her from making her own decisions. He just wished her the best and told her to be safe. Alicia left for California that following Thursday. My dad stayed with my mom that week, not as planned, but they were used to life throwing curveballs. They made do with what they had, and at least they had each other. Carolina came every day after class and stayed with them. I had lost all concept of time. The days seemed to draw out for all of us.

This entire time, I had no idea Alicia had a boyfriend on the West Coast, and quite frankly, I don't think my family had known either. It all happened too quickly for any of us to grasp, and they had spent all their time and energy on me. They disregarded their own lives to make sure they were there for me day and night. It's nothing I asked for, just something they did out of love. My mother kept telling me, as I kept getting better, that I owed them nothing. They would do it again if they had to. We were family. I don't think I ever saw her sleep during my time in the hospital. She was always awake watching over me while she let others sleep. Carolina and my dad were the ones driving at the time, so my mom always told them to rest. When they left the hospital, it was only to bring my mom food and clothes. There I was, lying in a hospital bed with no capacity to be anywhere else, and my mom was by my side every single day. She dropped her entire life to be with me. Though I had nothing but the best medical care at Shepherd, I felt I was going through hell, a prisoner in my own body...but I wasn't alone. If I had to walk through hell, my mom was going to walk it with me. We were on this journey together, and she made sure I understood that. "If you ever feel like you can't carry on, I'm here. I'll carry you the rest of the way. We are finishing this, one way or another," she would tell me. I don't think I could have asked for a better partner to walk this road with me. She felt my pain and cried the same tears. There was a connection between my mom and her children, formed at birth, that was unbreakable. The whole family understood she was never leaving my side while I was confined to those four walls. By my side is where she wanted to be, and that's where she stayed.

March went by a little quicker as I started walking more. Shepherd assigned a psychologist to my case who would see me every now and again to evaluate my mental stability. And in the short amount of time I talked with her, I felt a wave of emotions start pouring out that I had kept at bay for several days (trying to be strong for my mom). She asked me several questions I know were customary and routine, but to me they reiterated everything I had lost. Up to that point, my parents kept telling me to focus on the future and forget about what happened or my life before the accident. "This is a new Cesar, and you can do whatever you want," my mom said. "Not everyone gets a second chance after something like what you went through. I know you're destined for greatness."

The day I spoke with the psychologist, I'm not sure if she was evaluating my emotions or what, but she asked what I missed most about my life pre-accident. As I started looking back in my memory, searching for an answer, I stumbled across fun memories of things I couldn't do anymore, and I told her, "Everything. I miss everything, and it's not fair someone could take all that from me. I shouldn't be here." I said all this as best I could since the rubber bands in my mouth still made it difficult to talk, and the tears started rolling down my cheeks.

Sadness and anger were normally the only emotions I showed unless Heather was there. It was a weekday, so she wasn't. The psychologist didn't want me to get too riled up, so she said we should take a break and come back to discuss the answer. This allowed me to calm down, and once I regained composure, she proceeded to ask me what was the first thing I wanted to do once I recovered. "Hug Heather with both arms," I said. "I want to marry her, but I can barely stand. How will I ever be able to propose? It's depressing." She gave me a box of tissues to dry my eyes and then asked me what would happen if Heather one day left me. I'm sure these questions were meant to help or to evaluate me, but I think she saw how distraught I had become, so she decided to move on. She told me that my life still had meaning and that life is worth fighting for, so I should keep pushing forward.

But I was still angry at what she'd asked about Heather. "Tell me how you would feel if you were in my shoes," I said. "How would you feel if everything you had worked for was taken from you in an instant by some idiot? How would you cope with feeling useless every single day?" I nearly screamed the last part, but it came out as nothing more than a strong wheeze, with my mouth barely moving.

My mom placed a hand on my shoulder and told me to calm down. She said the psychologist was just trying to help. "Don't be rude," my mom said. "You're better than that." The psychologist said we were done and stepped outside to talk with my mom. I never knew what she told her, but I assume it had something to do with how my emotions would play an important part in my recovery and how to address them.

I didn't stop crying the entire way back to my room. My dad saw me and asked what had happened. I heard my parents say that the important thing was to make sure I focused on the future, not on the past or on the things I couldn't do anymore.

The nurse brought a few bottles of Ensure for me to drink. It was all part of the process to help me start eating again, and since I could barely open my mouth, liquids were the first thing to try. The bands in my mouth stretched enough for me to take a sip, but I still found it difficult to swallow. The next few speech therapy sessions revolved around strengthening my vocal cords and starting to try soft foods. My therapist, Deborah, was the sweetest. She never made me do something I wasn't capable of doing but always pushed me to get progressively better each time. I don't remember exactly when my sister or I showed her videos of me playing guitar and singing, but she took a keen interest in my case since she loved to sing as well. Every time I met with her from then on, we always attempted some singing. There was this YouTube video I uploaded in 2014 that Deborah would use to determine my vocal range and the vocal capacity I used to have. The video was an original song I titled "Don't Let Go Tonight." It became our goal to try to sing at least parts of it every session.

Near the end of March, my time at Shepherd was coming to a close. Every year Shepherd did a little spring festival at the hospital for the patients. I can say it's one of the few times I felt Heather and I actually shared a connection. She brought some Easter eggs and paint to color them with me. No one asked her to do this, nor did anyone expect it out of her, which is why it meant so much more, to me at least. It was her idea to spend the day painting the eggs with me before heading downstairs to the gym, where there were games and food for everyone. I felt a warmth that stemmed from her spending time with me rather than just sleeping. She pushed me around in my wheelchair, and for the first time, I didn't feel she was embarrassed. This only helped propel the false notion that we would end this horrible chapter just like we had started it—together. I desperately wanted it to be real. If only for that moment, I wish to think it was a genuine gesture and not just a networking opportunity for her to meet other therapists. We played a few games together, and even my parents were fooled that day into thinking perhaps she could be the one. I was genuinely happy and could have stayed in that moment forever. That's why I cherish that memory.

In the midst of my despair, there are a few moments here and there that shine through like a ray of sunshine in a storm. That was one of them. But like all things, everything must end. My happiness was short lived as the following weekend Heather was back to her old self. All she did was sleep when she visited, and I felt her getting more and more distant each day. She even asked me what would happen if one day she didn't come back. "It's a joke," she said afterward, but deep down we all knew it wasn't. She was testing the waters and wanted to see what I would do if she ever decided this was too much for her to handle. I didn't respond to her question. I simply told her, "I'll make it out of here . . . for us."

CHAPTER 7

An Old New World

I VIVIDLY REMEMBER GETTING DISCHARGED FROM SHEP-
herd Center. They removed the trach tube the day prior, and I was starting
to get used to breathing through my nose. The only thing remaining was
my feeding tube. The nurses told my parents if I was able to gain one pound
per week, they would remove it on the third week. My mother didn't care
about the feeding tube; she could deal with that. Her biggest fear had been
going home with the trach tube still inserted. She cried tears of joy when
the doctor said I was ready to leave the trach tube, and quickly removed it.
They also removed the bands on my teeth, and although I was still unable to
open my mouth more than a few centimeters, it felt nice to be going home
with my mouth unshut and with the hopes that speech therapy would only
help me improve further.

My therapists and nurses held a little going-away party for me in the
gym. They all hugged me, wishing me the best in my continued recovery.
I thanked them for all the support and for never giving up on me. Several

of the patients wished me the best as well, and I thanked them for giving me the strength to keep going by seeing their resilience every day. I gave everyone a one-arm hug before sitting down. They brought a keyboard to see if I wanted to play anything or if my sister wanted to play. Carolina started playing the intro to "Hallelujah" by Leonard Cohen and said she would sing with me so I wouldn't feel alone. I could barely move my mouth, but I saw Heather's parents watching, and I wanted to prove to them I was the same person who first fell in love with their daughter, that I could still do everything I did before. The strain I felt in my throat was huge, and when my voice cracked, Carolina made sure to cover it either with her voice or the piano. She knew very well how I felt.

All the therapists had tears in their eyes while my sister and I sang. Once we finished, I thanked them again before walking back to my room with my family. Tuesday morning came, and we all said goodbye to the hospital room that had been our home for almost three months. The therapists said I wouldn't be going home in a wheelchair but rather walking out of the hospital. I held my mom's hand, and we walked out through the same entrance they'd brought me in through on a stretcher months earlier. It was difficult to walk, but I had joyful tears in my eyes as I took each step. I told Heather I was going to walk out of the hospital and that I would be at her graduation, and here I was doing the first part. Walking out of Shepherd Center was the culmination of all the hard work I had put into my recovery because of the love I had for her. Not only was I leaving the hospital on my feet, but I was leaving without the trach tube that had been my misery for weeks. My parents felt relieved thinking the worst part was behind us and that better days lay ahead. I don't blame them for wishful thinking because not even I knew what awaited us. I just knew I'd be at Heather's graduation, and as I walked out of that hospital, that was enough for me.

My dad brought the car around so my mom and I could get in the back, and something shifted in me. I can't tell you what caused the change in my emotions because it happened suddenly. Only later was I able to tell my mom why I cried the entire car ride to my apartment. "It was a mixture of things," I said. "The sounds of traffic were overwhelming, but I also started to realize how much life had changed. I couldn't even tie my shoes without help, so how could I expect to be the man Heather wanted."

It was emotional being in my apartment. I hadn't been there in over three months. Carolina had spoken with Marley, the front office receptionist at the complex. She explained to her why I had been behind on February's rent and assured her that she would pay my bills. The entire time I was in the hospital, Carolina had argued with my mom, telling her not to take me back to Richmond Hill. She wanted me to stay in Atlanta, close to the therapists and doctors I was to keep seeing. I told my parents many times that I needed my apartment because I had promised Heather she could move in with me when she went to grad school. They didn't think it was a good idea because they didn't feel Heather was going to help me like I needed. Regardless, I had already made my decision.

I had an appointment in Macon the following day with the plastic surgeon who first reconstructed my face, Dr. Paul Syribeys. My dad took us, and it was the first time I was on I-16 since that horrible day in January. My mom sat in the back with me and studied my expression, trying to decipher what was going through my mind. She asked me what it felt like to be on the road. "Ironically, I feel fine," I said. "It doesn't give me anxiety. I feel like I could even drive if I needed to." It was a blessing I didn't remember the accident because it gave my parents some peace of mind knowing that one day, I would be able to drive again. We finally arrived in Macon. I was excited and wanted to first and foremost thank Dr. Syribeys for putting my face back together but also to ask him what the next steps were in getting my face looking like before.

He didn't recognize me at first, and I expected that. I'm sure the first time he saw me, I was a bloody mess, so I figured it might take him a minute to realize who I was. I thanked him for all the work he had done, and my mother gave him a hug. He said it was a miracle I was alive and recovering so well. He asked me to smile and proceeded to inspect my teeth and jawline. In the upper palate of my mouth, there was a metal plate he said he could remove. My upper jaw had been broken down the middle and he had placed the metal plate there to hold both parts together. "It did the job it was supposed to do," he said proudly.

I chuckled and asked him what he could do for me with respect to my cheekbones jutting out much further than before. "I wasn't fat before," I said jokingly, "but my face looks fat now." He laughed and said the front desk would get me scheduled to remove the metal plate in my mouth, but there wasn't much more he could do for my cheekbones. I can't even imagine all the work it must have taken to put my face together again. The accident had only been a few months before, so there was still some swelling in my face. Dr. Syribeys told me that after an event like I had been through, it's not uncommon for the swelling to take a full year to go away. Once the swelling and inflammation went down, he said, it would make a big difference.

I was silent on the drive back to Atlanta. My mom kept trying to talk to me, saying there were still doctors we had to see who could give us different answers, so I shouldn't worry. I just gazed out the window the entire way, wondering why life had done me so wrong. When we got back to my apartment, I decided I needed to keep busy and keep my mind occupied, so I started getting my bills in order. My mother asked me where Heather would put her things in the closet because there wasn't much room. The closet was big enough for one person but definitely not two. I had a lot of shoes that took up half the closet and probably more clothes than even Heather. I knew we would need a bigger closet. My lease was ending soon, so I told my mom I'd get a bigger apartment in the same complex. Marley knew my situation, and I knew she'd be willing to help. For the next several weeks, my parents and sister all slept in that one-bedroom apartment the best way they could. Carolina slept on my futon, and my parents slept on an inflatable air couch Sean had brought over.

Several boxes of formula were sent to my apartment to start the nutrition regimen. The goal was to gain one pound per week in order to get the feeding tube removed. My mom said she wasn't going to use the feeding tube. "You need actual food and nutrients," she said. "I'll cook your food and toss everything into a blender so you can drink it." The thought of taking everything in liquid form was a little nauseating, but I wanted that tube out of my stomach. I agreed to it. I'm not sure how many of you reading this have a Latin mother, but you'd best believe she fed me well. She spent every day cooking different meals and throwing it all in the blender. While she liquified my food, she cooked meals for my dad, my sisters, and even Heather when she came to visit.

My dad tried helping me gain weight by getting me a Chick-fil-A milkshake almost every day. Before the accident, my diet was balanced and consisted mostly of proteins and staying away from sugars and fats. I hadn't had a milkshake from Chick-fil-A in over a year, but I was now drinking one almost every day. It didn't matter to me where the weight came from; I just knew I needed to gain one pound per week to get the tube removed. I remember weighing myself at the gym the day of my accident and the scale had read 156 lbs. Leaving Shepherd Center, I weighed 124 lbs. In three months, I had lost over 30 lbs. and didn't have much muscle left. My six-pack was still visible but that was due to having almost no body fat on me with all the weight I had lost. My goal was to regain my strength and start working on my body, but I couldn't even think about starting to do that with the feeding tube still attached. I kept consuming everything I could in liquid form. I would drink two Ensures daily and eat everything my mom made. My dad would bring two milkshakes (one for him and one for me), and I'd use a spoon to try and eat it all. Within a month, I had met the requirements to have the tube removed. We kept the regimen going even after the tube was removed because we could see the progress my mom's food was making. I slowly started weaning off the milkshakes, but my dad would still get them. Today he jokingly blames me for making him put on weight as well. "I would do it all over again though," he says. "It all paid off, and we did everything to make sure you never felt alone."

It was still very hard to get food in my mouth despite not having it shut. It would take time to strengthen the muscles in my jaw and get them accustomed to moving again. When I did get the food in my mouth, I had to tilt my head back slightly to avoid the food coming out my left nostril. The extent of the damages in my mouth were more apparent one day when I tried some soup, and as I swallowed, half of it came out my nose and almost made me choke. Every time I swallowed, I felt the liquid shoot through my nose. I asked my mom to look in my mouth to inspect the top palate while I pointed with my tongue where the issue was. She could see a small black circle, which turned out to be a hole. The little fistula led to my left nostril, and it was the reason why liquid came out my nose when I swallowed.

The days continued with more therapy sessions. Shepherd understood I wasn't in critical medical condition anymore but still had a long road ahead to a full recovery. I started going to their outpatient rehabilitation program at Pathways. My therapies at first just included physical therapy (to strengthen my left leg) and speech therapy (to help my jaw muscles work on everyday functions). As time went on, I started once again getting music therapy, occupational therapy, and vocational therapy. My dad stayed for the first few weeks in Atlanta, but he had to go back to work. He wanted to stay with us until I was done with my recovery, but he knew the best way he could help was going back to work and helping with bills that were piling up. I remember meeting with my vocational therapist, Shelby, at Pathways and telling her I was ready to go back to work. She told me there was a process I had to go through before getting cleared to work. Thankfully I remembered everything I did at work, so I felt I could go back. Despite my knowing what had happened, I still didn't fully comprehend how much further I had to go in my recovery. I just knew that the medical bills kept coming and that I had to pay my apartment bills each month if I expected Heather to move in with me after graduation. Next time I met with Shelby, I explained this to her, and she directed me to my healthcare benefits. She went over everything with me and said the best choice would be to hold off going to work while I was still in the primary stages of my recovery. The next step would be to apply for Long-Term Disability.

I always left Pathways feeling like I'd be cleared to return to work the next week. But the days kept passing by and I was nowhere closer to getting cleared. My mom had gotten over her fear of driving back when she had to pick us up from middle school. What happened to me in 2018 completely washed away all the progress she had made. She couldn't drive and take me to my appointments, especially in Atlanta where traffic was worse than what she was used to. My dad told her it was okay and that it was one of the reasons Carolina was moving closer, so she could take us where we needed to go. I know whenever I was in the car, whoever was driving felt even more responsibility just by having me there. Nobody wanted to see me get hurt any more than I already had been, so they drove as cautiously as they could.

I was able to stand and walk more at this point but with obvious difficulty. My parents thought of getting me a walker to assist me, but I told them no. There was no way I was going to Heather's graduation with a walker. I wanted to be at her graduation like the independent person I was, so a walker was out of the question. As the weeks went by, my mom asked me if I ever considered using a cane. She said I could dress up nicely and use a stylish cane should I need help walking at Heather's graduation. Carolina had been searching online, and she showed me pictures of several different canes. I liked how two of them looked, and to my mother's surprise, I agreed to use a cane. Sean called it my "pimp cane" since it looked flashy and didn't offer too much support, but for me it was enough. I just wanted to look good for Heather at her graduation, so if I had to use a cane, it'd damn sure be a fashionable one.

In the meantime, I kept walking the hallways with my dad, trying to get my gait back to normal. I still had a limp, and I hated that. It was one of the main reasons I didn't want to leave my apartment and normally walked when no one was in the halls. The stairs at my complex were an obstacle course for me. I would always have to go up with my right leg and come down with my left. My left leg wasn't strong enough to allow me to go up the stairs regularly. It took a while for me to come down the stairs because the rail was on the right side; my right arm was paralyzed, so I couldn't hold on. My parents or Carolina would hold on to me as I walked down the stairs, to make sure I never fell. It had only been a few weeks since I'd left Shepherd Center, and no one wanted a medical emergency. The doctors told my parents my head was the thing they had to watch carefully. Any fall or blow to the head could cause more damage while my brain was healing.

I had frequent migraines, and the pain was so intense that at times, I couldn't function. I had been on all sorts of painkillers, antibiotics, and steroids at the hospital, so my mother wanted to refrain from giving me more hard medication. She instead gave me children's Tylenol and children's Motrin in liquid form. When I say children's Motrin, I'm referring to the one that says, "For Ages 2 to 11 Years," and here I was, taking it at twenty-five. She thought the liquid form would reach my bloodstream and alleviate the pain faster. It worked quicker than even I had anticipated. I took a full dose of Tylenol and Motrin every four hours for the first few months. The pain in my head would only subside for a few hours, so my mom always had to carry a bag full of Kleenex, Tylenol, Motrin, and soft foods for me to eat. It was as if my mom was taking care of a newborn again, with all the items she carried in case I needed anything. I couldn't help her much since I could barely walk, and she always wanted me to have my left hand free in case I needed to hold on to something or someone. I can't tell you how much money my family spent on children's Motrin and Tylenol, but I would have to put it somewhere in the thousands. Though it was children's Motrin and Tylenol, I was going through one bottle of each every day, and I did this the entire first year.

I had an appointment with the Multi-Specialty Clinic at Shepherd Center the following week to check if I had gained enough weight to remove the feeding tube. During the entire drive from my apartment to Shepherd, I started remembering more and noticing I had gone through Peachtree Road many times before. There were several auditions I had attended that made me drive past Shepherd Center; I just hadn't noticed it before then. My memories started offering a little more clarity about my life before the accident and also my life currently. In a way, the memories helped propel me to take my life back, but it also took a deep emotional toll on me. My emotions still ran rampant, and I couldn't stop the tears from flowing, which distressed me even more. Before the accident, I couldn't remember the last time I had cried. Again, I don't mean this in a macho kind of way but rather to express that I was always in control of my emotions. The gym and music had been my remedy for everything. If I felt angry, upset, or anxious I would go to the gym and work out for hours. If I felt sad or emotional, I'd take time in the evening to play some music. I'd write down what I felt and turn it into a song. Ever since I was little, music has played an important role in my life, and it got me through tough times. It always helped me deal with my emotions in a healthy manner. All I could do now was listen. They say music is life and that's what I wanted—to feel alive again.

There I was in the back seat of the car in tears as memories kept pouring back to me. It made me angry to know I couldn't control my emotions. I knew the gym and music were my cure, but my arm was paralyzed still, so there was not much I could do to cope. I think I cried enough that first year to suffice for a lifetime. When we reached Shepherd, my mom dried my eyes, and I noticed her eyes were watery as well. My dad was getting teary eyed too and said, "Cesar, you know how many nights this hospital was our home? How many nights this car never left this garage? To see you walking on your own back into the hospital, I can say it has all been worth it." He hugged me and wiped his eyes, and three of us walked into the hospital together for the first time since leaving it.

When I got to the clinic, the nurse told me to step onto the scale. I don't remember exactly what the scale said but she wrote down the weight and told me to wait in the room with my parents. The doctor finally came to talk with us and said I had gained enough weight to merit removal of the feeding tube, and they could do it that same day. The nurse said all it required was pulling the tube out of my stomach and covering it with gauze. We had expected it to be another surgery in which they would stitch the opening after removal. It turned out to be like the trach tube removal. They said my body would close the hole on its own. I would just have to clean and change the gauze every day. My mother's face showed how worried she was, so the doctor asked her to step out while nurses came in to remove the tube. My dad stayed with me and held my right hand as they got me ready.

They cleaned the area, and I asked the doctor, "How much is this going to hurt?" She smiled. "It's a pretty quick procedure, and it hurts only at first," she said. "Almost everyone who has had one removed says it feels like a bee sting." I'm not sure if she said that just to make me feel better and not get anxious, but it did the trick. I let the nurses do their job and just held on tight to my dad's hand. The nurse pulling the tube out asked me if I was ready. I tried to smile as I nodded. She said it would only hurt slightly but to try and hold still. Man, did they lie. That shit hurt so bad as it was coming out. They don't just yank it out, so it feels like an eternity as they try to pull and wiggle it out. There was a little bumper at the end that prevented the tube from slipping out, so she had to really tug on it to get it through the small opening. As it moved through the muscle, fat, and skin, it felt like it was ripping me open. I didn't yell or scream but rather just held my breath the entire time. My eyes were getting red, and tears started rolling down my cheek. As she finished the last pull to get it past the skin, I squeezed my dad's hand and just let out a whimper. She told me I did a great job and asked me if I needed anything as she started placing gauze on the opening. I didn't even answer because my body was in shock. She understood and just told me to take a minute to let the pain subside. I don't know why it felt so painful, and again, maybe it had something to do with my brain injury, but I don't fully know. All I know is there are two events, apart from the accident itself, in which my brain blocked from remembering how the pain felt. These two events are the stenosis removal from the trach tube and the feeding tube removal. One thing the doctor was right about was that the pain would quickly subside, and thankfully, it did.

We walked back to the car happy nothing was sticking out of my body anymore. I was scared, however, to consume anything; I thought it might come out of the opening in my stomach, but the doctor said that wouldn't happen. My mom made some chicken soup when we got home, and I hesitantly drank it. We noticed nothing came out from the feeding tube opening, so it gave my mom the green light to keep cooking and making more nutrient-packed food for me. The feeding tube had been a hassle for me. I'd had to tuck it into my pants so it wouldn't dangle and get caught on something. Sometimes it would retain liquid, which my parents had to rinse out, and it did not smell pleasant. I now had a hole where the tube used to be, but I was content and hopeful it would close on its own as the doctor said.

The first week of May rolled around and my dad took us back to Macon for a follow-up appointment with the doctors who had first seen me at Navicent hospital. The first doctor I saw was Dr. Daniel Chan, who had overseen my left leg. He had placed the titanium rod in my femur and was the reason I hadn't lost my leg. Dr. Chan was excited to see me and taken aback by how I looked now compared to how he had first seen me. They did X-rays, and my mom asked him how long it would take for my leg to heal completely. He showed us the X-rays to answer my mom's questions and said the bone was growing back but it was still only 65 percent healed. "You will have to give it time and continue with therapy to keep the leg improving," he said. My next question was regarding my torn PCL and what could be done about it. He said I should focus first on regaining the strength on my leg, and once the bone had fully healed, we could talk about options for my PCL. "If it's really bothering you that much, I can prescribe a brace you can wear that will give you a little more stability, especially during therapy," he said. I was a very athletic person before the accident, so I knew I wanted my PCL fixed when the time came. He prescribed me the brace and we left his clinic.

My next appointment was close by with a neurosurgeon, Dr. Igor DeCastro. They did some scans and imaging on my brain before the doctor came to see me. He was grinning as he came into my room and had the scans in his hand to go over them with my mother and me. "You had quite an impact on your head," he said, "but it looks like your brain is healing well, and your body will continue to absorb the small amount of blood that is still around the brain." That was the best news my mother could have received. I had to ask about the migraines I kept having every day. "That is normal and to be expected after the massive impact your head received," he said. He showed me the brain scan, and there was a dark outline around the frontal part of my brain. "That is blood from where your brain was hemorrhaging," he said. "You will continue getting those headaches until that goes away, but don't worry because your body will continue to absorb it and help alleviate those headaches. In time, you'll be back to normal, and the headaches will have gone away." Hearing that gave me some peace of mind that at least I wouldn't have to be taking children's Tylenol and Motrin for the rest of my life.

We were about to leave his office when my mother asked him, "When do you need to see us again, Dr. DeCastro?" He smiled at her and said my brain was healing well. There was no need to make another appointment because now we just had to let time do the healing. As crazy as it sounded, he was completely right. With time, I noticed my migraines occurring less frequently, and the number of times I took medicine started diminishing. Now I never get headaches. I've gone months without taking one dose of Tylenol/Motrin, and I'm happy I don't have to depend on any medication to function properly.

It was the first week of May, and we had to leave Dr. DeCastro's clinic for Richmond Hill because Heather's graduation was that weekend. It was my first time going back to my parents' house since the accident. I had been driving to Statesboro that awful day, to see Heather, but the plan had always been to head toward Richmond Hill afterward to see my family. My dad hugged me before we got in the car and told me, "That day, you never got to finish your trip to go see Heather, but look at you now. You are finishing that trip today." I thanked them both for never giving up on me. We had all persevered. I hadn't given up the fight, and they hadn't given up on me. And my dad was right. I was about to finish the trip I had once started.

CHAPTER 8

Promises Kept

EVERYTHING SEEMED BRAND NEW ON THE WAY HOME despite my having driven the roads many times before. It was a shock to my memory, and I quickly began to recall everything: the many road trips, where each exit led, where my usual eating spots were, etc. I was eager to go everywhere again and explore, but then I remembered my reality. These were not my memories. I mean, they were, but they seemed so distant, like they belonged to someone else. As we reached the house, I started reminiscing on past days. We had a nice yard, but on the side close to the garage, the grass would barely grow. This was due to my dad playing soccer with my sister and me after work. We basically destroyed that part of the yard, but the memories were worth it. What I wouldn't give to be playing with my dad in that yard again! Now the grass had grown where we used to play. It was all evidence of change. My dogs, Chispita and Canela, came running as I opened the car door. They stopped suddenly before reaching me and tilted their heads. They didn't recognize me and didn't lick me like they normally did. I lowered my head. Everything in my life was different. I tried talking to my dogs so they'd come closer, hoping they'd at least recognize my voice. Eventually they did, and I reached out to pet them. "Sorry I left you guys," I said. "I'm home now."

I took some time to walk with my mom around the yard and across the bridge overlooking the marsh before going inside the house. There was a newfound beauty I noticed, born from almost not being able to see it again. We went into the house, and I headed straight to where my room used to be. My parents had organized it and had it ready for me. They thought I would be coming home to live with them after being discharged from Shepherd Center, but Carolina made sure I had all my bills up to date so I wouldn't lose my apartment. I'm glad she convinced my parents to let me stay in Atlanta. Not only were all my appointments there, but I wanted to hold on to at least a fragment of the independence I once had. Regardless, it felt nice to be home once again.

My dad would come down every other weekend to check on the animals, but for my parents the house had stopped feeling like home for a long time. For my mom, home was where her husband and children were. The hospital had been our home for months, so there was a lot to organize and clean. I asked if they needed any help or if there was anything I could to assist them with. They just told me to sit on the couch and start thinking of what I wanted to write in Heather's graduation card. Writing on the dry erase board was a lot easier than writing with pen and paper. I was concentrating very hard on my left hand because I wanted it to be legible. After fifteen minutes, I was able to write one sentence, but my hand began to cramp. I felt frustrated and grabbed my right hand to write with it instead. My left hand had to keep guiding it, but after a few minutes, it got a little easier. I decided to finish writing with my right hand, disregarding the neatness of my penmanship. Every few minutes, I would take a break, but by the time my parents were done organizing the guest room, I was able to show them what I'd done. I had written everything with my right hand. At the very top, I wrote "Sorry for the crappy handwriting, but I wanted to personally write to you." I made sure to give it my best effort. It was for Heather after all.

It was May 5, and I woke up early with my parents to hit the road for Heather's graduation. Once on campus, I felt the same feeling I did when I saw the house. I started reminiscing about my time at Georgia Southern and all the good memories started coming back to me. We parked at the Recreation Activity Center (RAC), which is where I'd spent most of my free time in college. It's where I would work out every day. The intramural sport fields that had once seen me run through them were also there, beckoning me to relive those moments. I wondered what would be going through the gym's mind if it were an actual person. When I left, I was in incredible shape, weighing about 155 lbs. Now, I was face to face with that gym once again but a completely different person. I was literally broken, walking with great difficulty, and half the size I used to be, weighing only 128 lbs. After a few moments, I realized we were still one mile away from the football stadium where the graduation would take place.

The parking lot was full of families trying to get to the stadium early. There were campus buses shuttling people to and from the stadium. We were running close to the time the ceremony would start, and I saw the line of people waiting for the bus. I told my parents we would just walk to the stadium because I was not going to wait for the bus and be late. Thankfully, I remembered the way, but before we started walking, my mom asked me, "Are you sure you can walk this? We can just wait. If not, your dad can carry you when you get tired." I hadn't walked more than a quarter mile since the accident, but it didn't matter because I was not going to be late to Heather's graduation. I also didn't want to get on the bus for fear of running into someone who knew me and having to explain why I looked different.

We agreed to walk. Halfway there, we stopped so I could catch my breath and let the other families pass us. It was hot with the sun beating down on us, and every step I took required a lot of effort. When we finally made it to the stadium, the place was packed. I wanted to sit down, but the only available seating was in the top deck of the stadium. My mom told me we could just stand there on the little hill overlooking the stage and wait until Heather's name was called. I didn't feel like walking anymore, so I agreed.

Alicia and Cesar at Heather's graduation

They eventually called Heather's name, and she walked onstage with the dress and wedges I had bought her. No one could see the dress because it was all covered by the graduation gown, but I was happy I had contributed in some way to her big day. I tried cheering for her but couldn't; it hurt, so I tried clapping for her, but to no avail. My right arm was immobile, so I did the only thing I could think of to show my support. I just shook my left hand in the air. Once Heather returned to her seat, my mother asked my dad to get the car and meet us up front to avoid having me walk all the way back. Their goal was to get me out of the stadium before the ceremony finished and hordes of people started leaving. Once in the car, I thanked them again for making this happen. They knew how much it meant to me that they brought me back to Georgia Southern to see my girlfriend graduate.

We drove to Heather's place on campus and waited for her and her parents. After forty-five minutes, we saw her parents rounding the corner. The ceremony was finished, but Heather was still in the stadium, taking pictures with her friends. My parents got a chance to talk with Heather's parents and her older sister who had flown into town for graduation. Heather's dad, whom I'll refer to as Tito from here on out, asked my parents how my recovery was going. "No one would believe you went through something so horrible just from looking at you," he told me. "You look great, man." Tito spoke more Spanish than English, so all the conversations my parents had with Heather's parents were in Spanish. Though Heather could understand most of the Spanish she heard, she wasn't fluent in it. She finally reached her apartment, and we took turns hugging and congratulating her. I was last and gave her a kiss as well as the card I wrote in for her. To be at her graduation, despite everything that had happened, was nothing short of a miracle. While Alicia took pictures of Heather and me, my parents stepped aside with her parents to discuss a few things.

Tito told my parents they were all going to Panama City as a celebratory trip for Heather. "Cesar should definitely come with us," he said. "My wife and I will make sure he is well taken care of. I think it would be amazing to have him with us." Heather had mentioned the plan was to head to Florida after graduation, but I hadn't discussed it with my parents. It had slipped my mind, and I didn't think my parents would ever agree to it. We'd be gone for several days, and I knew that would be hard on my mother. The cat was out of the bag, and they knew what the plan was now. My mom and dad knew that out of Heather's entire family, Tito genuinely cared about me and my recovery. They knew if he was going, he would be responsible and make sure I was taken care of. I had already made up my mind awhile back that I was going but just hadn't spoken to my parents about it. After we took all the pictures, I limped over and joined the conversation with Heather.

It hadn't been long since the feeding tube was removed. The hole was almost closed, but I didn't want to contract some bacteria through the slight opening, so I told my mom I wouldn't get in the water at Panama City. Heather's mom, whom I'll call Bertha, spoke to my mom and said, "Let him go. Heather just graduated, and they deserve to have fun. Tito and I will take good care of him." If there is something you should know about my mom, it's that she hates when anyone intervenes and tells her what she should do with regard to her children.

Once Bertha finished talking to my mom, I interrupted before my mom had a chance to respond because I knew she was starting to get upset. I told her I was going, and my mom and I would pack everything I needed. My mom agreed, and it was settled. I was going to Panama City with Heather's family. It would not be until later I discovered it had been Tito's idea to have me go with them. He thought it would be a great way for me and his daughter to make new memories and have a nice change of scenery. My accident had affected everyone close to me in one way or another, but only some people were deeply affected emotionally. I consider Tito as someone who fits in that category, and he spent many days telling my mother and me this. He saw how my life had been turned upside down, and yet the determination and resilience I showed really touched him. It was the effect I wanted to have on Heather, but her immaturity, as reiterated by her dad, did not allow her to grasp the magnitude of everything that had happened to me. At that moment I didn't care. I had an opportunity to make new memories with Heather, and that was enough to keep me on the right path toward my recovery. We all parted ways, and as I rode with my parents, I had to listen to everything I could and couldn't do while in Florida. My mom reiterated all the stuff I was aware of, but I just listened and let her talk. My mission had been accomplished; she had agreed to let me go to Panama City.

It seemed as if everything was happening on the same day. Despite everything going on, my parents made time to meet Alicia's boyfriend, Greg, who was visiting from California. Nobody knew what the future held for anyone anymore, but Alicia did her best to continue living her life. For my parents and Carolina, life had abruptly stopped and hadn't picked up again. Alicia was somehow trying to hold on to some fragment of normalcy, despite everything that had happened. I never knew how the first meeting with my parents went for them because I was on my way to Panama City. The trip took almost seven hours, and during most of the car ride, I carried Heather's head on my shoulder while she slept. I wanted to sleep too, but unfortunately, my mind would not shut off. On the drive down, I spoke with her parents and thanked them for letting me join. We made it to our destination, and I barely had time to use the restroom before Heather started telling me she wanted a margarita, so she wanted me to hurry up. Alcohol consumption is known to impair brain injury recovery. They told me this at Shepherd and Pathways, so I knew not to consume any. Thankfully, I had never actually craved alcohol. I had always been more focused on my fitness, so it was easy for me to reject a drink. Heather, on the other hand, was constantly craving alcohol.

Before the accident, I often took her out and bought her drinks at the bar or club we went to. My parents don't drink, but ever since the accident, they abhor alcohol even more, and I don't blame them. They had seen first-hand what a drunken idiot did to their son. I felt the same disgust toward alcohol when I realized my life had been ruined by an irresponsible individual unable to control himself. Heather kept hurrying me so she could get her margarita. We made it to a beach bar with her parents, and she told me to get a drink with her. "I love it when you drink with me," she said. "You're a grown man, so get a drink! I promise no one will say anything if you do." I had explained to her before leaving the house why I wasn't going to drink, and I thought she'd understand. Instead, she got upset. But I still didn't get a drink. My goal was true and constant; I wanted to get better for us. If she wanted to have fun and take more trips with me, I knew I had to get better. Only later would I realize I was never truly a part of that equation. Regardless, I held my ground and didn't let anything steer me away from my goal. It's a little ironic when I think about it today. I would've done anything for her so long as it all led to a life together, but she was stunting that dream's growth by asking me to drink and impeding my recovery.

We left the bar and headed back to the beach house. I tried talking to her about my brain injury when we were alone in our room. "Everything I am doing is with you in mind. I need to get better so I can give you the life I promised," I said. "I didn't ask for any of this, but I am going to get better for us." She said she understood. My brain injury played a crucial role in this, and to be honest, I'm glad I didn't question her answer then. In hindsight, perhaps if I had, things would have ended a lot sooner than they did. This would ultimately prove to be a blessing, but she was my reason for sticking around in this world a little longer, and at the time, I don't think my brain and heart were in the best shape to handle another loss. As long as I kept my eye on the goal, I knew I would eventually get there. It just so happened my goal was getting further and further away as the reality I tried holding onto—a future with Heather—did not exist.

I took that time to also tell her she could move into my apartment if she still wanted to. Heather told me she hated living with her parents because she never got along with her dad or sister. "My dad never lets me do anything, plus I don't want to be around them all the time and hear everyone fighting," she said. She didn't say anything about wanting to help me with my therapy, but she said she wanted to move in, so I didn't care. The next two days went by quickly. We went on a boat tour with her family, and for a moment, I felt alive again being there with Heather and capturing new memories with her. The next day, we drove back to Atlanta.

We reached Macon and reunited with my parents at Chick-fil-A. Everyone talked for a bit, and I thanked Heather's parents again for taking me with them to Panama City. I gave Heather a kiss and told her she could move in whenever she wanted. My parents and I left shortly after, and my mom asked me how I felt during the trip. "Everything went well. We even went on a boat, and I didn't feel dizzy or lightheaded," I said. I didn't bring up the issues Heather and I had about drinking but instead told her she'd be moving into the apartment with us. My mom stopped talking, and my dad put his hand on hers as if to let her know everything would be okay. I know my mom's head was racing, wondering how four people would fit in a one-bedroom apartment. My mom and dad were already sleeping on an inflatable mattress, and Carolina would take the couch on nights she stayed over to help.

We reached my apartment and sat down to discuss a few things. My mom mentioned the promise she made to me in the hospital. "I promised you I wouldn't leave your side until you were 100 percent better. Your dad will eventually have to go back to work, but I've already told him I'm staying here with you," she said.

I didn't want her to go. "I'll talk with Heather and make sure she understands you'll be living with me until I fully recover," I said. She didn't tell me this at the time, but once my brain healed, she told me she also stayed for Heather's safety.

"No one knew how you would react to certain things, and Heather never understood or cared about the fact that you had a severe brain injury," she said. "The last thing we wanted was for you to be aggressive toward her or hurt her hand like you did to us. We are your family and we would go through anything for you, but that's because we love you. We never felt that from Heather, so I stuck around to make sure she would never be able to say you did anything hurtful to her." I can't thank my mom enough for having gone through so much hell with me.

When I called Heather that night, I told her I was getting a bigger apartment for us and that my mom would be staying with me too since I still needed a lot of help. I half expected her to say, "Don't worry, baby, we will both be there to help you with anything you need, and I can help you with your therapy." But what she actually said was "Okay, but she will leave after your surgeries are finished, right? You're a grown man, and I don't think you should have to live with your mom forever." It hurt me to hear her say that. I knew my mom was staying because she loved me. She would have never dreamt of leaving me at a time when I needed help the most. My parents had sacrificed everything to see me alive and on the road to recovery. There were still many procedures I was unaware I had to go through before reclaiming my life. I did not want to have to choose between my mom and my girlfriend, so I agreed with Heather. "Yeah, she will only be here until my surgeries are finished," I said. "Afterwards, you and I can decide where we want to live." I wanted Heather to move in with me because being with her made me forget my pain, and in those moments, I felt like nothing I had lost mattered because I still had her. As corny as it sounds, it was the truth.

That same week, I started looking at different floor plans available at my complex that were affordable but would also give Heather more space for her things. To say I picked the apartment thinking about my mother, and making sure she had enough space, would be a lie. I strictly picked the apartment with Heather's needs in mind, disregarding anyone else's, even my own. My mom understood my brain injury better than anyone and knew my recovery would be a long process. Rather than tell me it wasn't a good idea for Heather to move in, she sat down and started looking at floor plans with me. She treated me with love and heard my opinion whether it was crazy or not. All she said was "Will Heather be splitting the rent with you? Because you are not working, and despite the money you have in the bank, it will soon be gone with all the medical bills."

"I promised Heather she could move in with me. I was going to take care of her, but I wasn't expecting any of this to happen," I said, pointing to my body. "It really sucks, but I'm trying to prove to her that I do love her, and I never lied." That was all my mom needed to hear to understand I had made up my mind a while ago and there was no turning back. She knew I couldn't see a lot of the things everyone else saw. There was nothing anyone could do to help my brain injury but just let it run its course and hope it healed in a timely manner.

She knew I had lost every aspect of the independence I once had, so the last thing she wanted to do was take away the ability to make my own decisions. It was the only thing I had left, and she made sure to protect it. My mom had told my sisters and my dad that the money from my uninsured motorist vehicle policy was mine to spend how I wanted. I spent most of my money on Heather, and no one stopped me. When I spent a lot of money on Heather's dress and shoes for graduation, nobody said a thing. The best thing they could do was allow me to make my own decisions rather than to tell me "Don't do this or don't do that." I wasn't there, with all the knowledge I have now, to tell my family how best to deal with my brain injury. Yet my mother knew exactly what to do to ensure the best possible outcome for me. Even my sisters and dad had their doubts about my mom's methodology of letting me spend my money how I wanted, considering the financial storm we were in. Money never mattered to her. She would have given anything to prevent any of this from happening to me. It didn't matter to her that she was going to live with my girlfriend and me but have no room of her own. She left her house in Richmond Hill to be with me and didn't care if she had to sleep on the couch for the next year or however long it took. A mother's promise to her son cannot easily be broken. She never left me during the toughest battle of my life.

We agreed on a larger apartment, and I picked the one with the largest closet, big enough for all of Heather's stuff. The rent would increase quite a bit, but I figured it was worth it for the chance to start new memories with Heather someplace new. Despite the abundant closet space, Heather would still need her own dresser because mine wasn't big enough for both of us. Everything I had in my apartment was definitely not made for a couple. My next thought was, *What if I just buy all new furniture for the new apartment and make Heather more excited to move in?* I started looking at new furniture online and even went with my dad to Rooms to Go. I started pointing to the furniture I wanted. Looking back on that day and remembering my dad's facial expressions, I know he didn't think it was a good idea. He wanted to say something, but he never did.

I called Heather and asked her if she wanted to go with me to Rooms to Go and pick out furniture in the colors and style she liked. She said she would go with me to help but never did. It was obvious to her she could do no wrong in my eyes. Even if she didn't go with me and offered no help, she knew I would get it done for her. My dad and I picked out all the furniture. I spent over four thousand dollars on a bed frame, dresser, nightstands, and recliner couch. It may not sound like much, but I had no business buying four thousand dollars worth of furniture when I had hundreds of thousands in medical bills piling up. My mother always taught me to keep receipts and keep everything well documented should I ever need them. I listened and kept receipts of everything, including all the medical bills that were beginning to accumulate. If only my brain injury had healed sooner, I might've saved that money for the difficult times ahead. I left the store feeling excited that my new apartment would look great for Heather.

She would come to my place on weekends and slowly started bringing gym bags and suitcases filled with her belongings. One of those days, she told me a friend of hers was coming down from Philadelphia. "Can we please go and have dinner with him? It'd be cool if you guys met," she said. My confidence was long gone and I was uncomfortable being around anyone because of my physical appearance. I would have preferred not to go but I couldn't say no to her. She had spoken to me about him before my accident and we had planned to meet whenever he was next in town. I never got the chance. He would now only meet a fragment of the man I once was, or at least it's how I felt. There was no jealousy or distrust from my end. Ever since the incident at the hospital, I vowed to never again question Heather. I had not gotten in a car with her yet. Heather had a tendency to drive a little erratically. Thankfully the place where we were going wasn't far, but I was still nervous. Regardless, I agreed to go. The uneasy discomfort I felt stemmed from self-consciousness so I told her, "Please just let your friend know, if you haven't already, that I was in a very bad car accident." She said she had told him.

I asked for her help in getting ready. "Can't you ask your mom for help? Because I need to get ready too," she said. That should have been a red flag, but I didn't see it like that. Instead, I asked my mom to help me change and tie my shoes. Heather's car was a coupe, and it was hard getting inside since it was so low to the ground and my legs were still very weak. She got in the car and completely forgot I needed help getting in. She just sat in the driver's seat, texting. As we left, I could see the look in my mother's eyes. Back then it meant nothing to me, but now as I see it in hindsight, I know she was worried about my future with Heather.

It was my first time being on the road alone with her. Normally I was the one who drove when we went somewhere, and she would just sit without saying much or sleep on the passenger's side. How things had changed. When we finally parked, I took a moment to apologize to Heather for everything that had happened. I told her I was sorry for how the accident had affected our future. I was sorry I couldn't do everything I did before. I was sorry if this had taken a toll on her . . . on us. Even though none of it was my fault, and it wasn't what I had expected for 2018, I apologized. Life had really thrown me a curveball, and I was trying to do the best I could with what I had. Regardless of how things were at the moment, I promised her it was only temporary. I would get better and I'd make up for the time lost in which we didn't live the life I once promised. She just nodded as she touched my cheek and then asked me to help her find her friend. No matter what, I had said what was weighing on my mind.

Getting out of the car was more difficult than getting in. I couldn't open the door with my right hand, and I couldn't push off with my left leg to get out. For several minutes, I struggled while Heather texted her friend to see where he was. I left my cane because I didn't want to look weak in front of her friends even though I still needed it. We took a few steps, and I asked Heather to give me her hand as we made it down the sidewalk. My balance was still not great, and I feared falling. She hesitantly let me hold on to her while we walked down.

After finally locating her friend, we agreed to meet at the entrance of the restaurant. He was tall and young. As we walked towards where he was, I stopped holding onto Heather and put my right hand in my pocket so it wasn't dangling from my shoulder. Every step I took from that moment until we reached him took every bit of concentration and my mind was racing. It kept trying to picture me from his point of view. I could see myself hobbling down the street behind Heather with only one arm moving, and what a sad sight that was to me. We reached him and I pulled my right hand out of my pocket with my left arm and shook his hand. Heather introduced us and the waiter took us to a table. One of my bottom teeth was broken in half and had the nerve exposed. Any time food went past that tooth, whether it was solid or liquid, the pain was unbearable. I would writhe in pain for several minutes while my whole head throbbed. I wasn't going to eat much at the restaurant because I didn't want to run the risk of feeling the pain again. The waiter gave all of us a menu, but I couldn't hold it open. As I've mentioned before, I've never been one to ask anyone for help because I've always considered myself an independent guy. There, sitting at the table, I came to the realization that my independent days were over and I needed to lose the pride of not asking for help. It took all my effort to ask Heather for help in finding something to eat. She and her friend continued to catch up when they brought the food. I would chime in again, here and there but I was more focused on eating and making sure I didn't choke. Suddenly I started getting a headache that worsened by the minute. I told Heather we needed to go home soon because my medicine was there. "But babe," she whispered to me, "is it that bad that you really need your medicine?" If only she understood how bad those headaches were, she would have never asked. It felt like my head was about to explode every time. My pain tolerance was high, but I couldn't stand the headaches, and they made me feel dizzy.

When the waiter came around, I asked him for a to-go container so I could take my food home in case my mother wanted to try it. Heather did the same after she saw my headache getting worse. The waiter brought us one of those containers where the foil wraps around the cover, but you have to press it all along the edges. Once he set the containers down, I realized the obstacle in front of me. There was no way I could put my food in the container because I would have to lift the plate and scrape the food off of it with the other hand. It was either ask my girlfriend or ask her friend for help. In my mind, if I asked Heather for help and her friend heard, he would probably think me completely useless; I couldn't even pack my own to-go container. This was foolish of me at the time, but it's how my emotions were making me think. I was shaking, knowing asking Heather was my only choice. Though she couldn't fully speak it, she understood Spanish, so I asked her in Spanish, knowing her friend wouldn't understand. "Hey babe, me puedes ayudar a meter la comida? No lo puedo hacer," I told her. This translates to "Hey babe, can you help me put my food in? I can't do it."

I'm certain she heard me, but she pretended she hadn't and continued talking to her friend about her college days. Everyone had already put their food in the container except me, so rather than go through the embarrassment of asking Heather for help again, I decided to try and do it myself with just one hand. I tried lifting the plate with my left hand and then pouring it into the container. Because I couldn't use my other hand to scrape the food into the bowl, food started falling on the table and onto the floor. Only then did Heather move to help. "Babe, you put the food into the plate, not onto the table," she said, laughing. That was the first time I really got upset with her. She had heard me ask for help in Spanish but had chosen not to and then joked about me dropping food on the table. I was extremely embarrassed. I had to rely on the help of others, in this case Heather, who had completely ignored me. The world could've swallowed me whole that day, and I wouldn't have cared. I felt like the dried-up husk of the man I used to be.

Driving back to my apartment, Heather kept asking me why I was upset. She already knew. I stayed silent the entire drive and just looked out the window, wondering when my life would change. When she parked the car, I told her, "I can't go anywhere with you like this if you're never going to help me. I wish I didn't have to ask for help but look at me! I can't even tie my own shoe." I stopped talking because I had to concentrate on my breathing. Crying consumed a lot of energy, and the mucus was starting to clog my nostrils as I frantically wiped away the tears. We walked into the apartment, and my mom was there waiting. She immediately got up to see what was wrong when she saw the tears in my eyes. "What happened?!" she asked us. I just waved my hand as if to indicate it wasn't important and walked back to my room. My mom asked Heather why I was crying, and she stayed to explain. I could hear them from my room. After Heather explained what happened, I heard my mom say, "That's why I don't really think it's a good idea for him to go out and be with other people . . . at least not right now. His brain is still healing, and his emotions are all over the place. He needs help with a lot of things, so just be patient with him if you actually love him. It won't be like this forever." Heather didn't say anything after that, at least nothing I could hear. She must have silently nodded, or at least I hoped she did. My mom ended the conversation by telling her to look how far I had come in such a short amount of time. "There's nothing you both won't be able to do if you see this through together," she said.

I was able to talk with my mom afterward when Heather left. "I hate having to ask for help," I said. "It shouldn't be like this. I didn't deserve this, and I don't know why I'm having to go through it." My mom hugged me and told me I was right.

"You didn't deserve this, it's true," she said, "and it's why I'm in a constant struggle with my faith because it's not fair this would happen to you, to us.

But look how far you've come." She showed me photos of my time in the hospital that I hadn't seen before. My mom couldn't look at the images because it still affected her deeply, but she let me see some of them. "There are many more pictures and videos your sisters have," she said, "but just look at where you were and where you are now. Whether God exists or not, you're here with us still, and that's all that matters." I thanked her for never leaving me. "You never have to worry about that," she continued. "If you needed an organ transplant, I would give you mine without thinking twice. You and your sisters are my greatest treasure."

I wasn't upset anymore but rather deeply saddened after seeing the images, which kept replaying in my head. I didn't recognize the person in them. My eyes looked dazed and confused. My heart ached for that person, and even though it was me, I didn't feel like it was. There was a specific photo I couldn't get out of my head, and it was one in which I was looking straight at the camera. When I got to it, I felt like the picture was looking directly into my eyes and asking me, "Why? How could you let this happen to me?"

That's when I realized it: I was alive, but I didn't feel like myself. As I mentioned before, I coded several times. The paramedics were able to bring me back each time I coded, but parts of who I was still perished. I felt like the Cesar I saw in the photos had saved me, but at what cost? He had sacrificed himself to give me a fighting chance, and it broke me to think I wasn't able to protect him. The Cesar I was before the accident had given me so much and had helped me get to where I wanted to be. Now he was like a newborn baby, scared of the world and all the pain out there. He had been driving my life up to this point, and now it was my turn to take the wheel and take care of whatever was left of him like he had done for me. I started to cry. Perhaps he was fading away, but maybe he was still in there, just not ready to face the world yet.

When I was alone in my room, I closed my eyes and tapped my chest. I whispered, "I'm sorry, man. Thank you. I love you, and I won't let anything or anyone else hurt us again. I promise." If the old Cesar was still in there somewhere, I know he heard me. I meant it wholeheartedly and I knew I had to take care of myself because in turn I was taking care of him, and I owed him as much. I didn't tell my mom any of this until months later because it was hard trying to describe the feeling. No one could understand how I felt unless they had experienced it. I didn't want anyone to think I was bipolar or had multiple personalities because it wasn't that. My life as Cesar before the accident had ended, and a new one had started post-accident. I was a new person altogether in how I thought, acted, and behaved. I decided not to look at those photos or any pictures of me from before the accident for a while. No one in my family could look at them either because the emotions were still too raw. We all still needed time to heal.

The days blurred together, and every day felt like a repetition of the previous one. The only difference between the days was the doctors or therapists I saw. I didn't leave the apartment complex. After coming home from appointments, I would start doing the therapy for my arm, legs, and mouth. This is what my life consisted of now. I tried not to go out or be around people because I was self-conscious about how I looked, and I didn't want to have to explain to anyone what I'd been through.

Surviving the accident was only half the battle. The uphill climb was all resting on my shoulders. It would be a long and tiresome journey, but if I had gotten myself to where I was before, on my own, then there was no reason I couldn't do it again. Would it be easy? Hell no. Would it hurt? Damn right. Would it be quick? Oh God, no.

Coming to terms with that was the hardest part. I've never been the most patient person. All my life I've looked for ways to make things happen the quickest and most efficient way possible. This is one of the reasons I never liked asking anyone for help with anything because I believed it would take longer than if I did it myself. That's how I managed to develop a lot of my talents. I figured this was not only the fastest way but also the most efficient way in getting things done. I was in a completely different situation now. There was no way to make this recovery process go by quicker. Aside from consistently doing my therapeutic exercises, there was nothing else I could do. I had to let time do most of the healing, and it was hard to accept. No matter how much I hated it, though, I just kept watching the days go by, hoping the healing process was going down the right path. This started the beginning of one of the most difficult stages of my journey: the path to acceptance. It didn't happen overnight, but like everything else I was going through, I ate the proverbial elephant one bite at a time. I just kept putting one foot in front of the other, day after day.

CHAPTER 9

When It Rains It Pours

HERE IS TRUTH IN THE ADAGE THAT WHEN IT RAINS, it pours. It definitely didn't make my path to acceptance any easier when it felt like things just kept piling on top of each other. At some point after Heather's graduation, I received an email from COX's HR department saying that the sports verticals branch (the one I worked at) was being terminated. I read it over several times because I couldn't believe my luck. I had left the hospital only two months earlier and had a substantial number of procedures still pending. How was I going to get the care I needed without my work benefits? My mom said if push came to shove, my dad would cover me with his insurance; I could still make the cutoff because I was only twenty-five. I was saddened to think I wouldn't see my coworkers again. We had become family over the previous sports season. I loved my job. I had found a place where I felt I belonged and could contribute all my great ideas. That was one of the last straws that made everything unbearable. Even if I were cleared to go back to work, there was no work to go back to.

I panicked and started submitting my resume to every company I could find in which I would be a good fit. I spent the following days at my computer, filling out applications. One day, I suddenly stopped when I saw my reflection on the screen. *Even if someone gave you an interview, who would hire you looking like this, man?* I thought. *You can't drive, let alone move your right arm, so who is really going to hire you when you limp into an interview?* I stopped applying that day and hopelessness weighed heavy on me. Nothing was going my way. I spent the next few days looking back at my life, trying to determine what horrible thing I had ever done to deserve any of this, but I came up with nothing. If there was at least an explanation, it might've been easier to accept, but there wasn't. I emailed the HR person in charge and told him my situation. I asked him what I could do to retain my healthcare benefits. It was all I could do at that time. I sent the email and waited to hear back.

My coworkers had heard a summarized version of my accident, but I knew I'd have to learn how to tell my story without reliving the pain each time. It was tough; I'm not going to lie. At first, my emotions were still too raw, and I would break down or start crying every time I would try to tell my story. Only once my brain started healing did my emotions start getting back to normal and I could tell it from beginning to end without shedding a tear. It took long nights talking with my mom to learn how to control my emotions again. She was my therapist, nurse, and psychologist all in one, but to put it in the simplest of terms, she was just being my mom.

I found it hard to sleep because my mind never shut off. Images kept replaying in my head and I'd have nightmares of the accident. I didn't remember it, but at night my mind would recreate the sequence of events and I'd witness it all as a bystander. Not only would I experience it firsthand, but I'd also see it from a third-person point of view. It was weird and disturbing. Nightmares also kept my mom awake at night. She would hear me crying and meet me at the door with tissues as I came out of my room. She asked me if Heather was asleep or if she had talked with me about why I was crying. I shook my head no. I can remember the way she looked at me. She was concerned about what the future held for me if I stayed with Heather. Back then, though, all I saw was a tired face wishing for past days.

My mom did what I had hoped Heather would do. She asked me what was wrong. I tried talking to Heather many times, explaining what I needed from her in our relationship. She was my number one priority, and I treated her as such. If ever she needed anything, she never had to ask because I was always there before she had to. To me that was the entire premise of a relationship. My needs and wants came secondary to hers because in the end, I just wanted her to be happy. She knew she could count on me for any type of support and care; I just wanted the same from her. The many times I talked about this with her and the many arguments we later had about it ultimately didn't make a difference. I explained my nightmares to my mom. "I just can't shut my mind off," I said. "I should have never left that day. I don't have a job anymore, so what if I lose my healthcare benefits? I have so much that needs to be done."

It's crazy how one action can change your life forever. If I had left the next day or even a few minutes later, I wouldn't be telling you this story. Every action you take in life has a consequence, and this is one of many key points you should take from this. The drunk driver that hit me made his choice and caused a horrible sequence of events that not only affected his life, but everyone involved and their families. It was my decision to leave Atlanta that day to go see my girlfriend. My mom told me to stay home because she feared there'd be drunk people on the road due to the long weekend, but I decided not to follow her advice. These were all decisions that could have changed the lives of many people if we had made different choices. Obviously, there's a difference between the severity of the consequences, but it just goes to show that no matter what decisions you make, they will have consequences. Whether they are good or bad consequences is up to you and the choice you make.

I was twenty-five and I felt like a baby again. I needed help brushing my teeth, changing my clothes, going to the restroom, and eating. There were many nights I would wake up and walk out of my room to talk with my mom. I would lie down on the air mattress or couch she was sleeping on and just talk while the tears kept flowing. "If you need to cry, just let it out, Cesar. Don't feel like you have to be strong all the time," she would tell me. My mom, battling her own demons, would find some peace in seeing me slowly start to accept what had happened. Maybe it sounds weird that a grown man would fall asleep next to his mom like an infant again, but that's how I felt. The world was a cruel place, and nothing made me feel more loved or protected than my mother's embrace. I wished nothing more than to feel love and affection from the person I loved more than anything (Heather), but that was all it ever turned out to be . . . wishful thinking.

I had bought everything for Heather to feel comfortable at our new apartment. I didn't want her to worry about anything. All I wanted in return was for her to care. Before we moved into the new apartment, she told me her mom was giving her eight hundred dollars a month since she wasn't working or in school yet. It blew my family's mind that she never even offered to help with any of the bills. None of them ever asked her to because they didn't feel it was their right to do so, seeing as she was my girlfriend and it was my apartment. The decision was mine to have her live with me, so the responsibility of asking her to help fell on me. In the beginning, I was completely against it because it had always been my plan to take care of everything and give Heather a good life. That dream was shattered, and I was in a completely different situation now. Heather knew the bills I was facing—we talked about them—but never once did I hear what I would have said if we had traded places: "Let me help you." It wasn't until months later that I asked her to help with some of the bills. "If anything, at least help me pay for your phone line," I said.

I wasn't working because of my accident. "What's her excuse?" my dad asked the week we moved. I told him she had just graduated and didn't have a job lined up yet. There was a lot going through my mind at the time. Fear of losing my benefits was stressing me out, but my focus remained on making sure Heather moved in. "I don't want her to use the fact that she has to help me with bills as an excuse to not live with me," I told my dad. "I was always going to take care of her before, and my goals haven't changed with her." Still, eight hundred dollars a month could've at least helped with utilities or something. When I was attending college with my sisters, my mom would give us each twenty bucks a week and it was a major sacrifice for her, given our economic situation. We never complained. We were grateful. We had to pay for our housing off campus and all the utilities with our hard-earned money while going to school full time. Here was Heather, getting eight hundred bucks a month, with no bills or expenses, and she'd complain she didn't have enough to get her hair done. This really rubbed my sisters the wrong way, but they never let it show.

No one would make Heather feel uncomfortable because everyone knew she was what I wanted more than anything. They figured it would only push me away, so it was an unspoken rule: they'd only say good things about Heather so she'd feel comfortable living with me, with us in the apartment. No one in my family ever asked her to help; they didn't want to cause any stress for Heather that might ultimately affect my relationship with her. The last thing they wanted to do was give me a reason to say, "She left because of this," when in reality, she left because she didn't feel the same way anymore. My family knew where our relationship was headed, but all they could do was hope my brain would heal in time so I could see it too.

Carolina moved to Dunwoody and got yet another job to help me with my bills. She hated that Heather did nothing and everyone thought she was helping just because she was all I ever talked about. People assumed she had moved in with me out of love and that because she "loved" me, she was helping me. I never spoke about my private life with anyone after my accident and tried to stay away from social media so no one really knew what I was going through. I never spoke ill of Heather to anyone. On the contrary, I told all my therapists she was the best and the reason I was improving so much. In a way, I wasn't lying. She did provide me with the motivation, a goal to strive toward, but she never did more than that. I painted a picture of Heather to everyone, perhaps not a realistic one, but the one I was dying to see. I can't blame anyone but myself for this. She was my world. I wanted everyone to see her through my eyes, and my family did just that. It's crazy how foggy my mind was back then. I was out of the hospital and slowly recovering, but my mind was a mess of emotions. Things about Heather that should have been a red light for me did not register as such. The motives were there; I just couldn't see them.

When it was time to move out of my old apartment, I took time to say goodbye to a room that had seen me go through a lot. It had seen me soaring high in every aspect of my life, but it had also witnessed how far I'd fallen and how broken I'd become. My dad picked up the furniture I bought. It was a lot, but thankfully my friend Peter, his brother Steven, and my other friend Chris were visiting and helped move everything. Once everything was settled, I realized it was the start of a new chapter. I took one last look at the rooms and said goodbye to apartment 9021. I walked out of there with red eyes, my cane in my left hand, my dad's hand on my shoulder, and my mom holding my right hand.

Heather and I were about to be living together, and it was the start of our life as a couple. It was not like I had initially planned, but I was trying.

Heather's parents came over and they noticed all the new furniture I had bought. I told them, "She is all I want, so I want to make sure Heather has everything she needs."

Bertha said, "I know she will be fine here with you. We can see how much you love her. I just hope she helps you with everything." That's what everyone thought Heather would be doing: helping me. It didn't matter to me though because at the time, all I wanted was to be with her. Even Heather's parents agreed that my mom should stay because they didn't think Heather would be much help. As much as I hate to admit it, they were right. I had no idea what the future held.

To put it in perspective, I was paying over sixteen hundred dollars a month so Heather could live comfortably with me. I was not working and had no idea if I could get on Long-Term Disability. The bills kept piling up, and the bills were huge. One of them alone was over forty thousand bucks, and it wasn't the only one I received. My family tried to help the best they could with the bills, but there were just too many and not enough money to cover them all. The only money I had at that time was my uninsured motorist vehicle policy. That money was going quickly and not entirely on medical bills. I had just spent over four thousand dollars on new furniture and moved into a more expensive apartment. My sisters shook their heads at my mom and questioned why she didn't take control of my money and make sure I spent it wisely. "It's his money, and it's the only thing he has right now that makes him feel some sense of independence," my mom said. "I can't take that away from him. We have to let time heal his brain." Honestly, if I had been there with no brain injury, I would have argued with my mom and told her she was wrong. Little did I know she was the only one who knew how to handle the situation, and not because she understood the science behind my injuries but rather because she listened to her heart. Her heart had been broken just as much as my body had, and all she wanted was to see me recover. I didn't understand my mom's reasoning at the time because I was in my own little jumbled world. Now when I go back and analyze how I was feeling, what I was doing, and why I was doing it, I can finally understand how genius my mom was in her method.

You see, I was as independent as I could be before the accident, and I really thought things could only get better. On January 12 everything changed. Before, I was the guy who could do it all. At the gym, people would stop and watch me do my "crazy pull-ups" as they liked to call them. My routine involved a variation of commando pull-ups, windshield wipers, body rows, around the world pull-ups, typewrites, L-sits, and walking pull-ups. When I went out, people would always ask me about my acting career and what projects I was working on. If there was a guitar in the room, everyone would ask me to play and sing a song for them. At work I was the only one capable of doing the type of design/video elements our clients needed. Now...I couldn't get dressed or tie my shoes on my own. My parents bought some stretchy laces that would always remain tied so I could just slip the shoe on. One of my OT therapists, Jana Candia, had given my parents the idea after seeing the frustration tying my shoes caused. They made a big difference, but it still made me feel depressed knowing I had to rely on special laces to feel somewhat "normal."

After the accident, I didn't know if Heather would stick around through my recovery, seeing as so much of me had changed, but I desperately hoped she would. My acting dreams went out the window. I couldn't move my right arm, so I couldn't be a musician. There was no way I could even think of being a singer if I could barely talk. My body, which I had trained so hard, was a mere shadow of what it once was. I looked like a little boy needing all the care in the world. Let's not even mention the hopes I had of proposing to Heather in 2018. We had spoken about it before the accident, and we seemed to be on the same page. It made me bitter and angry knowing I could never live out that dream the way I visualized it many times before. There was no way I could kneel down, and there was no way I could open the ring box to propose. *I'll be damned if I propose and have to ask Heather for help opening the box and then ask her to put the ring on*, I thought.

I spent many days and nights telling her how much she meant to me and how happy I was that she was with me, but it never registered. Her smile was never as bright as when I bought her things. But the money was finite, and as my mom told me when I was at Shepherd, the best way I could show her I loved her was to recover—for both of us. I decided to do just that and use proposing to Heather as my new motivation to keep pushing myself. My goal was to propose to her on my own without help. I was going to make sure I did that, even if, in the back of my mind, I wasn't sure she would accept my proposal. Keeping my eye on the prize kept my fighting spirit strong.

CHAPTER 10

The World Breaks Everyone

I T WAS PROBABLY INEVITABLE THAT THE ACCIDENT would cause more than just physical injuries. For my mom and me, my accident shook our beliefs to their very core, but for my dad it reinforced them. His faith was unbreakable. He never faltered for a second and picked up the faith my mom and I had thrown away. I consider my dad my best friend, and I know he feels the same way about me. I'm sure seeing me lying lifeless on the hospital bed in Macon stirred a lot of emotions in him. After seeing the remains of the vehicles, he knew there was no other explanation to why I had survived. I remember him telling me in the hospital, "You're a miracle, Cesar." To him, God existed and had proven His power in keeping me alive through it all. No one could shake that belief from him, and when people saw pictures of the vehicles, they too agreed. I was a miracle. I hated hearing the words because they made no sense to me. "God kept him alive for a reason. He has big plans for him." Every time someone said that, I would think, *Oh really? God has big plans for me? So, His plan for me was to take two trucks to the face, basically die, but not fully...and then live through it and struggle with everyday life? Maybe He should've asked me first because I would have told Him I wanted nothing to do with this plan.* I'm sure if I had asked anyone who said that if they'd be willing to go through what I went through for a "big plan" God had for them, they would've said no. No one would have traded places with me at that time besides my parents, and they would have done it out of love, not belief.

My mom had always been the most religious of my parents, but something changed in her the day of my accident. She wondered if everything she had believed up to that point had been a lie. Her parents had raised her as a Christian all her life, and she used to believe God heard all her prayers. After my accident, I'm not sure what my mom believed in anymore, and I didn't fare much better. We were both fighting our demons and fixated on the most important question: Why? It's true we live in a fallen world that often falls on us, but this was something on another level. If misery and desperation had a measuring index, I had surpassed it, and my journey was just beginning. All the good I ever did in my life couldn't save me from this pain. I was falling further than I ever thought possible, and the end was nowhere in sight. My descent into the black abyss that was now my life pushed me further away from everything I believed. I decided God didn't exist for me. *What's the point in being a decent human being if in the end, you get the worst of what life has to offer?* I thought at the time. *There's no point in living right if it doesn't matter in the end.* If I was wrong and there was a God, what more could He take from me? My life? Not sure if I even cared at that point. More pain? I was getting used to it. When I told my mom this, for the first time, she didn't fight me on it and told me it was my right to believe what I wanted. "I'm not going to make you believe in something or someone I don't fully know is there," she told me with tears in her eyes. I knew she was broken too, but her break was deeper. Everything she had believed for over forty-five years had been shattered.

Regardless of how each of us felt, one thing was certain: my parents weren't leaving my side. My dad kept carrying the weight of all our faith since we wanted nothing to do with it; he knew it was just the pain talking. My dad didn't try to change our minds. He felt we had to get through the pain before we were ready to accept the truth. It used to be my mom who would lead us in prayer at the dinner table, but she couldn't do it anymore. My dad took over and said grace out loud every time before we ate. I didn't care anymore and didn't participate. My dad would always end his prayer by thanking God for saving me and giving the family an opportunity to be whole again.

Our time together would be short lived, seeing as my dad had to go back to work and Alicia was moving to San Diego. Everything was happening on the same weekend. My dad had been by my mom's side since the beginning, giving her the support she needed during the toughest time of her life. It was far from over, but life doesn't play by our rules, and my dad had to go back. He had been the first person to make me laugh back when my mouth was wired shut. I couldn't laugh normally, but I was grinning from ear to ear. Hearing me try to laugh at a time when our world was at its darkest gave my parents newfound hope. Maybe we would make it out of this.

My mom spent several days talking with my sister, making sure she understood it would be hard for all of us to see each other living on opposite coasts. The medical bills continued to grow, and our hands were full of medical appointments, therapies, and surgeries. Heather didn't offer any help, and Carolina was already working two jobs, trying to keep everything afloat. With my dad going back to work, my mom would need help getting me to my appointments.

That following weekend, we left Alicia at the airport and said our good-byes. I don't fully know when she even started dating Greg, but she looked happy. My parents both had their thoughts on the matter and would have preferred if she stayed to help us as we battled with my recovery, but they didn't try to change her mind. I didn't think much about it, and not because I didn't care about my sister, but rather because Heather took up almost every one of my thoughts. I wasn't happy or angry that Alicia was leaving. My parents told me several weeks prior, and I had taken it just like any other news. It didn't affect me like it should have or as it did once my brain began to heal. For Carolina, it was a different situation. She was angry Alicia was leaving when we needed her most. She knew my parents couldn't count on Heather for help since she never offered any. When Alicia was here, my mom at least had three different shoulders to rely on when needed. My dad and Alicia were leaving the same weekend, so that placed all the responsibility on Carolina. She didn't think it fair Alicia got to live out her life like she wanted when the family was still in pieces.

Carolina resigned herself to the fact she was not living life like she hoped. She never thought she'd have to be her brother's keeper, but when the time came, she never faltered or complained. If there was ever a more selfless person aside from my parents, it was her. She saw how close I had been to fading away, and she vowed, the same as my mom, to never leave my side until I was better than before. Nothing mattered to her but my parents and me. She abandoned finding love, chasing her career goals, her savings, and happiness in general. Like my mom and me, something had broken inside her that was not easily repairable. I know she went through some dark times as well in which she thought nothing in life mattered. My parents tell me they were worried about her being suicidal even months after my accident. Now when I speak with Carolina about those moments, she tells me the only thing that kept her going was seeing me push forward and continue to fight. The fact that I was determined to come out of the darkness I had been placed in made her see she had no reason to give up. "That, and I couldn't leave Mom to deal with this on her own. I knew she could break down at any moment, so I needed to be her rock," she tells me. We had been each other's rock at one point or another, providing each other with the strength to carry on when giving up seemed all too tempting. It's the only way we survived and realized we were truly unbreakable.

I don't blame Alicia for leaving. Many months later as my brain continued to heal, I asked my mom why Alicia left when I needed her most. She had done a lot for me and the family while I was in the hospital, but no one had any idea that the worst parts still lay ahead. She started the GoFundMe page, stayed in contact with the paramedics and EMS crew that pulled me out of the wreck, made sure Heather always came to see me, and kept family and friends up to date with my progress. I don't know if my parents or Carolina would have been in the right state of mind to do any of those things, and Alicia knew this, so she took control. My family was the best team anyone could have put together, and I am the result of all their efforts and sacrifices.

I got a chance to talk with Alicia a year later when we visited her in San Diego. Several questions plagued me as my brain began to heal, and I needed to address them with her. "Why did you go?" I asked her. "We needed you there... hell, I needed you. It was only the beginning of all this shit."

I turned to look at her and tears rolled down her cheeks. "I'm sorry, man," she told me. "When you got discharged from the hospital, I thought the worst part was over. I didn't know everything that was still ahead."

I said I had come to terms with her decision and didn't blame her for leaving anymore. "Look, I forgive you. I do," I said. "To be honest, I don't know what I would've done if we had traded places. I want to say I would've stayed, but I know I would've probably done the same." She then told me she had asked herself that same question at the hospital, *What would Cesar do in my position?*

"I know you would have followed your dreams," she said. "I chose to follow mine, knowing you would have probably made the same choice if a life-changing opportunity came up." I couldn't disagree with her even if I wanted to.

"You're right," I said, "but you don't need to worry about apologizing to me. It's Mom, Dad, and Carolina you need to talk to. You and I are very similar in how we make decisions, but all they do is love unconditionally. They would've done the very same thing they've done for me had you been in my situation. They would've never left."

I finished by thanking her for everything she did when I was in the hospital and for making sure Heather came to see me. "I'm sorry I couldn't do more to help, man," she said, "but you know I'll always be there for any one of you guys. I'm sorry I left, but you know I love you with all my heart." She gave me a big hug, and I felt the tears break loose. I had finally stitched up the small wound Alicia had made—albeit unknowingly—the day she left for San Diego. It was a big deal because it was the start of my internal healing process. At that point my body was healing well, but internally, I was still a mess. No one knew if I was capable of forgiving, not even me. That day was a breakthrough as I let the anger go and learned to forgive again.

It would be a long time before I reached that forgiving stage. I didn't fully comprehend the emotions that would start to develop as my brain healed. When we were at the airport, saying our goodbyes to Alicia as she left for San Diego, I was nowhere near that point and I didn't care that I wasn't. I remember giving her a hug and saying I'd keep her updated on my recovery. Heather was still there with me, so my world was intact. So long as she was in my life, the world could go up in flames and I'd be okay. I didn't feel what my parents or Carolina felt as they watched Alicia's plane take off. My mom was wiping her eyes as my dad held her close. He told her everything would be okay and they just needed to focus on making sure I completely recovered. Alicia had left and now it was my dad's turn to say goodbye. He only stayed that extra day to drive us to the airport and tell Alicia goodbye. The difference between both departures was that my dad would only be a four-hour drive away, and he would come to Atlanta every weekend. Alicia would be on the opposite side of the country, and we'd be lucky if we got to see her once a year.

My dad entrusted Carolina to accomplish the driving tasks in his absence. She didn't ask questions and just told him that's what she was there for, to help. We all said goodbye to my dad. He hugged me. "Thank you for fighting to stick around with us a little longer," he said. "Now just continue pushing forward. That's the reason your mom and sister are staying, to help you with anything you need. I would stay too, but one of us has to continue providing. I'll be coming up every weekend." I thanked him and promised to continue pushing myself in my recovery. Before getting in the car, he kissed my mom and hugged her tight. If there was a gesture that said more than words, that would have been it. They embraced each other, and I'm sure neither of them wanted it to end, but time was ticking, and my dad had to hit the road. This was the first time my parents would be separated for a long period of time, and I'm sure it was a new and scary feeling for them. "If you guys need anything—seriously, anything—just call me. I'm only four hours away, and I won't hesitate to leave everything and come up," he told my mom before driving off. It was tough for my mom saying goodbye to my dad, but there's always a first time for everything. She swallowed her tears and focused on her current goal, which was seeing me get better.

My dad tells me now how he felt driving away that day. "It was heart wrenching having to leave your wife and return to an empty house that had once been filled with laughter from you, your sisters, and your mom." We were all my mom and dad had ever known. I can only imagine the difficult and emotional moments my dad went through being in that big house by himself, a house that had long ago stopped feeling like home. He never showed any weakness, and if he ever cried or felt emotional, he had to go through it alone. Every weekend he came to Atlanta, my mom would be waiting for him with a genuine smile. The days would seem to go by quicker, and for the first time since I can remember, we wished the days would go by slower so my dad could stay longer. Two days were just never enough for us, but we made the most of our time together. When he was with us, we felt alive again. It was like having him there refueled us with the energy we'd need while he was gone. On the days I had surgeries, my dad was there to help my mom when I woke up from the anesthesia. He told his boss the dates I had surgeries and let them know it was his duty to be there with my mother and me. Thankfully, they understood.

Our world had become a little more jumbled, but my mom and Carolina stepped up to the challenge. They ensured I stayed on the path to recovery and that I never felt alone. I didn't exactly make it easy for them. The metal plate on my top palate was removed in the following weeks, and Heather asked me to take her to the fair at Perimeter Mall. It had only been two days since my surgery and I could barely talk, but I couldn't say no to her even if I tried. Deep down, I knew it wasn't the best idea but I told her I'd go. My mom shook her head but went with us anyway—not because she liked the fair but because she wanted to make sure nothing hindered my healing process. If Heather asked me to do something, my mom knew I'd do it, and that frightened her.

Once we got to the fair, she begged me to think of all the progress I had made and to not risk it by getting on any rides that spun or had sudden drops. I should've listened to her, but I didn't. Heather sat in one of the pods on a spinning ride and tapped the seat beside her, telling me to get in. The operator had to help me up three stairs and looked at me dubiously, wondering if I should be riding it. I sat down and closed my eyes, holding tightly to the security bar. Spinning rides had never bothered me before, and I hoped that hadn't changed. As the ride gained momentum, I started to feel dizzy, but I just pushed through it.

As we headed home from the fair, Heather was happy, my mom was angry, and I was worried as I felt new blood soak through the gauze. I never liked fair rides. They had never appealed to me with all their sudden drops, twists, and turns. The only reason I had gone was for Heather, to see her happy, but I would definitely pay the price that night for my decision. I felt my nose begin to drip as I lay in bed that night. I wiped it away but it did not stop. With great difficulty, I got out of bed, trying not to wake Heather, and went to the bathroom. Once I turned on the lights, I saw that my nose was bleeding profusely. In the morning when Heather woke up, she complained that I had bled on the pillowcases and through the mattress. Despite everything being mine, she acted as if I had offended her by ruining the mattress. She had a way of doing that, making me feel like everything I was going through was more of a tribulation for her.

I apologized and walked to the bathroom to check my nose again. My mom helped me drain out the remaining mucus in my nostril and clean out any dried blood. She asked me how I was feeling when she finished. I felt fine, with no pain. "I think it bled all it needed to," I said jokingly. "I think it's done for good now." We went about our day as usual. Oftentimes we would take walks by the complex to strengthen my leg and get out of the apartment. We decided to walk toward the DSW about a mile away. I've always been fascinated with shoes, and my mom knew this. Sometimes we'd go to DSW to see what new shoes had arrived. We would always invite Heather to join us on our walk, but she never did. "I have some things to do," she would say, but when we'd come back, she'd be asleep on the couch. At the time I found it funny, but looking back, it would've meant a lot to me if she had taken the time to walk with us since it was about the only thing I could do.

My mother and I went on our walk. I hold these moments very dear to my heart. It was just me and her against the world in those moments. She would talk to me the entire walk, trying to get an idea of how my brain was healing and how my emotions were doing. I knew she worried about what was going through my mind, but it was never easy to explain because it was a whirlwind of "what ifs" tossing around in my head. What if my arm doesn't get better? What if Heather leaves me because of what happened to me? What if I get nothing from my lawsuit? What if I have to give up acting? What if I can never play or sing again? What if the doctors can't fix my facial bones? All of these were just a few of the questions darting in and out of my mind every second of the day. My answer was more of a question. "Why me? Why did this have to happen to me?" It's a question we had all asked ourselves at some point since my accident. "I don't know," she said. "I just know you're here with us still, and that's all I need to know." She tried turning her face away, but I could see the tears in her eyes. I had several napkins in my pocket, and I reached out and gave her one. We walked a few minutes in silence and I felt something wet in my nose. I thought nothing of it and kept walking. Later, I saw a drop of blood fall on the pavement.

I touched my nose, and sure enough, it was bleeding profusely again. I didn't want people looking at me in the store, so we walked back to the apartment. My mom shook her head. She and I both knew the only explanation was that ride at the fair. It was the only thing I had done out of the ordinary that could have caused it. We reached the apartment, and I called the doctor's clinic to ask about the bleeding. They asked me if I had done anything out of the ordinary, and I was going to tell them about the fair but decided not to. If the bleeding didn't get better by the next day, I would have to call them or go see them. They were in Macon, so I hoped it would stop on its own. After about twenty minutes, it finally stopped. We went through the cleaning process, and I knew I'd have to sleep on the couch again. It bled some more the next day, but that was the end of it.

All I did was stare at the ceiling as I lay on the couch that night. It was summertime, a reminder that time had not stopped. It kept moving forward and that was all I was trying to do, but change was slower for me, and the days drew on forever. Change wasn't evident in me like it was in the color of leaves or their falling to the ground in the fall. There was nothing to indicate I was rounding the curve into another stage of the healing process. It was not apparent to me, but changes were occurring. Perhaps not at the rate I would've liked, but time didn't care about what I wanted. I just had to be patient and endure. There was a lot of healing yet to do. I tackled what was dependent on me like my brain, muscles, lungs, etc. Learning to forgive and restoring my faith would be a much more difficult battle.

So many things had broken in January, and it would take time to heal. As I write this, I'm reminded of a Hemingway quote: "The world breaks everyone and afterward many are strong at the broken places." I was broken, true, but I was alive. There were some breaks that went deeper than others, like my faith and my ability to forgive. It would take years before the healing bore fruit, but at least the seed had been planted. I just had to care for it and wait. In the following years, I would refortify those broken parts and make them stronger than before. Now they are a part of what makes me unbreakable.

CHAPTER 11

A Little Less Dark

T'S REMARKABLE HOW WE CAN SHOW LOVE FOR OTHERS, even when we are not "obligated" by a familial bond. I was the recipient of so much love. Clearly, my own family made massive sacrifices. But I also received love from some very unexpected sources. I had numerous procedures, surgeries, and therapy pending in the following months. School was starting soon for Carolina, and she wouldn't be able to take me to my appointments. Although I hoped Heather would offer, she didn't. It would have meant the world to me, even if in the end I'd have taken Uber so she didn't have to take time off work.

The next time Heather's parents visited us, the subject of my transportation issues came up. Unexpectedly, her dad offered to help whenever Carolina couldn't. "Let me know whatever days and time you have your appointments, Cesar, and I'll come down and take you," Tito said. "Even if Heather is able to take you, call me because I know she drives crazy, and I don't want your mom scared." My mom felt more at ease. Tito wasn't working so he had the ability to come down any time of the day. Since Carolina could take me after school, I tried scheduling all of my appointments for after 3:30 p.m. so Tito wouldn't have to drive an hour just to pick us up. The days in which appointments coincided with Carolina working, Tito picked us up and took us. When the appointments were early in the morning, I'd take an Uber to prevent Tito from waking earlier. I will forever be grateful to him for helping me get to my appointments when my sister or dad could not. In all honesty, I can say I received more care and consideration from him than I ever did from the rest of his family, including Heather. He helped my mom ease away from her fear of the roads and highways. They would talk the entire ride about life back in El Salvador, and it helped my mom take her mind off our current situation.

For me, it wasn't the drive or appointments that kept me anxious but rather not knowing when I would go back to work. I had always been a hardworking individual because that's what my parents were. At the time, I had some money in the bank, but my mom and I weren't working, and I knew the medical bills would only keep growing. I had been paid all my PTO days from my job prior to leaving Shepherd Center. After that, I stopped receiving income but thankfully kept my health insurance. The worst part, however, was receiving that email in May stating that they would terminate the branch I had been working in and that the last date of employment was June 30. When I got that email, I felt like my whole life was unraveling and burning to the ground. What drove the decision? I don't know, but the decision wasn't made lightly as it affected a lot of my coworkers as well.

I got in touch with my boss and asked if I could stop by to greet everyone and return my equipment. It was a bittersweet moment the day I walked back into the building that had once seen me working hard and just . . . happy. It was surreal walking back through the entrance I had gone past so many times before. Carolina drove me there and went inside to assist me with anything I might need. The security guy was the same one who'd been working when I was there before, but he didn't recognize me. I mean, how could he? I had lost roughly thirty-five pounds, I couldn't speak well, and I sure as hell did not look the same. After giving him my name, he called the top floor to let my boss know I was there and then he let me pass. I'm sure he knew who I was after I told him my name, but at that point what could he do? "You can go on up, Mr. Pérez," he said as I gave one last look at the entrance and made my way to the elevator with my sister.

I remember how happy I was that the elevator was working that day. Everyone at work knew I was very much into fitness, and I had always made it a point to take the stairs. It felt odd getting into the elevator, but I was happy nobody would have to see me attempt to climb the stairs that day. I was dressed like I would've been on any given workday. Somehow, I hoped it would help me feel like nothing had changed. I took one deep breath as the elevator doors opened. As I adjusted the sling on my right arm, I felt tears forming in my eyes. The doors shut, and I stayed inside the elevator to catch my breath and control my emotions. My sister said nothing; she understood I just needed a moment. She put her hand on my shoulder and just waited.

Only when I knew the tears were no longer coming did I push the button to open the doors. I looked at Carolina and nodded to let her know I was ready. We turned the corner to where I would've normally worked. Everyone was gathered there waiting to see me, and I received the warmest welcome. They expressed how glad they were to see me and how happy they were that I was recovering well. No one treated me differently, and for that I was grateful. They were so kind at a time when I really needed kindness. They joked and played around with me like nothing had happened, and it gave me a sense of normality that had long faded from my life.

While I spoke to people individually and caught up with them, every-one directed all the deep personal questions to my sister with regards to how I was feeling and if we needed anything. We thanked everyone for never giving up on me and for all their support. Before leaving, I went to the studio where we did all the sports shows and took it all in one last time. "I'll be back," I whispered before walking out. I wouldn't come back to the same place, of course, since everyone was being let go. "I'll be back" meant I would one day be back doing what I loved.

After saying goodbye, I walked down to return my work equipment. All of it had been in the car with me the day of my accident, but ironically, only my personal laptop was damaged. I returned my work computer without a single scratch on it. As I returned it, I was a little hesitant because I knew I needed a laptop, and mine was broken. My job was no longer there, and I needed to keep updating my portfolio to apply elsewhere. A laptop was something I desperately needed, and I was scared of letting it go. I took a deep breath and reminded myself that doing the right thing still matters.

The future was uncertain. My whole life, I had taken pride in being prepared for every situation, yet here I was not knowing what tomorrow held for me, and to be honest, I don't think I really cared. I was frantically reaching, trying to hold on to remnants of my past life that reminded me of better days. I found it difficult to exit the building after returning my equipment. There was a sense of nostalgia hidden in the walls for me, and my sister knew it. As she saw me taking everything in one last time, her eyes got red, and she turned away as I walked by and pushed the doors open one last time.

I thanked her for bringing me and staying the entire time. "You know you never have to do anything alone," she said. I nodded but rode the entire drive home in silence. The issue of no longer having a job was gaining traction in my mind. I knew neither my parents nor my sister could afford my medical bills, so I needed to find a solution. My mom didn't want me worrying about work or my benefits because she was afraid any stress would impede my recovery. But I couldn't just ignore it.

As soon as I got home, I started googling places that were hiring designers or producers and began applying again. Deep down, I knew I wouldn't hear back from anyone for a while since the hiring process was a long one. But what scared me most was the possibility that someone *would* get back to me. Even though I hadn't revised my resume or portfolio, I knew my work was good and could stand on its own. But I literally couldn't stand for too long, and the idea of a face-to-face interview frightened me. I knew my confidence was not the same. *That'll be evident in an interview,* I thought. *I'll just cross that bridge when I come to it.* Days turned to weeks, and I grew more anxious, knowing my benefits would terminate soon and I had no income. The medical bills never took a break and kept coming, unbothered by the anxiety brewing in me.

Fearing the worst, I decided to call HR at COX and ask if there were positions in any of their other branches to which I could easily transition to. I told them I didn't care much about the salary. I just wanted to make sure I kept my health coverage and benefits due to everything that had happened. They had me get in touch with the HR manager in charge of my case, Carl Davis. I had met and spoken with Carl a few times while I worked there before, but I had no idea just how big of a role he'd end up playing in my recovery. It was because of him that I truly learned what Short- and Long-Term Disability were. He agreed to sit down and talk things out with me to see how he could help. Although he knew my story, I told it to him again. He got a first-hand account of everything I was going through. He empathized with me because he had been in a terrible accident as well when he was younger. We both understood my biggest concern was health insurance and the fact that I still had countless therapy sessions and surgeries pending. "The best option for you right now is to be on Long-Term Disability," he told me. "Obviously there is a protocol to follow, so you will have to apply for Short-Term Disability first and be approved. Then your case will get reviewed, and if you meet the requirements, you will get transitioned into Long-Term Disability."

I looked at him with an expression indicating I understood, but the word disability made me cringe. There were a lot of things I couldn't physically do, so I knew I was impaired, but I didn't like to view myself as disabled. As a matter of fact, on all the applications I had submitted I put down that I didn't have a disability because that's how I felt. I didn't want anyone feeling sorry for me, and I sure as hell didn't want anyone's pity. The person I was before: that's who I wanted everyone to see me as.

"Once you've been approved for Short-Term and Long-Term Disability, you will start receiving a monthly payment that's a small portion of what your salary was. I know it may not be much, but I think it will help, and most importantly, you'll get to keep your benefits, which is what we want." I felt a huge wave of relief wash over me, and he must have noticed because right after that, he said, "COX would be more than happy to have you back once you are fully recovered. Don't rush, but just know if a position arises that you think you'd be a great fit for, don't hesitate to reach out, and I'll make sure your application reaches the hiring manager." I thanked him repeatedly for helping me find a solution. Neither Carl nor COX were obligated in any way to help me. I was once again benefiting mightily from the kindness of others.

"If you guys ever need anything, even if I'm not fully recovered, just know you can always count on me and I will help the best I can," I said as I got up to leave. He smiled and wished me continued success in my recovery.

I felt reinvigorated that my life wasn't completely crumbling as I walked out of his office. For a second, a faint smile danced across my face, and I knew there was no reason to give up fighting. Upon getting home, I told my mom the good news and said I would be applying for disability with the hope of having some income and retaining my work benefits. "I told you things had to get better," she said. "There's no reason to give up now.

Fully focus on your recovery and don't let anything else stress you out or drain your energy." I stopped applying for other jobs, knowing that even if I was hired, I wouldn't be able to maintain a full-time position. My focus was now on fully recovering and getting the most out of my therapy. I still had various questions regarding Short-Term disability, but Carl always got on the phone or sent me an email with an answer.

When I met with my vocational therapist (VT), Shelby, she would address any questions I had about getting back to work. The goal was ultimately to get me back to where I was before my accident. She strongly supported me in applying for Short-Term disability and was sure I would meet the requirements for Long-Term. "This will definitely give you some peace of mind," she said, "and if you need any help filling anything out, or if they need anything from your doctors or therapists just let me know, and I'll make sure to get it to them."

According to the handbook Carl sent me, after two years on Long-Term Disability, my case would be evaluated to see if I still met the disability requirements. If somehow I did meet the requirements, I would be transitioned to permanently disabled. I freaked out when Shelby told me this because permanently disabled meant I would no longer be able to do what I did before. "Yeah, it would be nice to retain my benefits, but I don't want to be labeled as permanently disabled," I told her. She understood and said we didn't even have to worry about that yet because I needed to apply and get approved for Short-Term disability first.

With the help of both Carl and Shelby, I was finally approved. Shortly after, I began receiving my monthly check in the mail. Even though it was a small portion of my salary, it helped so much and kept me from going crazy, stressing over bills. Most of the time, that monthly check would go toward meeting the deductibles. Carolina and my mom had been trying to find other organizations that could potentially help us. That's how I came to know about Mothers Against Drunk Driving (MADD). My mother read the organization's humble beginnings and could fully empathize with all the mothers who had or nearly lost a child to a drunk driver. She told me to reach out to MADD and ask for help since we were in dire need of it. Thankfully, I agreed and got on the phone with Shermaine Johnson, who at the time was a victims service specialist at MADD. She listened to my story as I nearly broke down telling it, and she told me I should apply to the Georgia Victim Compensation Program. There was no doubt in her mind I would be eligible for it and it would at least help with all the medical bills and some of the lost wages. Shermaine told me it was a lengthy process but that MADD was there to help me get through the toughest moment in my life. I thanked her and ended the conversion by letting her know once I made it out of this darkness, they could count on me to help. I wanted to help in any way and make sure no one else would ever have to go through this.

One of my ex-managers at COX, Christopher Smith, contacted me to check up. He was one of the people I interviewed with for my previous position. We got along great at work, and our relationship got stronger as the sports season progressed. He was the host of a sports betting show I helped produce. When COX sold most of its media, everyone went their separate ways and found work elsewhere. Chris stayed in contact with me through it all and came to see me a few times at my apartment. He mentioned he was moving to Orlando. I got a call from him one day that summer, asking if I would like to do some freelance design work for a sportsbook company he was working for. He had the ability to get any designer he wanted, but he chose to give me the opportunity since he was familiar with the type of work I produced. I'll forever be grateful to him for giving me a chance to prove I could still do my work. The job was remote, and it made me feel whole again. I was finally doing what I did before my accident. Aside from the financial aspect, which helped a great deal, my life was not in complete darkness anymore. Chris had faith in me and in my abilities despite my injuries. He didn't treat me like I was disabled; he saw me as the same person he had met the day he first interviewed me.

Though I had filed a lawsuit against the drunk driver and the big rig company, I never expected a handout. All my life, my parents had taught me to work for everything. Nothing came free. My thought process was no different now, even with a brain injury. I wanted to work and earn my living again, pay my bills, and be independent. My lawsuit was handled by Karsman, Mckenzie & Hart. Jeremy, my lawyer, told me cases like mine took a long time. I felt frustrated when he told me this, but it made no difference. I set the lawsuit aside and put it out of my mind. I would have to find a way out of this financial crisis. "It could take years," he said, and in the end my case could even get thrown out. The only way forward was finding a way to earn some income. I was willing to work for it. When Chris came to me with the offer of working with him and MyBookie on a freelance basis, I could've hugged him through the phone. It made life a little less dark for me.

Not only did this give me the opportunity to ease my way back into my working rhythm, but it also helped me perfect my skills. I knew I'd have to one day go back to work full time, which is why I wanted to keep learning new things to make myself more marketable. If hard work got results, then I would be the hardest working person in the room at any given time. I could do nothing and feel sorry for myself, or I could work toward a goal. Robert H. Schuller once said, "Tough times never last, but tough people do." Was I tough enough to withstand everything that was yet to come? I honestly didn't know but only hoped I was. I mean, what other choice did I have?

CHAPTER 12

Rebuilding the Man I Was

AS TIME PROGRESSED, I THANKFULLY KEPT IMPROVING —not all at once, not always constantly, and certainly nothing drastic overnight. But I kept moving in the right direction. One doctor my mom had been adamant I see was a specialized ophthalmologist. She wanted to make sure my vision wasn't compromised. I've always had myopia, which caused me to be nearsighted, but my eyesight got slightly worse after the accident. The change was minimal considering what I had been through, but my mom wanted to make sure my peripheral vision had not been affected.

After some exams, the ophthalmologist let me know my peripheral vision had not been affected. The next step was getting an updated prescription for glasses. My mom and I spoke to the optometrist and told her our concerns, my story, and why I was there. She asked how bad the accident was, and I showed her the photos on my phone so she could judge for herself. She looked at the pictures, put down her phone, and hugged me. "You're a miracle," she said. "I can only imagine the pain you both have gone through." By the time we left the store with my new lenses, everyone who worked there had heard my story. They hugged me and told me not to give up because I was an inspiration.

I didn't view myself as an inspiration. Back then, my goal was strictly not to break—to just keep holding on. I told myself this every day, but it wasn't until I reached the other side of the proverbial mountain that I was able to see the immense courage and determination it took. I was striving to take back my life, and I was walking on a razor-thin ledge toward that goal. More than once, I almost fell off, only to look back and see my mother, father, or sister had caught me. We kept marching forward. And once I reached the other side, I knew I had to share my story with the world. You, too, can do the unthinkable, beat the odds, and become unbreakable. It's not easy but definitely worth it. You need to realize that each day you have on this earth is a chance to change your life, for the better if you desire it. Leave all the excuses behind, and know that you are capable of changing the trajectory of your life toward what you want it to be. We all have choices to make, so make them count, and ensure everything you're doing is helping you reach your goals or achieve your dreams.

Aside from checking my eyesight, we were also concerned about a pimple that kept coming back under my right brow. The pimple wasn't the issue but rather how big and painful it was. My face had started clearing up after the metal plate was removed from my mouth, but the pimple always kept coming back. Sometimes it would pop, and my mom and I would clean it with alcohol, hoping it would stay away. I made several appointments with the ophthalmologist to see if I could get the pimple removed or prevent it from returning. "It just keeps coming back and I don't know why," I told him. "It hurts when I press it too." He told me he could cut it, inspect it inside, and cauterize the incision to keep it from coming back. When the pimple first started bothering me, my mom told me it was the body trying to push something out because I was never one to break out in that area. She spoke to me from experience and what she had seen in her life. Her dad had been in a bad bicycle accident when he was young, and had gashed his leg. She said he complained about pain in his knee, even after it had healed. It wasn't until a few years later that his leg pushed out a piece of gravel that had remained stuck since the accident. In her mind, that's what was happening under my right brow. I listened to her but didn't think it was possible.

Next time I saw the doctor, I was taken to the procedure room. He told me he'd inject local anesthesia into my brow so I wouldn't feel anything. The injection was the worst part of the entire procedure. It hurt but I pushed through it. After he dug around a bit, he said, "I don't see anything out of the ordinary or any foreign body." I was relieved, until he said it was time to cauterize it. Having already felt the initial injection of local anesthesia, I found it best not to ask for it again and just push through the pain as he cauterized the area.

I left the clinic feeling good the pimple had been removed. As the days went by, I kept an eye on the area and continued to clean it, but one day, it started hurting again. After several days, it came back just as big and painful as before. Not only was it not aesthetically pleasing, but the doctor had said it shouldn't come back. I was riding in the back seat with Heather one weekend and scratched my right brow. The pimple popped. I squeezed everything out and cleaned the area with alcohol. What followed next is something I never expected, and to this day, I find it hard to believe. As I cleaned the blood and puss from the area, I felt what I thought was a scab from when it was cauterized. I pulled on the scab and felt a severe pain that caught me off guard. Again, my mentality at this stage was no matter how much it hurts, just get through it. I pulled on the scab again, harder this time.

What was meant to be a quick tug took several seconds. The longer I pulled, the more it hurt. When I finished, I held a twig about four centimeters long in my hand. "See, this is what I was saying," my mom said. "I knew the body was signaling there was something that shouldn't be there. I'm surprised the doctor couldn't find this."

As my brow recovered from the pain, I kept turning the little twig in my hand, mesmerized at what had been under my skin for months. Heather inspected it as well. "We've got to name it," she said jokingly. I laughed.

"Alright," I said, and for some reason, I thought of the movie *Guardians of the Galaxy*. "Let's call it Groot." The pain subsided and I smiled. My mom had been right all along.

Twig removed from Cesar's eyebrow, months after the accident

We cleaned the area, and she put the twig in a glass jar. To this day, my mom still has the little twig in a small container, a remnant of the dark times we went through. I showed the ophthalmologist the twig the next time I saw him and told him the pimple had not come back since then. He said he hadn't seen it when he dug inside but perhaps the antibiotics I was taking helped push it closer to the surface where it eventually came out. "You're done with me," he said. I thanked him for his care and paid my fifty-dollar co-pay for that day. Despite paying for an appointment in which the doctor hadn't said or done much, I was in good spirits knowing my brow was good now. You can still faintly see the little scar of where it used to be.

Over time, my leg got stronger, and I was able to do a lot more. I was still overcompensating with my right leg, but it had improved. After a while, it wasn't my legs slowing my progress but rather my paralyzed right arm. To put it into perspective, my arm weighed somewhere between six to eight pounds. Now imagine running with an eight-pound grocery bag just dangling from your shoulder. That is how it felt for me. The human body is a perfect machine, and I saw how important every part of the body was in making sure it functioned properly. You never stop to think how important your arms are when jogging since your legs technically do all the work. Only when I grabbed my right arm to create a bend in my elbow did my balance get better and I overcompensated less. I got cleared to start jogging on the treadmill, and I made sure to do it every day. I knew it was all about repetition and getting the body accustomed to the work again. The more I tried, the more my legs grew accustomed to it. My mom went with me to the gym in the beginning, fearing I could fall. Before, I could run a mile in under six minutes just as a warmup before my workouts. Now I was struggling doing a mile in nineteen minutes. How things change so quickly. I had to watch my legs and make sure I ran properly, all the while holding on to the handles.

Every day, I made sure to get it done. I had trained my body before to look past the pain, so I pushed past the throbbing in my left hip. It was hard, and eventually my mother stopped coming with me as she saw me getting stronger. I actually wanted that time to myself. Aside from creating music, I viewed the gym as my other sanctuary where I could release my emotions.

God, I had so many to deal with. Several times, I would go to the gym and jog/walk on the treadmill until I had expelled every tear. It was the perfect place for me to let go of the anger, pain, and sadness since the gym was always empty. I would tend to go in the afternoons before everyone got off work and made it back to the apartment complex. There I channeled my emotions. The anger and pain pushed me further each day. I chased the person I used to be. Every step I took was painful, but I never stopped. I'd have a good workout one day, and two days later it would be painful to even walk. I still jogged regardless. I was forever chasing the shadow of yesterday, and I felt it would elude me every time I got closer. Still, I kept running after it.

My friend Chris Evans gifted me a book he thought would resonate with me. I had more time on my hands, so I decided to read it and add to the checklist of things I wanted to do every day. Aside from therapy, exercises, French lessons, and working on my portfolio, my checklist had one more thing now—read ten pages of David Goggins' book *Can't Hurt Me*. His story inspired me. Although our stories and situations were completely different, we both had to push past the literal pain even when we thought we couldn't and just take one more step. Some people say his way of thinking and living life is too drastic or extreme, but sometimes that's what it takes. When you have nothing else to lose, there is no reason to hold back. What resonated with me was how he said the mental battle was far more difficult than the physical one. It was the truest statement. Physically, I knew I could handle anything; my body had proven it time and time again, but the demons in my mind were something new. It was something I had never experienced before and had no idea how to control. My body before the accident was a result of hard work and determination, but I had no idea how to apply that to my mind.

My situation was different not only in how broken I was but with how the accident had affected my brain. I took Goggins' approach and decided to callus my mind. The mirror became my daily therapist. I talked to myself in the mirror and addressed the areas I needed to fix that were under my control. I came to accept my reflection in the mirror because the facial trauma was not something I could fix, at least not on my own. Getting my body back was something I could do. I had done it before. "Let's start there," I'd say, and I would hit the gym. It was a different connection I had with my body. I pushed myself harder than I ever had, but it was with the utmost love and care. I felt I owed myself that. Every step I took was both austere and nurturing. Like raising a child, I was trying to rebuild the man I once was.

Ideally, the goal is to not be at one extreme or another but rather the in-between, where you're striving to better yourself but also enjoying life. I didn't have the leisure to do that. Sometimes you have to enter that extreme mentality in order to come out better, stronger, and to get through all the changes as quickly as possible. I knew if I kept repeating my workouts and therapies, and kept callusing my mind, the pain would eventually subside. Every second was a second I progressed, or one in which I stayed the same, and I was not about to let that happen.

The days I didn't do my therapy or make it to the gym were the days Heather wanted to do something. It was either go out or stay inside watching TV. I was never one to watch much TV and always found it hard to stay still for too long. The entire time I watched a movie with Heather I thought about what I could be doing instead to keep progressing. She never had that mentality, but I didn't complain. In the beginning, I asked Heather to come with me to the gym and help me. Carolina also offered to come along and assist. I always started with my leg exercises. Though my right arm still wasn't functioning, I would try to strengthen what I could. Heather told me to try lat pulldowns on the machine, and obviously I obliged. She set the resistance at the bare minimum. It was so weird feeling my left arm doing all the work, and no matter how much I tried, my right arm didn't respond.

I barely moved the weight and felt both angry and embarrassed. Heather's chuckle didn't help, but the worst part was what she said next. "Babe, come on, that's bitch weight. Don't think about it. Just do it."

I remember the thoughts going through my head at that moment: I know it's bitch weight. I could do it before, but is this what my life is now? I'm trying. If I can't move this, does that make me a little bitch? I wasn't angry at Heather when she said it. My anger was always at life, for taking everything from me and placing me in that position where I felt like half the man I used to be. My sister saw the change in my emotions and told Heather to go back to the apartment so she could stay and talk with me. I didn't want to finish my workout, especially since I had "failed" in front of the person I loved. Carolina tried to downplay what Heather said, but then just told me to forget about it. "Heather is still young and has a lot of learning to do. She doesn't fully understand everything you went through, but we're here," she said. The interesting thing is that what Heather said would have never bothered me before, but seeing how different my life was now, her comment just made me focus on what I had lost.

I'm sure she meant no harm, but she never fully grasped nor understood how much my brain injury affected my emotions. I promised to never again ask Heather to go to the gym with me, at least not until I was a lot better. It was embarrassing for me to let her see how weak I had become. I kept going to the gym every day by myself and always attempted to do some lat pulldowns, hoping one day I could surprise Heather and move that "bitch weight." That day wouldn't come for a long time, and when it finally did, she wouldn't be around to see it. In the beginning, that would've devastated me, but my brain had healed enough by that point to understand I deserved better. On days I couldn't go to the gym, I went to bed feeling I had unfinished business. It wasn't something I could explain to anyone. No one understood where this need to push myself was coming from; they couldn't feel what I was feeling. Not even my mom understood at first, but for a different reason.

She would tell me to rest and take it easy. Her eyes were always teary when she said it. My mom knew the pain I felt jogging and doing any exercise, and the last thing she wanted was to see me suffer more. A mother's love knows no boundaries, and she would have traded places with me without hesitation. But this was something no one else could go through except me. I had seen pictures of my car and the crushed metal it had become; I knew I was made of something stronger. "Tomorrow is another day," I kept telling myself. But tomorrow came around and nothing really changed. This would've driven anyone crazy. I was giving it my all, and nothing was changing. To the untrained eye, there was no evident or immediate change happening, but the change was occurring inside. I knew the toughest battle was in my mind: learning to be patient and trust the process all over again.

We all chase after something. I heard Matthew McConaughey give a speech about chasing his hero. "My hero is always ten years away. I'm never gonna be my hero. I'm not gonna attain that. I know I'm not, and that's just fine with me because that keeps me with somebody to keep on chasing." As ironic as it is, I wasn't chasing me in ten years. I kept chasing the Cesar of yesterday, from before the accident. Every day that passed felt like I was getting closer to him, though I knew I would never reach him. Regardless... I kept chasing. If you asked me today what I gained from this traumatic experience, I would tell you it is patience.

This new virtue I possess came at a high price. It wasn't something I was looking for but rather something I held on to, to survive and not drown in depression. In gaining this newfound virtue, I learned to appreciate every moment since time was moving so slow for me. Every morning I took a breath, I got the chance to chase my goals again. Regardless of the pain, I was still alive and lucky enough to be able to keep pushing forward, and that's what I focused on.

I had the chance to recover, no one knew to what extent exactly, but there was a slight possibility I could recover everything. For my family that was enough, a light glimmer of hope. My dad tried to make me see that. He would always tell me that as long as there was hope, there was still a possibility. As weeks turned to months and surgeries kept piling on, I felt like hope was not saving but rather poisoning me. I clung to hope in despair, always thinking tomorrow would be better, but it never seemed that way. As long as there was hope, I would keep trying, but what if almost all my hard work was for nothing? What if in the end I couldn't get much better and my life would never be the same? Then hope is the cruelest thing for mankind, always reaching for something that's forever out of reach. I told my mom this one night after my therapy session. "What if we are all hoping and holding on to something that's never going to happen? It's so hard pushing forward when each step I take feels like I'm going nowhere," I said.

My eyes were red from holding back the tears, but when my mother hugged me, the dam broke, and the tears flowed. Her tears mixed with mine once I realized she, too, was crying. "We love you as you are. I know you are going to get better," she said. "Just know I will always be here, whether you push forward or not. But I know you will because you're my son."

I did press on despite the weight of my incredulity and uncertainty of the future. *Fuck it*, I thought. *If I don't get better, it sure as hell won't be because I didn't try.* If my therapist told me to do my exercises twice daily, I'd go home and do them four times. My goal was to get through this stage of recovery as quickly as possible because I was in misery having lost almost all my independence.

As 2018 came to a close, two big surgeries were approaching. The first one was my arm surgery scheduled for September of that year. Dr. Peljovich would do some nerve transfers to restore movement in my arm. Nerve regeneration occurs slowly, at a rate of approximately one millimeter per day, and patients may not see results for several months. Dr. Peljovich and the nurses made sure to hammer this into my brain before going through with the procedure. They didn't want me to have false expectations of having movement in my arm again any time soon, even after surgery. Still, I decided to go through with it. "I'm all in," I told them.

Before the accident, I had no idea what a brachial plexus injury was, but I made sure to study it day and night so that by the time the surgery date came around, I was well versed. They prepped me for surgery, and all I remember seeing were two big lights coming at me before I blacked out. I was used to anesthesia; at that stage, my body had a long history of use and had been put down several times. When I awoke, my parents were standing over me with some ginger ale. My right arm was bandaged from my shoulder blade to just above my elbow. The doctor came and told us how to take care of the incisions and when my follow-up would be. "Will I start therapy next week?" I asked, still coming off the anesthesia. He told me to take it easy and that therapy would start later. He explained the procedure then, and even in my dazed state of mind, I was able to capture most of it. What stuck in my head was that he had performed an Oberlin's nerve transfer. I later went home and read about the procedure. Dr. Peljovich had used my ulnar nerve to help restore function to my musculocutaneous nerve— which powers elbow flexion.

I remember just thinking how lucky I was to be born in an age where this was all possible. Never did I think I would need a nerve transfer, and here I was leaving the hospital with several. I left the hospital content that one more surgery was behind me, convinced that something positive would come from it. But that feeling faded as the days passed, and I continued sleeping upright on the couch. I wasn't allowed to get the area wet, so showering was an odyssey. My mom would wrap my arm in plastic to make sure no water droplets fell on my incision, and then my dad would hold my right arm outside the tub while she bathed me. The worst part though was not being able to put on deodorant. Plus, they had shaved my armpit for the procedure, and the itching was unbearable. Dr. Peljovich removed the bandages at the following appointment and cleared me to shower. I was able to meet my future OT, Sherri, and we discussed how slow nerves took to heal and why it was going to be a lengthy process. My eagerness to start therapy was evident because she told me we had to wait some time still. As the weeks kept rolling by, I started feeling depressed again, thinking I went through that entire procedure for nothing. Every day, I tried to move my arm to see if there was a connection forming, but it was all in vain.

I spent most of my days on the couch recovering from my procedure. I remember one of those days watching the movie *Wonder* on Netflix and crying my eyes out because I related to the little boy in the movie. The film is about a ten-year-old boy, Auggie, who has a facial deformity called mandibulofacial dysostosis. I felt what he was going through and wanted an astronaut helmet like his, so people wouldn't stare. He dealt with the very emotions I was experiencing. Auggie says he has had twenty-seven surgeries that have helped him breathe, hear, and see better, but none of them have made him look ordinary. Little did I know my own surgeries would be in the double digits later that year, and although they addressed certain issues, I never did feel normal or like myself.

Yeah, Auggie and I were fifteen years apart in age, but I easily needed all the help a five-year-old needs. I was like a child again, relearning everything in life. *Wonder* spoke of just one part of my life that had been affected. My confidence was long gone, but I knew what true love and friendship were when I saw my family and friends who stuck by me. Julia Roberts plays Auggie's mother in the film, and she never cared what her child looked like because in the end, he was her son. That was the only thing that mattered.

Just like her, my mom always told me she wouldn't change a thing about me. She didn't want me to have any more surgeries to "restore" my old features because each surgery signified more pain. "You don't have to change a thing," she told me. "You're perfect as you are." I knew she meant it because she said it from the truest of places—her heart. The world was not my mom though, and I knew they'd see something different.

Christmas used to be my favorite holiday. However, Halloween was approaching, and now it had a new meaning for me. "I wish every day was Halloween," I told my mom. It was the only day I could be someone different, and that was what I wanted. Just like the kid in the movie wanted to hide his face all the time, I too wanted to cover up and hide my trauma from the world. Heather didn't think anything of it and said she wanted to go to a bar with me for Halloween. If we had to dress up, I told her we would go as Dia de los Muertos so we could use face paint. The trauma I went through was not something I wanted to show the world yet. At least this time I would look different because I had made the decision to do so. That same day, I came across a quote online that echoed what I was feeling. Richard Paul Evans said, "The greatest disability is the inability to love those who are different than you." That was me. I was disabled at the time and looked different than everyone else. Not only that, but I had yet to come to terms with loving myself for who I was at the time. Yeah, I looked different, but the person I was before my accident was still there. I just had to see it.

That was my greatest disability, being unable to love and accept myself just because I looked different. The sad thing was, Heather suffered that same disability. She couldn't come to terms with the fact that externally I looked different, even though who I was inside remained the same. Yeah, I had a different perspective on life post-accident. How could I not? My world had been turned upside down and lit on fire, so my viewpoint was drastically different than everyone else's. Yet my love for Heather had not diminished.

If anything, it had been amplified. She knew this and kept biding her time, knowing I would never tell her to leave or ask her to do more.

Knowing I found it difficult to say no to her, she asked me to go with her to the Tapas bar on Halloween. We had gone the year prior. It was called Eclipse Di Luna. Every year, they threw a Halloween party that got so packed you couldn't even move on the dance floor. We walked to the place with Carolina, and Heather immediately went to the bar and ordered shots. Neither my sister nor I were drinking, so she drank them all on her own. It was bizarre seeing her drunk and trying to dance because she had no rhythm and there was no room. She gave up after a few minutes and ordered more drinks. I just took in the environment and tried to keep myself calm and collected because I still felt uncomfortable in crowded places. After she had yet another drink, Heather pulled my arm and asked me to dance salsa with her. I would have liked nothing more, but I just couldn't physically do it. The best I could do at the time was a two-step, and even that took a lot of concentration. I gave up after a few minutes and just held her close. "I'm sorry it's not like last year," I told her. "I'll make it up to you next Halloween. I promise. We will dance the night away." Did she even hear me or perceive what I told her? I don't know. She was already several drinks in. My thoughts and emotions, however, were raw and sober.

Midnight came around, and I signaled to my sister it was time to leave because I didn't want Heather puking. "The walk back should help sober her up," I told Carolina. We walked back to the apartment with Heather leaning on my left shoulder. Despite my being unable to dance with her like before, I was happy I could still take care of her and make sure she made it home safe. That was always my goal and what I had promised her before my accident. "I will always take care of you." Not even two trucks to the face could break that promise. When we made it home, she fell asleep as soon as she hit the bed. I went to the closet and grabbed a blanket, and as I covered her, I couldn't help but smile. I didn't care if she didn't help me with my recovery, my appointments, or the rent. For me, it was enough that she was there. I kissed her cheek and closed the door so she could rest. My mom and Carolina were in the living room talking about how the evening went. Once I stepped into the room, they quickly changed the subject, and my mom asked me how I had felt being in a crowded place. I told her it was the same place I took Heather the year before, so I was just glad I got a chance to do it again.

Heather was hungover the following morning with the biggest headache. We didn't have an electric kettle, so I went to the kitchen and tried to boil some water to make her chamomile tea. My mom got up to help as soon as she saw me in the kitchen with a pot on the stove. She said she would make her tea and cook her some soup so she could recover quickly. The day Alicia left for California, my parents told Heather at the airport, "One daughter leaves, but we gained one more. Always five." They treated her like they did any one of us, with the utmost love and care.

Once she felt better in the evening, I asked her why she wanted to drink every time we went out. I wanted to know why, after seeing what a drunk guy had done to me, she still felt the need to get drunk. My brain couldn't comprehend it. I never thought something similar would happen to her because my case was extreme, but what if she got into a wreck because she had been drinking? I tried to make sure she never drank when she was driving, but sometimes she went out by herself to hang out with friends. Those moments I wasn't with her scared me the most, thinking something could happen if she didn't make the smart decision not to drink and drive. I couldn't be there with her, so I would just hope she made it home safely, back to me.

"You know I don't have a drinking problem," she told me, upset I had asked. "My dad was the biggest alcoholic and my older sister also told me she had a drinking problem at one point. So I know what a drinking problem looks like." I sat down and just tried to analyze the situation Heather and I were in. My mind went back to the days before the accident when I would take her everywhere and buy her a drink whenever she wanted. Those days were long gone, but I didn't need a drink to enjoy my time with her, so why did she? I couldn't arrive at a sensible conclusion, so I just let the thoughts go.

There have been studies done to determine what drives or motivates people to consume alcohol, and although the motives vary, there are two broad categories into which most people fall. One of the categories is to avoid or escape reality. The second is to fit in or have a good time with others. I felt neither of these should be reasons for Heather to drink every time we went out. If anyone wanted to escape reality, it was me, and yet I was adamant about not drinking because I wanted to recover, for us. I had heard of several cases in which people, recovering from their own trauma, turned to alcohol for answers, only to fall deeper into depression and never recover. That's not what I wanted. I knew I didn't need a drink to have a good time with Heather. The moments I was with her, I didn't want anything to hinder my senses. I wanted my eyes to see her, to remember her as she was in that moment, because I had come so close to not sharing it with her. Did Heather really want to escape her reality, this new reality we had been thrown into? *That can't be it*, I thought . . . but mostly hoped.

It wasn't long before I found myself in another surgery room. The needles were less and less painful as I continued undergoing more procedures. They were part of my routine now. This surgery was to repair the fistula in my upper jaw and fix my septum that was still out of place. My otolaryngologist was Dr. Dockery, who had performed the stenosis removal while I was still at Shepherd Center. He felt my mother's pain and wanted to do everything he could to help us. After surgery, Dr. Dockery told me that what he had found was worse than what he had expected. There was a lot more bone missing than he initially thought, but he fixed it the best he could. At the end of surgery, he had stitched gauze to the roof of my mouth where the fistula was located, to prevent me from playing with the area. Aside from that, I had two plastic tubes in my nostrils keeping the septum in place. They wouldn't come out for several days, so I would have to breathe through my mouth. It should have come as no surprise to me when he said I would have to sleep upright for several days. I was just starting to get accustomed to sleeping in my bed again, and now it was back to the couch. It was nothing but liquid or soft foods for me until the gauze fell off or he removed it.

Thanksgiving and Christmas were around the corner, but I wouldn't be able to enjoy any of the holiday food. I had planned for this, and my mom kept me on a well-balanced diet with home-cooked meals and smoothies. My headaches had improved drastically, and I would only take Tylenol and Motrin every three to four hours, but the headaches had returned with a vengeance. The days continued to drag on, and the headaches kept getting worse and worse. They were coming faster and more intensely. I started taking pain relievers every two hours, children's Motrin and Tylenol. "Why does it seem like your headaches are more frequent and getting worse?" my mom asked me. It was something that had puzzled me too. I wasn't doing anything differently. Before answering her, I took one deep breath, and I smelled the mucus and blood that had been collecting inside my nose around the splints. It was nauseating.

After cleaning my nose, I told my mom I knew what the problem was. "These tubes are so far up my nose that all the accumulated blood and mucus is causing my headaches to be more frequent and intense," I said. "Just smelling it makes me want to throw up, and I am smelling it all day . . . making me nauseous."

She took my head, tilted it slightly, and tried to see if she could smell it. "I can't smell it from outside though," she told me, "so at least you don't have to worry about other people smelling it." I couldn't blow my nose, so there was no way to remove anything that was lodged inside. I just had to push through the headaches until Dr. Dockery saw me to remove the splints. This was my life for several weeks—a constant agony that felt as though my head would explode. I got through it somehow, with my mom next to me and my two best friends: Tylenol and Motrin.

The day finally arrived when Dr. Dockery would remove the splints from my nose. The gauze on the roof of my mouth was dangling by a thread, so he cut it off and told me not to play with the area. Next was my nose. My eyes teared up every time he moved inside my nostril, but then he finally started pulling the gauze and plastic tubes he had placed. He started pulling everything out, and just when I thought he was done, he kept pulling more. Once he finished, I felt alive again. "I can breathe better now," I told my mom. After I took a look at everything he removed from my nose, it all made sense. I could not believe all that had been in my nose. Even my mom told me she could smell the horrid odor when he removed it from my nose. No wonder my headaches had been so intense. We made it to the car, and Tito asked us how it all went. He had taken us to the appointment and waited in the car. My mom filled him in on all the details. He said he was really glad we could cross one more thing off the list. "Where do you guys want to eat?" he asked us. I chuckled and told him I still was on a liquid/soft diet. Even though the doctor had removed the gauze from the roof of my mouth, he told me to not touch it. I told Tito to stop by Chick-fil-A so he and my mom could get something to eat.

It was an unspoken agreement that after Tito took us to my appointments, lunch or dinner was on me. Chick-fil-A was always Tito's go-to place, and it was my mom's favorite fast food too, so it all worked out. I enjoyed the time we got to spend with him because he kept my mom distracted from the internal distress of seeing me go through so much. He and my mom continued to bond, spending the entire time talking about life in El Salvador. He would always finish by asking her how Heather was behaving or helping out at home. My mother never spoke ill of anyone, and she damn sure wasn't about to do it in front of my girlfriend's dad. Her answer was always, "Yeah she's doing the best she can and helping wherever she can." My entire family knew that was a lie. My mom was the one who cooked and cleaned, and Tito took me to my appointments. So what was Heather actually doing? She wasn't helping me with my therapies or bills. Really, living with me was a means to an end. She had told me several times she couldn't stand being at home with her family. The worst part, however, would be when she told me she was only living with me because I was closer to her school. She said it was a joke, but behind every joke, there is some truth. If free housing was all I was, I didn't know it yet. The ending had no space for me, and yet I kept chasing that illusion in which she and I made it through the storm together. I continued holding on to that hope for a long time, and my parents continued to see Heather through the lens I saw her—love.

Many of the first responders connected with my sisters. Now that I felt stronger, I wanted to go see them and personally thank them for saving me. One of the first responders on the scene, Treutlen County firefighter Josh Cammack, reached out to me through Facebook, and I asked him if I could stop by and see everyone who had played a part in my rescue. He told me it would be amazing and that almost everyone who had played a part in my rescue would be there. They all wanted to see the miracle their hard work had produced. That's what I was to them, a miracle.

I didn't want to go empty-handed. I wanted to give them something and a thank-you card in my handwriting. It was nothing huge, but I figured it would mean a lot to them. Heather was invited to come, but she stayed home instead to meet up with her friends. None of us were surprised. It's weird, but we all felt a little relieved we were the only ones going. Heather wouldn't be able to speak about my pain, surgeries, obstacles, or emotions because she was never really there. The only ones that could attest to my resilience and determination were my family because they had been with me every moment since the beginning. Sure, it would've been nice to have Heather join me in thanking the men and women who saved me, but the fact that she wasn't there didn't make it any less special for me. I wasn't alone; my parents and Carolina went with me, which in the end was all I ever needed.

There was no way they were going to miss seeing the heroes who saved their son/brother. I spent all day writing their cards and fixing their gift bags with coffee bread and coffee. It was nothing compared to what I wish I could give them or what they deserved. All I know is every bag was filled to the brim with love. Heather wasn't there, and for some reason I didn't miss her. I was focused on the mission at hand, thanking these men and women for everything. Everyone was waiting for me at the fire station. They looked at me like I wasn't real. Seeing me walk in and talk was nothing short of a miracle to them. I knew they were touched after seeing me fight for my life that dreadful night, and although they had all prayed I'd make it through, no one really knew what would happen. We hugged, and I told them about the procedures I had undergone and the ones still pending. Then we talked about January 12.

I asked them to tell me what happened that day and what they experienced since I didn't remember anything from that night. Each one of them recounted their point of view. There was something different about my rescue, and it had touched everyone involved. As they were pulling me out from the scrap metal my car had become, they told me they had never felt so much fight in one person. The irony of it is that it's all a dark void in my memory. Jokingly, I told them if I had been coherent, I wouldn't have fought them off since they were trying to help. The massive impact to my brain had caused me to act irrationally, and I had no idea what was happening at the time. My fight-or-flight response was evident. At least now I knew I was a fighter through and through. I was a strong guy, and it had taken several of them to hold me down so they could extricate me from the vehicle. One of the most interesting things they told me was that I had fought them off with both arms. I looked down at my paralyzed right arm and smiled. I realized I'd never go down easily. Even in the chaos of that desperate moment my mind had chosen to erase, I hadn't given up. Now that I was healing and coherent, what wasn't I capable of accomplishing? Never would I run away from anything. I would stay and fight my way out of this darkness.

Cesar visiting the first responders who rescued him

We went outside and they showed me the equipment used to roll the dash off my legs. My vehicle was a compact car, and they had to be careful rolling the dashboard off since my femur was protruding from my left thigh. The extrication took roughly forty-five minutes. I'm sure it was a chaotic scene with me fighting them and them trying to find the best way to free me from my vehicle. What surprised me most was knowing most of these heroes were volunteers. They had full-time jobs, but they did this because they were passionate about helping others. In an open field out front was the air evac helicopter that had transported me. They took me out to see it, and the pilot let me get in it once again, only this time, I wasn't on a stretcher.

I thought some memories might return to me after seeing everyone and being inside the helicopter once again, but my brain still recalled nothing. We walked back inside the fire station, and I gave everyone the gift bags and thank-you cards I had prepared for them. They all smiled, and I realized they were a part of my family now. They didn't know who I was that day, yet they did everything in their power to save me and give me a fighting chance. How can one repay that? You can't. All I had for them was the deepest gratitude, love, and a gift bag with a handwritten card. A firefighter named Lee Henry said, "That's the only payment we need, just seeing you walk in here." My mom just kept saying thank you. She didn't know what else to say. She was at a loss for words being amongst the angels who had given her son back.

We said goodbye and told them they could count on us for anything. I noticed my mom looking out the window as we headed home, smiling with tears rolling down her face. I asked her if she was okay. "They'll never know just how grateful I am," she said. "All I could say was thank you. I hope they felt my gratitude."

As 2018 came to a close, I thought about what a crazy year it had been. Honestly, I couldn't even make this up if I wanted to. It was like my life was an emotional drama you see on TV. The movie script was all laid out, and I was eager to know how it would end. There were all these twists and turns, but the biggest surprise came on December 20. All this time, the only thing I had known about the drunk driver who hit me was that he was Latino. No one had told me where he was from, and frankly, my family didn't care. They just wanted him to pay, whoever he was. That Thursday, I received an email from my lawyer's paralegal, Tiffany. She forwarded me the PDF mini depositions of the drunk driver and the big rig driver, on two separate files. I wasn't ready for what I found. As I read the deposition of Alexander Lopez Vasquez (the drunk driver), I got to the part where they asked him his age and where he was born. He stated he was born in El Salvador, and I swear I read that sentence four times just to make sure I was reading it correctly. I couldn't believe it. My eyes started tearing up, and I couldn't read any further. I needed to get some fresh air.

It was a small world after all. My parents had brought me to the United States to avoid the violence and poverty back home. Was this destiny? Was it fate? Was all this predetermined by a higher power? I had so many questions. Life wasn't fair. I knew that now, but it was more absurdly ironic. Somehow everything had come back full circle; all the suffering my parents wanted to avoid we were now paying tenfold. All the paths we took to avoid struggles back home somehow all led to this moment where nearly nothing but pain existed.

Growing up, I was always proud of who I was and where I was from. Though El Salvador only saw me the first three years of my life, I didn't care. I was Salvadoran, and I made sure the world knew. People often viewed El Salvador in a negative light, due to all the gang violence and poverty. I wanted to change their view of my country, so they would know of people like me and my family. We weren't all gangsters or thugs. We had talented people with great work ethics who would no doubt be successful if given the opportunity. My sisters and I tried to shine a different light on El Salvador and show everyone that you can't paint people with a broad brush. That was easier said than done, but despite all the adversities we faced in life, I was always proud to be Latino and Salvadoran. Something changed in me that Thursday. I felt disgusted. Never again would I be able to call myself Salvadoran, not if people like him (Alexander) were associated with it.

The drunk driver being a different ethnicity wouldn't have made things any easier, but knowing we were both from the same place just poured salt on the wound. This was all happening at a time when the president was calling for a wall on the southern border and stronger security to halt immigration. How could I ever advocate for my people if people like Alexander gave us a bad name? I wasn't the only one feeling weighed down by the news. My parents were shocked when I told them, and my mom just closed her eyes as a tear rolled down her cheek. We had spent all our lives trying to be outstanding citizens in this place we called home. It was filled with opportunities one only dreams of in El Salvador. The Declaration of Independence states everyone has the right to life, liberty, and the pursuit of happiness. That's what Alexander took from my family and me that day. He almost succeeded in taking my life. Happiness was now just a distant memory, and what good was liberty when I felt like a prisoner in my own body? Why had I ever tried to be different? Why try to break the glass through which all Salvadorans were seen?

We went to Piedmont Park one day, and I found the answer to my questions. As I walked with my parents, I turned to look at them and realized we weren't like everyone else. We were something different entirely. My dad was not the typical Latino everyone thinks of as being machista. He is the most caring and devoted husband, father, son, uncle, and my best friend. They don't make many like him nowadays, and I am blessed to call him Dad. My mom is an all-encompassing love, and her priority was always family. She cared not for looks, money, or material things. So long as we were all good, she was content. Looking at both my parents as they held hands in the park, I realized how different we were. And I was okay with that. This was just another trial we had to endure. *Many people would never come out from something like this*, I thought. *But dammit, we were different*. We would make it through somehow, some way. Everything we had lived and sacrificed for couldn't be for nothing. It just couldn't.

Heather's parents invited us over to their place for the holidays, so we spent Thanksgiving and New Year's Eve at their house. I was prepared to miss out on the Thanksgiving food but was still disappointed I wouldn't be able to try Tito's tamales. Regardless, I drank my soup and enjoyed the moment. What was I thankful for that year? When it was time to say grace, I looked around the entire table and thought—this. This is what I'm thankful for. I got to spend more moments with the people I love. That Thanksgiving had an entirely different meaning to me. I felt no one had more to be thankful for than me. My life had changed dramatically, but I was alive, and for that I was grateful.

I started pondering how life would be if I were not in it. How would my family have coped, survived, endured it? They wouldn't have. You can't overcome such a tragic loss, and it's something I wish no one ever had to experience. I think losing someone you truly love has to be the most agonizing pain, knowing there is nothing you can do about it. Time only moves forward. As I write this today, I can say the pain my family felt, seeing me on the precipice of death, was far greater than anything I had experienced. I have survived and endured almost every physical pain you can think of, and yet I don't think I could handle losing someone I love. There's no medicine to make that pain go away as it is fueled constantly by memories of moments past. I know I'm battle-ready, prepared for anything life may throw at me, but not that. I don't think you can ever be ready for those moments. They come, nonetheless. That's why every day, I try to live with purpose, making sure I take full advantage of every moment I get to spend with the ones I love.

I tried explaining this to Heather but don't think she fully understood how much it meant to me to be spending one more holiday with her. Although it might've been her twenty-second Thanksgiving, for me it was my first. Life had given me a second chance, and I was starting over.

Everything meant so much more. My parents understood, and they enjoyed every moment to the fullest because I was able to share it with them. That's all that mattered.

New Year's Eve came and went in the same fashion. I was happy to be closing a year that had brought me and my family so much pain. I was positive the worst parts of my recovery were over, but life had different plans. The year was ending, and I just felt a sense of gratitude. Heather's sister was visiting for the holidays with her newborn baby, and as I looked at him, I thought of my future children. Ever since high school, I knew I wanted to be a father and start a family. I was a family man through and through. That's who my dad was. It was the example I had seen every day growing up. If I ever had children, I wanted them to know their dad fought to the end and never gave up. *When it's all over, my children will say their father is unbreakable*, I thought as it was my turn to hold the baby. I gave Heather her midnight kiss and stepped into 2019 with high expectations. No one knew what tomorrow would bring. I just knew I had to keep moving forward. There was only progress to be made, moments to remember, and some to forget, but many lessons yet to learn.

CHAPTER 13

One More Reason to Continue

SOMETIMES IT FELT LIKE MY RECOVERY STOOD STILL, even though overall I was still making progress. I didn't really know when my recovery would be complete, and every day brought new challenges. Each day started and ended the same for several weeks. My mother and I had steadily been going to different doctors/surgeons the year prior to see what they could do to fix my facial bones. We saw a few professionals and almost always received the same response. Everyone thought my case was too complicated. The doctors would either decline or refer us to someone else who might take my case. I had seen so many doctors by that point, so I don't remember who it was that recommended I see Dr. Stephanie Drew at Emory Hospital.

I met Dr. Drew and shared my story with her, half-expecting her to turn me away as well, but she didn't. My mom showed her pictures of who I used to be, and I could see the emotions stir within her. She had children of her own who often made the long trip to see her in Atlanta, and she could only imagine the pain my mom and I had been through. Dr. Drew agreed to take me in. She told me it would be a lengthy process and that I'd need to get braces first to align everything.

She referred me to the Georgia School of Orthodontics, where I was able to get my teeth aligned before my surgical procedures. It would take quite some time to get my teeth in position for surgery. Seeing how out of place my teeth were, it didn't surprise me. I already felt self-conscious about my appearance, and now I'd have to add braces to my troubles. Invisalign was my first request, but because of the damage my face had sustained, they told me metal braces would be the best and quickest option for treatment. That's all they had to say. I was on board. The quickest way I could put all this behind me was what I would do. I had already had several root canals done, so thankfully my teeth weren't as susceptible to the pain the braces caused. My orthodontist, Dr. Savage, said I would have braces for two years or more, which meant I had to adjust my expectations. I wouldn't be done with my recovery any earlier than the start of 2021. Even that was being optimistic.

Only surgeries or procedures would make my days different, but for the most part, each day was a carbon copy of the previous one. The only difference was I now had braces. I learned to cope, with time, and became a patient man. I decided to trust the process and keep pushing myself, knowing someday it would all be worth it. My parents told me to document everything and to keep track of my progress. They always thought my story could help others someday.

When I first found out about my brachial plexus injury, I went online to find similar cases of people with the same injury. The stuff I found helped me better understand my injury, but none of it told me how to better my chances for a full recovery nor let me compare before-and-after pictures. I figured my experience could someday help someone like me, and that was motivation enough. I compiled an Excel spreadsheet of all the therapeutic arm exercises I did every day. In the end, I knew the surgery would only get me so far. I had to put in the work. Anyone who saw my Excel spreadsheet would see how much work it took. Every other Thursday, I took pictures of my arm from various angles to showcase any improvement.

So many things happened in 2019, and none could've brought us more joy than the birth of my nephew, Antonío. Alicia had told us she was pregnant near the end of 2018. Neither one of my parents could believe it and thought it was a joke at first. We were all living through one of the darkest moments in our lives, so it sounded too good to be true. Months later, she called to tell us she was having a boy. Alicia said she wanted to name him Antonío after me—my full name is Cesar Antonío Pérez Mancía. They had all been so close to losing me, and now another boy would come into our family.

Alicia's due date was on March 30, my birthday. I don't think it could've aligned any better. God and the universe were trying to tell us something. Life goes on. My sister didn't want to name her boy Cesar because she thought I might want to name my future son that, and she wasn't having the baby to replace me. It meant more than that. She wanted my parents to have something more to live for. Even though she was on the opposite side of the country, Alicia also craved that. Like I said, I wasn't the only one broken down after my accident. We had all changed.

March was quickly approaching, so I decided to buy my family's and Heather's tickets to California with some of the money I had left. Heather would only be able to go for a week as opposed to the two weeks my parents and I were staying. It cost me more to book them on different days, but I had helped Heather get a part-time job at Shepherd Center, and I didn't want her taking too much time off from work. When she had been looking for a job, I kept telling her to apply to any position available at Shepherd because it was the best place for a future therapist. Eventually she applied at the outpatient clinic. Every time I went to Pathways, I spoke about her and how much she was "helping" me at home with my therapies. No one knew it was a lie, and I always vouched for her, trying to make sure the hiring manager would see her application. I just wanted to help her. They finally hired her, and I hoped she would cherish that job because Shepherd was a place for second chances.

We flew to California just two days before my birthday. I had never really cared about my birthday before. In the end, I was just getting older, and my life was passing me by. My family knew this wasn't exactly a vacation. We'd be at the hospital, for the most part, making sure Alicia was okay and that the baby was born healthy.

This was my first time being in a hospital where I wasn't the patient. March 30 came and went, and the baby still hadn't arrived. Antonío, just like me, enjoyed being fashionably late, and on April 3, 2019, my nephew was born. Lee Henry and his wife Victoria gave us a baby onesie from the fire department for my nephew, and we placed him in it. Here was a little baby on the other side of the country, representing the Treutlen County fire department.

We got home and I sat down to hold my nephew. They had wanted to let me hold him at the hospital, but I still didn't feel strong or confident in my right arm. As I held Antonío, I couldn't help but feel a strong connection to him. After the chaos my life had been the past years, here was a little ray of light that bore my name. I wouldn't have been able to enjoy it had it not been for everything the first responders did to get me out of my car. Earlier, I explained how I felt I resembled a newborn baby, just like Antonío. The connection I felt with him was on a whole different level. I wanted to shield him from all the cruelty of the world. The innocence I saw in him I vowed to protect.

Cesar holding Antonío for the first time

Antonío hadn't a care in the world, no worries, and no trauma as he lay on my sister's chest. That innocence is one of the greatest losses we experience as humans through the years. I was content being in the moment with my new buddy.

We all had yet another reason to continue as we left for Atlanta the following week. The sad realization was, being on opposite coasts, we wouldn't be able to see Antonío grow. There wasn't much time to dwell on anything since there were plenty of appointments, therapies, and follow-ups waiting for me as I got back. The time we spent with my sister in California was the only change of pace we had.

I wanted to get my PCL reconstructed; this much I knew despite people telling me I could live my life without one. The goal was always to get back on the soccer field and play, so I knew I wanted it done. I was referred to Dr. Scott Kimmerly, an orthopedic surgeon who specialized in sports medicine and trauma. The first few times I met with him, he told me to let my femur heal first before talking about PCL reconstruction. It had been over a year now since my accident, and we could finally start discussing options. When I tore my ACL in college, they reconstructed it using my patella tendon, and it had healed amazingly. Dr. Kimmerly told me that because of the injury and trauma my body had sustained, he would recommend using an allograft (tissue from a cadaver). We scheduled and planned for surgery to occur sometime in July, and in the meantime, I'd just have to continue strengthening my quad. After surgery, I'd be on crutches for a while before starting physical therapy again. He said it was my choice where I'd like to do my PT, but he recommended Peachtree Orthopedics.

All the while, I kept going to Pathways for all my other therapies. Carolina or Tito would take me. My dad was still driving back and forth from Savannah to Atlanta every weekend. Having him on the road so much kept everyone on edge after everything I'd been through on I-16. We kept telling him to just stay in Richmond Hill and only come see us once a month when he could. The only two times he didn't come to Atlanta, it was due to extra work he took on to earn more money. My last PT session was coming up at the end of June. It was one of the weekends my dad couldn't make it to Atlanta. He had been hired to cut down a few trees at someone's house, so Carolina took me.

It was late in the afternoon, and we were on the way to Pathways when my mom called my dad to check on him. They liked to video chat since they had never been apart this long. As soon as my mom saw my dad's face, she asked him what was wrong. He is one of those people who can't sit still and always has to be doing something, so my mother knew there was a reason he was sitting down. Like the man he is, he insisted everything was fine and that he was just tired. My mom asked him to stand up, and he just smiled and shook his head. After a few moments, he tried standing up. He couldn't, so he decided to confess what had really happened.

While cutting down a tree for someone in Richmond Hill, the branch he had been standing on broke. He fell sixteen feet through a roof and broke his tibia. Thankfully he landed on his feet, but that impact caused a fissure in his bone. He had the chainsaw with him when the branch broke off, and he threw it away immediately, or else he would've been injured even worse. My dad kept smiling while trying to talk through the pain, and my mom kept listening, her heart beating faster. My mother lost it as my dad began throwing up. She told Carolina to keep on driving to Richmond Hill because my dad was injured. I called Pathways and canceled my appointment. My dad had been there for me all this time, and now it was my turn to be there for him.

We rushed to Savannah, and one of my dad's coworkers took him to the hospital. That car ride felt so long, and Atlanta traffic didn't help. My dad got to the ER, and after several x-rays, they told him he needed surgery. By the time we got to the hospital, it was nighttime. The staff let us see my dad, and we camped out in his little room. There was only one comfortable chair. Carolina and my mom both told me to take it. If my dad wasn't having surgery until morning, we would sleep there by his side. One of the nurses during that shift came into the room and saw Carolina and me nodding off. Hannah Hall brought my mom and sister another couch where they could rest better. People like her remind me there's still good in humanity, and people who want to help others. I'm sure anyone who's been in a hospital room with us can feel the love my family radiates. It's something magical, priceless, and above all, true.

My dad was upset that he broke his leg before my surgery. He was supposed to help my mom and me while I was on crutches, but he was about to be on crutches himself. Unlike me, my dad had never undergone a surgery, and I could see he was nervous. As someone who had multiple surgeries under his belt, I felt it was my duty to calm him and let him see the positive side of things. He always made me laugh and helped me keep a positive attitude, so it was the least I could do for him. The following morning, they took him to surgery. Before he left, we all hugged him and thanked him for working his whole life for us. It was our turn to take care of him now. My mom was nervous and anxious about both my dad's surgery and my upcoming one, seeing as my dad would be out of commission. They had spent so much time taking care of me, so I told my mom it was time to focus on my dad.

She and I walked the hospital halls. She did it to keep her mind occupied; I did it to continue strengthening my leg. I wanted to make sure I had the best chance at a speedy recovery after my PCL reconstruction. The nurses let us know the procedure was over and we could visit my dad in his recovery room. We rushed to his side and breathed easier as we saw him smiling. He laughed and said he understood why I'd undergone so many surgeries, "That's the best sleep I've ever had," he said. "I see why you like anesthesia." My mom could finally smile and laugh again. I started joking and playing around with him like nothing had happened. That was important.

He didn't know the emotions of feeling like a prisoner in your own body, but I did. It was important we made my dad feel like nothing had changed. That was the only thing that had kept me from going crazy. My mom always treated me with love but always allowed me to make my own decisions, so long as they didn't impede my recovery. I spoke to my mom shortly after and told her my dad would probably struggle and might feel depressed—that it'd be difficult for him, not being able to do everything he did before. She laughed and said my dad wasn't the type of person to get depressed. I just smiled and hoped she was right. But I hadn't been that type of person either, and it still hit me hard.

We stayed that first week with my dad in Richmond Hill to take him to his follow-up appointment in Savannah. He hated having to use crutches and keeping his leg elevated. Just like with me, the couch became his bed.

My mom slept on the couch next to him just like she had done for me. It was like life was showing me a mirror image of days I had already lived. I thankfully knew how these days played out and how to help my dad. He had the staples removed from his leg, and the doctors didn't prescribe any PT, which I found very odd. Physical therapy had been essential in my recovery, and I felt my dad would need some once he left the crutches behind.

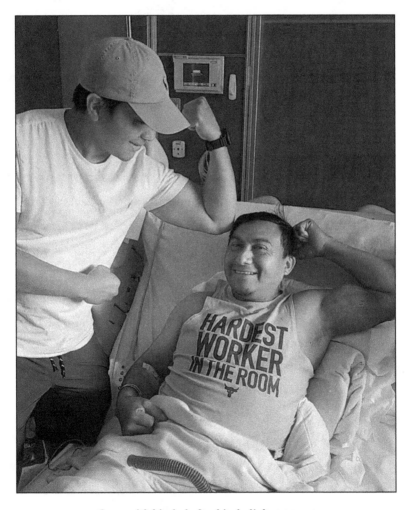

Cesar with his dad after his dad's leg surgery

Cesar and his father, both after their leg surgeries

There wasn't much we could do for the moment because my surgery was fast approaching, and we just had to let my dad's break heal. We brought him to Atlanta with us so my mom could take care of us both after surgery. That's when emotions started weighing down on my father. Thoughts of "what if" started calling his mind home. He had taken the side job to make more money and help us, yet he had paid almost double for his surgery than what he made from that job. My dad kept pondering. What if he had just driven to Atlanta instead? What if he had said no to that job? These were similar to the thoughts I had experienced time and time again. I expected my dad to have them as well. He mostly regretted that he had put more responsibility on my mom's plate. As if taking care of me wasn't enough, the woman now had to take care of us both. My dad and I were the only men in our family, and we could do nothing to help the women in our lives. That weighed heavily on his mind. He started feeling hopeless and useless, something I knew a lot about.

I think this was one of the events, aside from my accident, that marked our lives. My dad is the strongest man I know, and it broke my family's hearts to see him struggle. With him staying in Atlanta with us, the big question was what we would do with our two dogs and sixty chickens. There was no way we could bring them with us to the apartment and no way we could drive back and forth to check on them. Sadly, we had to give everything away. My parents had started off with twelve chickens, and my mom had named each one that hatched. It had been their little pastime while my sisters and I were away. With no children in the house, my mom had dedicated her time to raising healthy chicks, but now she'd have to let them all go. Carolina cried for several days, not for the chickens but for Chispita and Canela. They had come into our lives years ago, and now we had to give them up.

One of my dad's friends agreed to take the chickens and dogs off our hands. When we went back to Richmond Hill for one of my dad's appointments, it was eerie seeing the house empty. In the backyard, where my parents built the chicken coop, it was just dirt and overgrown grass. It was a sunny and breezy day as we stood on the bridge overlooking the marsh. What should've been beautiful scenery weighed down on us heavily. It seemed like we were slowly losing everything, and it had all begun January 12, 2018. I hugged my mom. We were still alive, and we had each other. Everything that truly mattered was still intact. Really, we had lost nothing. Our family still held on; we continued to become unbreakable.

Obviously, my dad got injured by a chaotic sequence of events, but we started considering perhaps our family was cursed. Look, I've never been one to believe in witchcraft or curses, but even I started to have my doubts. How much more could my family endure? What had we ever done to have so many calamities befall us? Alicia brought up the idea when she called to check on my dad. I gave it a moment's thought. Yeah, what happened to me and all of us sucked, but we could not let this moment define us. "There's no way we're cursed. I'm alive, Dad is here, and we're together," I told my mom. "We will make it out. If someone or something cursed us, they fucked up." I tried not to cuss in front of my mom, but I had to get my point across. My little speech invigorated me, and I was ready for what came next.

Carolina drove us to the hospital on my surgery date, and again my family waited until I was out. I felt bad for my dad because he was feeling worse each day about not being able to help. The nurses wheeled me out to the car, and I rode in the back with both my parents. What a sight it was. My mom sat in the middle with a pillow on her lap where both my dad and I elevated our legs. We were both injured but on opposite sides.

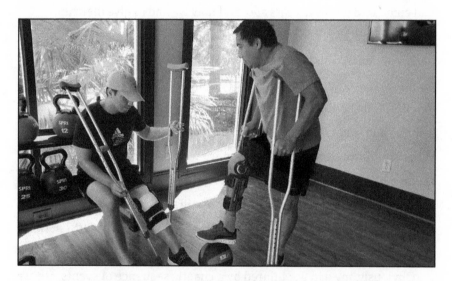

Cesar with his dad at the gym, showing him some leg exercises from therapy

Thankfully, I was prescribed PT. I was an athlete and my therapist Sean, at Peachtree Orthopedics, followed the protocol but also continued to push me harder. That's what I needed; it's what I craved. There was no taking the easy way out because I had never let myself do that. I went a step further in every session, aiming to recover as quickly as possible. My crutches were still the most dangerous part. My arm still wasn't fully functional, and it would sometimes lag, causing me to stumble and nearly fall. I decided to walk more and get my arm accustomed to the crutches. I was damn sure not about to waste my days on the couch when I had been desperately trying to get my body back and exercising daily. My dad was cleared to stop using the crutches, and since he wasn't prescribed therapy, I taught him therapeutic exercises I had learned throughout my journey to strengthen his leg.

I took him to the gym with me, and that's when I realized my determination was motivation for everyone around me. We had been through hell, and yet I was still fighting for what was mine. My dad said seeing me hit the gym despite my limitations inspired and motivated him. I kept going to my therapy sessions with newfound energy, knowing my grit also motivated my dad to get better. Every other day, I'd come in saying my calves looked bigger and that women at Walmart had been eyeing them. Sean would laugh and tell me I'd have to do more work because I was lying. It was a running joke, but I started feeling like myself again. When they'd tell me to do ten jumping squats, I'd do fifteen because even though it hurt, I knew it was the only way to get to where I wanted to be.

My leg healed well, although not as quickly as I would have liked. But by this point, patience was my friend. We kept driving back and forth between Savannah and Atlanta to my appointments for my dad and me. He could not have been happier when they finally cleared him to drive and work. My dad tells me he felt useless and helpless at not being able to do anything. I just nod because I experienced that and more, not just for a few months but for years. We made it out though, and that's what counts.

Everyone at Peachtree Orthopedics saw my determination and hard work. Near the end of my prescribed sessions, they called me "The Energizer Bunny" because I just kept going and going. I could've stayed there with

Sean and the other therapists all day. They made it a fun atmosphere, and I knew I was being taken care of, so I pushed myself harder every time. Sean gave me a shirt when I was discharged, as my reward for making it through all my sessions. I thanked him and everyone who had played a pivotal role in my recovery. "The world will know my story," I said as I walked out after saying goodbye to everyone. I told them I hoped to see them again but not as a patient. "Next time you see me, even you'll be like 'damn, those calves are sexy!'" I told Sean. I didn't realize how soon I'd be seeing them again.

CHAPTER 14

The Fog Lifted

WITHOUT A DOUBT, MY MOM DESERVED THE MOON after everything she had done for me. She deserved more than what life had given her thus far, and certainly didn't deserve to keep sleeping on a couch. I always wanted to help anyone I could, and that was especially true of those dear to me. As my brain continued to heal, I began to notice everyone's sacrifices even more. My mom never complained, but I told Carolina she deserved better. She and I kept discussing buying a house together because the apartments were also not doable forever. So, as 2019 was coming to an end, we were heavily focused on buying a house to avoid paying rent for something that would never be ours.

I had spoken with Heather several times, telling her Carolina and I would be buying a house big enough for everyone. "With me not working, there's no way we'll be able to afford the apartment," I told her. "Plus, I'm done with having my mom sleep on the couch. She deserves more." Every morning, I'd wake up and see what my mom's life had been reduced to, but she never faltered. I knew something had to change for the better, and maybe buying a house was the change we needed. Money was running out, and with my dad having been injured, our funds were running low. Carolina and I agreed that whatever house we bought had to be close to Dunwoody since she was working at that high school and COX was headquartered there in case I ever went back.

I helped get Heather into the university of her choice by going to the interview with her. Whatever house we bought in Dunwoody would not be a long commute to school. She had done several other interviews, but they had not gone as planned. The interview I attended with her was the best one she had. The woman doing the interview knew the doctors who had worked on my case. This allowed me to establish a rapport with her. I told Heather to talk about my recovery and how she had helped me with my therapy. I felt accomplished when we left the interview because I had managed to help in some way. That always made me happy, like I had a purpose. Tito thanked me the following weekend for going and helping her as well. Everyone was happy when she got the acceptance letter. I told her not to worry about the cost because I would help pay for it. Don't ask me how the math worked in my head. I would find a way to pay for her schooling despite the huge bills in the mail each week.

Heather hadn't been helping with rent, and it wasn't until I asked her to help with the utilities that she actually started paying the power and water bills. I didn't think it fair Carolina and my dad were busting their ass to help me with bills when Heather could easily help with the money her mom was giving her every month. One day, I was looking at houses on my computer and decided to call Heather over to see them. I wanted her to be a part of the decision-making process. "Why are you looking at houses in this area?" she asked. "It'd be nice if it was actually closer to school for me." She looked at two houses and then left. I let her leave. Her comment rubbed me the wrong way. Not only did I feel like she was being selfish but also inconsiderate. I had told her she wouldn't have to worry about anything since the mortgage would be split between my sister and me. That's why we were looking for a house close to her job and potentially mine.

My headaches occurred less frequently, and I was starting to think clearer. I could see the big picture and see everything my family had sacrificed for me. How could Heather not think of anyone but herself and what was more convenient just for her? I kept thinking, *I know she's young, but even when I was her age, I was mature and tried to think about others and how I could help. Is this how it's going to be with us?* That question had been answered for me already, but I was just starting to see it. Everything Heather had said during the past year started coming back to me.

One day, I asked her what she saw in our future, and she let her true intentions slip. "Well, I know I'll definitely have my doctorate, and that's when we can go our separate ways," she said. "I'm only staying here because I don't want to live with my parents and you're closer to school. So . . . in three years, we can split." She immediately caught herself and started laughing. It was an awkward laugh, as if she had unwittingly spoken the truth and now had to fix it. My mom and Carolina were there in the living room and overheard, which is why Heather acted like she had just told the funniest joke. They just looked at each other but said nothing before stepping out of the room. They had been talking about my appointments and Carolina's schedule, but once they stepped out, their topic of conversation changed to Heather and me. Now they tell me what they spoke of, and it was basically the fear they had always had. They knew Heather wouldn't see me through to the end of my recovery, but how much longer before I saw it?

Back inside the apartment, I was laughing awkwardly too because I didn't want them to think she was serious, even though I didn't fully know. As I've said before, there's a grain of truth in every joke. It wasn't just a grain with her; she poured it all on me then and there. I just chose not to see it because I couldn't handle losing something else, especially not her. My brain and emotions didn't allow me to pick up on all the signs, but my memory retained every bit of information so I could analyze it in the future, which is what I did. Had I been in the right state of mind, I would've revisited those comments and not feared her answer. Everything in my life had changed, so I was desperately trying to hold on to what remained. I chose not to bring it up. I hoped sweeping it under the rug would make it disappear. It didn't.

In November, Josh Cammack, one of the Treutlen County firefighters, got in touch with me again. He invited my family and me to a holiday dinner. They were holding the dinner to also raise money for more equipment, such as the equipment needed for my extrication. Not that they would ask, but if I'd had a million dollars and they asked for it, I would've given it to them. If I had the funds and wasn't facing huge medical bills, I would've donated all my money. What they had done for me meant that much, and of course I wanted to help in any way I could. Josh asked me if I was willing to share my story with everyone at dinner because I was a prime example of why these donations mattered. They saved lives. I told him I'd be willing to help in any way.

The last time I had seen them all was near the end of 2018. Almost a year had passed since then. I wanted them to see a more improved Cesar, so I hit the gym even harder. Getting the opportunity to see them again gave me more motivation to get better and show them all their hard work in getting me out of my vehicle had not been for nothing. I focused on moving my arm more. I figured I'd be meeting new people and might have to shake several hands. We drove to Soperton for dinner, and I immediately felt the love and warmth from everyone. Several of the first responders I had met the previous year were there, as well as new recruits. Though we had only met twice, they were like family to me. They gave me something for which

I could never repay them...my life. Everyone came up to me and said how amazing my recovery had been. Although I'd prepared for handshakes, I only got two or three. Instead, everyone hugged me. *I guess I should've prepared for this*, I thought, since my arm still couldn't hug properly. But it didn't matter. They were just glad to see me again, and I was glad just to be there with them.

I answered all their questions as best I could, even though I didn't know the answer to some. One question they asked me was "Where is your girlfriend?" I had invited Heather to the dinner, but she thought the car ride would be too long and decided not to join us. I didn't tell them this. I didn't want them to think poorly of Heather, so I told them she had to work late. They knew I had a girlfriend but had never met her. She didn't come the first time I went to thank them, nor was she there for this moment. After the meal, Josh, Justin McNure, and Lee Henry all took time to say a few words.

Lee pointed at me and said, "This is the reason why we do what we do." I closed my eyes, trying not to get emotional, and just concentrated on my heartbeat. Then I was asked to speak and tell everyone a little bit about myself and everything I had been through. The pictures themselves spoke volumes as they showed images of my car, but I got on stage and told them my story. "Thank you would never be enough for what you guys do," I said, "but truly, from the bottom of my heart, thank you." It was the first time I had spoken to a large audience about my accident. Everyone told me afterward how moved they were by my testimony and resilience. As I gave back the mic, Josh and Justin asked me to stay on stage because they had a gift for me.

Justin spoke first because he had a few things he had been wanting to tell me for a while. "That night, you had courage and you had fight. I could feel it," he said. "It's an unwritten rule not to get attached, but Josh and I talked about it, hours after and days after. We had to get in touch with your family. We couldn't stand not knowing because we saw how you were fighting. So that's why Josh has something right there for you." Josh presented me with a glass trophy. On it was my name and the fire department logo, and it said Honorary Member. "Cesar, we want to make you an honorary member of the Soperton, Treutlen County Fire Department. You've been such an inspiration to us," he said. "I mean, the will power you've got. Thank you for your friendship we get to enjoy, and we will get to enjoy your recovery along with you. We appreciate it, bud." He handed me the award. I thanked him and did my best to hug him tight. I've received many awards and accomplished a lot in my life, but nothing meant more to me than getting that award from a group of real-life heroes. It still has a special place in my house. I'm proudest of that award. The story and meaning behind it are unrivaled by anything else. I told them this that night because I wanted to make sure they understood what an honor it was to be standing amongst them. They say I inspired them, but truly they inspired me.

They brought me a guitar afterward. "I know the magic you can produce on that thing," Josh said. "Play us a little something if you can or are up for it. No pressure though." They had seen videos of me playing and singing. I couldn't sing like that anymore, and I sure couldn't strum like before, but I took the guitar and tried. My sister and I had decided if they asked me to play, I would play "Hallelujah" again so she could help my voice when it faded. I could always count on her to back me up and never let me fall. It was a repeat of the performance we had done when I left Shepherd, but I was much stronger this time, and my voice was beginning to take shape.

When we finished, I told them I'd come back and perform for them once my arm and voice were better. I felt so much love and appreciation in that room that I found it hard to say goodbye. It was a new holiday season for my family and me. Everything had new meaning. We had the opportunity to spend one more Christmas together, and we had these heroes to thank for that.

The drive back to Atlanta was pleasant as we all basked in the experience of being surrounded by such amazing individuals. When I got home, I showed Heather the gift they gave me. She said she was glad I got a chance to spend time with them. "I just didn't want to sit in the car that long," she said, trying to excuse her absence. I told her I had covered for her. It would've meant a lot to me if she had gone.

Every year since college, I had made sure to decorate for Christmas and create a winter wonderland. My family had a running joke that every year, I went into Martha Stewart mode and wanted everything to be perfect. They did their best to uphold my tradition and decorate the apartment like I would have before. Even though she didn't help, Heather took pictures and sent them to her friends to show them all how the place looked. Everyone loved it.

The following week, Heather told me one of her friends wanted to come over and stay for the weekend. "She can come, but she can't spend the night," I said. "Where would she sleep?"

What Heather said next made me realize just how selfish people can be: "Well, I was thinking your mom could just go to Carolina's place and sleep there for the weekend." I was silent, dumbfounded by what I had just heard. My mom was living in my living room not because she didn't have a house to go back to but because she wanted to make sure I was taken care of. She knew Heather wouldn't take care of me or be there for me when I needed, so she stayed.

"What makes you think you have the right to suggest my mom finds somewhere else to sleep?" I asked. "She's the only person who has been there for me 24/7. You definitely haven't. Has your friend been there for me as well? No, I didn't think so. So, if you want to spend a weekend with your friends, then go rent a hotel or something because I'm not telling my mom to leave."

I was genuinely angry with Heather. I knew this wasn't the life I had promised her, but dammit, I was doing the best I could. When I told my sister what Heather said, she wanted to tell her to get out. "How can she be so fucking selfish? She hasn't done shit for you and has no right asking Mom to sleep somewhere else! Cesar, you better not ask mom to go," Carolina said. I just looked down and nodded in agreement. Hearing my sister cuss was always weird because she never did it. I knew she was livid. I spent the next three days trying to figure out what Heather and I were, exactly. She hadn't done anything since I'd left the hospital to make me feel like I was her number one priority like she was mine, and it hurt as I began to see it. I knew what unconditional love was. My parents were the living incarnation of it. My mom relinquished her own life to be by my side every day because love doesn't seek its own way. I had been to many weddings, and I knew the scripture read at almost every ceremony, 1 Corinthians 13: 4–8, which in the New American Standard Bible reads:

Love is patient, love is kind, it is not jealous; love does not brag, it is not arrogant. It does not act disgracefully, it does not seek its own *benefit*; it is not provoked, does not keep an account of a wrong *suffered*, it does not rejoice in unrighteousness, but rejoices with the truth; it keeps every confidence, it believes all things, hopes all things, endures all things.

Love never fails....

That passage kept replaying in my head, and I tried time and time again to squeeze Heather into that definition, knowing deep down she would never fit.

If love was patient, then where was it when I asked Heather to weather the storm with me while I continued getting better for both of us? If love endures all things, why was it unbearable to see me learn to walk, talk, and eat again? In the end, if it was unbearable to anyone, it should have been me since I was the one going through it. Heather couldn't and never would understand the pain and storm raging inside me, so how could I expect her to endure this hell with me? I had given her everything I possibly could to keep her close, and instead, I felt her getting further and further away. "Love never fails" is the ending to that passage. So if it fails, was it ever truly love? I didn't want to answer that question, knowing the answer would trouble me. Could everything I had done thus far be in vain? If it all leads to the same place—a life without her—should I have just given up earlier?

Everything with Heather was slowly starting to make sense. All the while I was in the hospital and many months after, Heather had been my everything. My brain may have been severely impaired at the time, but for some reason, the musical side of my brain was not. I knew what I was feeling in that moment was something very few people got to experience: the pain and despair of not knowing what the future held, even for the few things remaining in my life. Every day felt like it could be my last, and all I asked God, or whoever was listening at the time, was for a little more time. Eventually, I wrote down all the thoughts I'd had in the hospital and added my guitar. Though I couldn't play like before, I wanted to gift Heather a song that had been forming in my mind long before I even opened my mouth to say "I love you" again. Everything I felt for her was wrapped up in this one song, titled "I Love You Like I Did."

★　★　★

You see the way you look tonight, girl,

Couldn't dream of something better.

You're what I want to see as I close my eyes.

Should tomorrow never come for me,
I pray that you'll be strong

Because I won't be there to dry your eyes.

All I ask is for a little more time.

So give me just a moment, to hold her in my arms again.

Let her know this love I feel won't fade.

And though I'm halfway to you,
Lord, give me peace of mind and let her know,

Just let her know.

I love her like I did before.

I started writing that song for her in August, and I felt December was as good a time as any to play it for her and let her know how I've always felt. It was one of my last attempts at trying to make her understand what she meant to me. When she got home, I asked her to sit down, and I took out my guitar. "I'm still working on it," I said, giggling. Then I played and sang her the song. It was just her and me in the living room.

I don't know what reaction I expected, but definitely not the one I got. "You're definitely gonna marry a white girl," she said. "That's more her style, probably. But thank you for the song, baby, I appreciate it." She kissed me and went to the bathroom to fix her makeup. To say I was stunned would be an understatement. My singing and playing were not what they used to be, but I was baring my soul to her, trying to make her see nothing I felt for her had changed. I wasn't expecting a standing ovation or anything, but to say I was going to marry someone else, when she was all I wanted, made me feel hopeless. It was the proverbial straw that broke the camel's back. She had long ago started chipping away at the image of her I had created in my mind, and now she stood before me in true form. How much longer could I try holding on to something that had long ago stopped being mine? I tried to brace myself for what I hoped would never come, but it was inevitable.

After that, I decided not to include Heather in any future plans because she was no longer a constant in my life but rather an unknown variable. My family was the one constant, so naturally I made sure to include them. Two weeks before Christmas, I began to order presents for Heather and her family. We were going to spend it with them, and I didn't want to go empty-handed. Before, I would get Heather whatever she wanted, disregarding the price. Now, I had a different perspective.

I had spent so much time and effort doing anything and everything I could to help her, and continued to get better, for both of us. I was still that man who wanted to help anyone however I could, especially those I loved. But it soon became apparent to me that some people take advantage of that quality in others. What if she didn't stay? I had planned several months earlier to get her a new MacBook Pro laptop. That idea didn't sound good anymore, so I started thinking about what I could give her instead. Something less expensive. She always called me her little moose, and I did the same. I figured I could buy her a bedspread and bed sheets with moose on them. If she chose to leave, I would at least be left with new bedding that I liked and could use. If she took it with her, well at least it wasn't a MacBook Pro.

As the fog lifted, I was finally able to see Heather clearly. Did she stay this long out of convenience, self-interest, or perhaps both? I don't know. But I finally began to see it wasn't love. No one wants their love for others to go to waste, and I was no exception.

CHAPTER 15

Perhaps I Was Never Alone

EVERYTHING HAPPENS FOR A REASON. IT WAS A statement I had heard repeatedly since the day of my accident. I'm sure some of the folks who said it believed it, but for the most part, it was just something people said when nothing else would do. I was in a situation no one should be in, and there was no justification for it. There was no explaining it. Every one of us is born with free will and though God may establish our steps, we choose what path we want to take. I had not chosen this. This was not the path on which I wanted to take my life. I was paying the price of someone else's actions. There must have been outside forces at play, something bigger than us that no one could understand. But it still didn't take the anger away. Who in their right mind would let this happen to someone who's always tried to do right? It couldn't be God's plan, could it? The God I knew—the God I prayed to—was a loving God. But this wasn't love.

This was pain in its purest form. Life is a ledger, a collection of everything we've done. Yeah, I've had my faults, but I've always learned and tried to fix them. The world was filled with bad people, and yet, some were living a grandiose life, with no repercussions for their past indiscretions.

None of what happened could ever be justified "for a reason" or as something that was meant to happen. We decide what trajectory our destinies take. Alexander Vasquez was not destined to get on the road drunk and ruin my life for a greater purpose; my life already had one when he came into it. It was his choice, however, and we are all just paying the price. No, everything doesn't happen for a reason or purpose, but we can definitely give purpose to our life, decide where it goes, and make the best with what we're given. That was my only lifeline, my only choice. Otherwise, why continue? I knew I didn't deserve this, but life was never meant to be fair. It's unpredictable and comes in a mixture of moments filled with distress, exultation, or both. Despite all this, life can still be beautiful, and it's worth living every second of every day. Trust me.

I survived what no one thought possible, and maybe, just maybe, that's where God was. He hadn't let me slip away because He, too, didn't think it was fair. I didn't come to this realization right away. Two years had to pass before I even began contemplating the idea that God never left me. He had not abandoned me like I initially thought. Where I needed Him, there He was. He may have taken His time, but He was never late. I began to see how things would fall right into place just moments before I thought no solution would come. I'm not here to preach to you or make you a believer; that's not my goal. These are just the words of a man telling his story in hopes that it might help you realize that, yeah, life can be difficult, but there's still a chance of finding peace in the storm. In doing so, you might even find what everyone seeks in this world: happiness. I definitely had to go through some healing, piecing together all the broken parts. It took time, sweat, blood, and tears, but in the end it was worth it. Becoming unbreakable was the culmination of all my hard work, persistence, and determination to not give up.

I forget the exact date, but in late 2019, I finally got scheduled for my driving evaluation at Shepherd. We all thought the evaluation would just be me driving in a simulator and testing my reflexes. I asked Heather to come with me to the evaluation since she was free that day. Thankfully she agreed to it, and Heather, my parents, and I made our way to Shepherd. When we got there, I filled out some paperwork, and they tested my vision and my understanding of road signals. After the first part was complete, they came to get me and told my parents we'd do the last part of the evaluation on the road. My mom turned pale. I hugged her and told her the same thing I had heard so many times. "Everything will be okay." I said it with confidence. I wanted to make myself believe it too. Normally I don't get nervous, but as I walked to the car and got in the driver's seat, the nerves started making their presence felt. The driving instructor sat beside me, and someone else sat in the back seat, taking notes.

I put on my seatbelt and adjusted the mirrors, and once I felt comfortable, I asked him where we were going. He pointed straight ahead and said we would go for a little drive and he would tell me where to turn. My heart was beating fast. I realized how hard it was staying relaxed when my right arm couldn't fully move. As I was about to get onto Peachtree Road, I remembered my blinker. I had been waiting for this moment for so long, and they were not about to catch me slipping. Reminding myself about the blinker made me feel more confident. I knew how to do everything; I just had to get used to doing it again. We drove around for about twenty-five minutes and then returned to Shepherd. The only thing I did incorrectly was switch lanes as I crossed a traffic light, something they advise against. Aside from that, the evaluation went smoothly, even though I drove with just my left arm.

I was amazed my driving instructor could be so calm when this was my first time driving after a severe brain injury. He told me he was passionate about helping patients reclaim their independence, and he had done it so many times. It's hard finding people who are truly passionate about what they do, but that's what made Shepherd Center such an amazing place; all their employees are like that. This made the biggest difference not just in my recovery but for every patient who got to call Shepherd home, even if just for a bit. The following week, I received a letter in the mail stating I had passed the evaluation. If there was ever a moment for confetti, this was it. I felt like I had just won an Oscar. It was the biggest accomplishment thus far in my eyes. Crazy to think something like this would make me feel so special when it was something everyone did, and I had done it so often before. I took it all in with gratitude and an acknowledgment that perhaps everything would be okay.

As 2019 was ending, so too was my Long-Term Disability (LTD). Carl and Shelby had gone over the requirements I needed to meet for LTD, but back then, when they had said two years, it seemed so far away. Here I was rounding out my second year on LTD, and I started feeling anxious about my future again. Would my benefits be terminated? How would I be able to pay for the pending surgeries? Was there a way to extend it? I wasn't trying to beat the system, and I didn't care if I didn't get my monthly payment. I just needed to keep my benefits; shit, I would pay it out of pocket if I had to. Time. I just needed a little more time. I got on the phone with the insurance company and tried to get my LTD extended. "I just have about three more surgeries that'll have me out for several weeks," I said. "There's no way I could go back to a full-time position just to be gone for several weeks."

The representative told me the only way it worked was if I were transitioned into Permanent Disability. "You would have to meet the requirements, and we would talk with all your physicians," she said. "This means you'd be permanently disabled from doing any job, not just yours." I knew that wasn't me, and hell, I didn't *want* to be labeled permanently disabled. That's why I was busting my ass, working hard so no one looked at me differently than before. My arm still wasn't fully functional, but I knew I would never meet the requirements. I got off the phone and prepared myself for the worst, hoping for the best.

The best option for me was to apply for job openings at COX and hopefully get accepted before my LTD expired. The other option was to get on COBRA, which meant instead of paying the employee rate, I'd pay the full amount for my healthcare. It was a big jump in numbers, and I knew I couldn't maintain that rate given our financial circumstances. COBRA was out of the question. I kept taking all the freelance work I could get, knowing tough times lay ahead.

This is where someone was looking out for me. I call Him God, but He might go by another name for you, or maybe you believe in the power of the universe. Whatever the case, I know I wasn't alone. I received a letter soon after, detailing how my LTD would terminate at the end of the year. It was the letter I never wanted, but it came, nonetheless. My parents said not to worry. We had been through worse, and we'd always made it through. We all assumed I would lose my benefits, but COX kept me on the employee rate. It was that one-in-a-million probability of getting what I had hoped for rather than what I had expected that made me realize I wasn't alone. They didn't have to do that, but they did. They did it out of appreciation for me and because they wanted to help get me through this horrible time. I will forever have a deep appreciation and respect for COX. They showed me they put their employees first. Once again, I benefited from the kindness of others. It made me feel optimistic. Maybe I really could make it out of this nightmare. I didn't know for how long they would let me do this, but it gave me new energy to keep pushing for a full recovery. There was no excuse to give up now. I felt—for the first time in a while—blessed. There was finally some peace returning in my faith.

Things weren't particularly looking up, but they could have been worse, so I took the small victories wherever I could. If money had been an issue this year, I could only imagine what 2020 had in store for us. The only positive I could think of was the fact that we had a house, and Carolina could cover the mortgage on her own should it come to that. The fear of eviction or homelessness was gone. It would be a numbers game now. Heather would have to help this time. Right before the end of the year, I asked her if she could help by starting to pay for her phone. "When you can't, I'll gladly pay it for you," I told her. "Who knows if I'll have LTD next year? I need to start cutting down on some costs if it comes to that."

I'm not sure why she took it badly when I was just asking for help in paying *her* phone bill. She turned it into an argument and said she didn't know if she could help. I knew her parents were giving her money, and she wasn't helping with the rent. She said she needed to make a budget before agreeing to pay for her phone. I took that as a step in the right direction and asked her if she needed help making a budget. "I'll get to it when I get to it, babe," she said sharply. "You're not my dad. I don't need you telling me how to spend my money." I swear I felt my blood boil when she said that. I couldn't have cared less what she was spending her money on; it wasn't my business. I was just asking her to pay for the phone she was using, which I had bought her. The anger in my face must have been evident. She tried to make a joke and divert my attention. It was useless.

"I'm not trying to be your dad. All I was asking for was some help," I said, "but then I don't know why I'm doing 'dad' things and paying for everything you use. You're not my child either, so grow up. The phone bill is yours now, and I'll even speak to your parents about it." I was so angry, and deep down I had a feeling none of this would end like I hoped. We didn't speak much for the next few days, and it was odd. We lived and slept together but were like strangers again. I had bigger problems. A cloud of uncertainty loomed over my head as 2020 rapidly approached. The following week, before she left for school, I told Heather, "You know this is only for the moment; it won't be like this forever." I must've uttered that last sentence a couple hundred times. I was always trying to make her see that things would eventually turn around for us. I didn't know how long "this moment" would last, but I needed her to weather the storm with me for one more day. If we could do that, we would be invincible when it cleared. She told me she loved me, but the words seemed hollow. She spoke them, but with no intent. Like an empty promise, it left me wanting more.

Her parents invited us to spend New Year's Eve with them again. We went to their place, and I had a sudden flashback to when I had first met them in 2017. It seemed like ages ago and like that memory belonged to someone else. It was around the same time of year that I had met them, and the juxtaposition between this moment and that one was so clear. When I first met them, I was unstoppable, and they knew I'd go on to do great things with Heather by my side. That was then. The now was definitely unclear and uncertain, at least to them. Almost two years after my accident, I was still picking up the broken pieces of my life and putting them back together. No one knew, but I was reinforcing the broken parts with steel derived from my conviction, hard-learned lessons, and determination. As we all gathered together for the holiday, I foolishly thought the next year I'd be done piecing together the broken parts. I didn't know there were still parts left to break. Moving in the right direction was all I could do. I accepted that. It would be a long journey still, but whatever it took, it was worth refortifying myself to become unbreakable.

CHAPTER 16

If Only

THE YEAR 2020 WAS ONE FOR THE BOOKS. IT'S A YEAR almost everyone wants to forget for many reasons, but especially due to the challenges of COVID-19. That year brought so many changes to my life. I went into 2020 with the highest expectations, always thinking positively and hoping it'd be the year I fully recovered. Was it just wishful thinking? Perhaps, but I had to keep hoping. At this point, I started understanding what everyone meant when they told me I had survived for a reason. I still didn't think it fair, but I knew I was made for something more. This was not how my story would end if I had anything to say about it. I started to feel it in my bones and truly believe it. It couldn't have all been for nothing. I wanted to use my story for good. I knew I could inspire people and change lives.

Something good must come out of this. That thought is what made me start growing my hair. Part two of the facial reconstruction would involve cutting my head open from ear to ear to make sure everything was symmetrical. I would probably be required to shave or cut my hair very short. My mother and I had spoken about it several times, and I told her I wanted to grow my hair until the day of surgery and donate it to children with cancer. That was my goal. In the end, if I didn't look like the old me, at least I could change someone's life for the better. I had good, healthy hair, straight but thick, so it was the perfect plan to do good in someone's life.

It was new for me. I had never let my hair grow out. I now have a new-found respect and admiration for guys with long hair because it's not easy getting through that awkward stage. There were so many times I wanted to cut it when I looked in the mirror. I looked like a mushroom because my hair had so much volume. Every time though, I would remind myself why I was doing it and just wear a hat to tame the mess. Along with my hair, my patience grew, and for that I'm grateful. Even after I explained to Heather why I was letting it grow, she told me to cut it. "You look better with short hair," she said. I knew this, but letting my hair grow until my surgery gave me a reward to look forward to. Not only would I be able to cut my hair and donate it for a good cause, but I would also be getting my face realigned.

The old Cesar probably would've cut his hair when Heather said to, but I was now even more goal-oriented than before, and nothing could deter me—not even Heather. Her mom thought I should cut my hair too. "There is this great barber in town," she said when we visited. "I can take you so you can cut your hair. That way you won't look so Mexican." I don't know what her issue was with Mexicans, but I just laughed it off and told her I would keep growing it. In a way, I was insulted, and not so much by her Mexican comment but because she still didn't understand I wasn't doing it for looks but rather to do some good. Some of my closest friends were Mexican, so her comment also rubbed me the wrong way, but it was Heather's mom, so I let it go. I thanked her but declined. Growing my hair also helped dispel the anxiety as I awaited my second facial reconstruction. Now I wasn't merely waiting for my surgery but also waiting for my hair to reach a certain length.

It's weird how the brain works, but it helped. It diverted my attention. I realize now that my body was always in survival mode, searching for the best way to get me through the toughest moments.

In early January, I received a casting notice for a commercial filming in LA. I had not submitted for any project since my accident. First, because I was still recovering, and secondly, I didn't feel confident yet. This project was a little different from others I had received, so it caught my eye. They wanted real people (not actors) who were immigrants and Verizon users. I knew my IMDb acting credits would make me ineligible, but I thought of my family and how beneficial the money would be if they were cast. What persuaded me to submit my family was reading they would pay for travel and lodging to California. It had been several months since we had last seen Alicia and Antonío, so without hesitation, I submitted my family and told our story. Yes, we were immigrants and Verizon users, but beyond that, we had a raw and authentic story to tell.

Communication was critical the day of my accident. Had Carolina not had good reception to get in contact with the hospitals, my parents wouldn't have found the hospital I was transported to. I sent pictures of my vehicle so they could see the magnitude of the wreck. Our story was too real to ignore. They did a second interview with us the following week, and then I got the call I had received several times before, but this time there was a new joy tied to it. I was getting the chance to do what I did before. My parents were right; everything was starting to come back. The casting agency got in touch with me and said they wanted to use our story for the commercial and that if we confirmed, they would fly us out to Long Beach, California. My mom was more excited about seeing Alicia and Antonío again. To be honest, I don't think we would've seen them until the following year since I still had pending surgeries and no full-time job. We were running low on funds, but we managed to scrape by each week. There was no way we could've paid for the four of us to go see Alicia in California. It was too expensive. This opportunity presented itself, and was the best chance we would get to see my nephew again. Everyone agreed to do it. I was just happy I could do something for my family and that I had taken the first step to getting back in front of the cameras.

On January 13 we flew to California. It was such an amazing experience getting to travel with them. Though we would all be working on set, it still felt nice to break the monotony of our lives thus far. This was something none of us had been expecting and we planned to make the most of it. Being reunited with my sister and getting to play with Antonío was the best gift I could have asked for. Having my family all together again under one roof felt like Christmas in January. It's those little moments in life that truly give it meaning.

None of my family knew what to expect on set, so each day was full of surprises and funny moments. My dad and I were paired together to get fitted for the wardrobe. He was excited to be doing this with me. They told him to try different outfits and pose for a picture so they could decide which wardrobe was best. He would come back into the fitting room, saying, "I was made for this. They know a star when they see one." He never could say it with a straight face. His goal was always to make me laugh.

They gave me a large, red button-down shirt and jeans cuffed at the bottom. My hair was at that awkward stage where it was long but not long enough to tie together in a bun or ponytail. They combed my hair in a way I would never wear it. When Carolina saw me, she said I looked like a miniature George Lopez. I couldn't help but laugh because it was true. I wasn't the only one looking different though. Alicia walked out and we all laughed together. This was to be seen by a lot of people (if our commercial got chosen) and everyone would see Alicia in a flowery dress, the thing she never wanted. None of us ever dressed like this.

Cesar's dad holding Antonío

I discovered that the commercial would air during the 2020 Oscars. Alicia was so excited. She would be on live TV during the 92nd Academy Awards. "Only if they decide to use our commercial for the spot," I told her. "There are several families auditioning." Regardless of whether our commercial aired, we were together, and that's all that mattered. We were also getting paid for our time, so no one complained.

On our last day in California, we tried to spend the entire time with my sister and Antonío. Who knew when we would get another opportunity to see him? He would have to get to know us through video chats. We went to dinner, and I felt like perhaps the sun was finally beginning to smile down on us. Two years earlier, I was tied to a hospital bed, desperately trying to survive. Now here I was in California with my family, doing what I love. Though I wasn't done with my recovery, I looked around at all of us gathered at the dining table. "This is what it's all about. This is why I've pushed myself so hard every day. I didn't want to miss moments like this," I told them. My mom just hugged me and said nothing would have meaning if I wasn't in their life. They all thanked me for having submitted us for the casting call and knew how big a step this was for me, getting back to what I did before.

I got to hold Antonío after dinner, and something clicked inside me again as he looked up and smiled, just as it had when we visited before. I can't put it into words nor accurately describe what I felt. When he smiled at me, he unearthed something I thought had been lost forever. Remember how I said I felt I had let the past Cesar down since I had not been able to protect him? I felt like a part of me did perish the day of the accident, and it forever haunted me. Old pictures would motivate me but also deeply saddened me. I didn't have a multiple personality disorder before, but now (post-accident) I felt like the old Cesar was a completely different person, and he had sacrificed himself so I could live. That's why I was caught off guard when Antonío smiled at me. I felt a strong connection between us. It wasn't just the connection of uncle and nephew. That was obvious. No, this was something different. In Antonío, I saw the part of me I thought had died. I don't know why, but as I mentioned before, something about his pure innocence made me want to protect him from all the pain this world had to offer. "I wasn't able to do it for me, but I promise I'll be here for you and help you where I failed," I whispered to him.

Cesar spending time with Antonío after filming
Verizon commercial for the Oscars

I couldn't protect the old Cesar, but here was a chance to make amends. If some part of me was living in Antonío, I knew how to find some peace with the ghost that had haunted me. Antonío shared my name, but now we had a connection thicker than blood. He was, in my eyes, a second chance. We were both just starting to make sense of what life was—him, because he was only months old—me, because I had been born again (figuratively speaking). My mother saw Antonío as a second chance as well, a reminder that life keeps going and there are still reasons to live and cherish it. I had lost nothing. The only thing I lost was time, but I decided to make the most of every day I had yet to live.

It was hard saying goodbye to them both. We boarded a flight back to Atlanta the next morning, and I was sad to go but excited to get home to Heather. She had stayed because of school, and the director had only interviewed my family. I told her all about the trip and that if they chose our commercial, it would probably air during the Oscars. She seemed to listen but appeared more distant, and I had no idea why at the time. Carolina and I had bought the house and we were just waiting to move at the end of January. Several times, my sister and I had invited her to go see the house, which was only fifteen minutes away. But she never did, and there was always an excuse as to why. We had only one week left in the apartment after I got back from California. My dad had been coming up every weekend to pack things so we wouldn't fall behind. Everything was ready to go by the time we moved out, except Heather's things. She never packed her stuff. Finally, on the last day, it was my sister and dad who did the packing. She laid on the bed and watched Netflix while Carolina and my dad moved everything. I sensed something was off with Heather. I tried talking to her, and she just stared off toward the TV, not really paying attention to it. "Babe, I'm excited to start somewhere new with you," I told her.

She turned to look at me. "I didn't sign up for this," she said. "I wasn't expecting all of this when we started dating." I know she immediately caught herself, but by then the words were out and the damage was done. She came toward me to kiss me, but this time, I pulled away.

She hadn't signed up for this? Did she think I had signed up to take two trucks to the face and spend the next couple of years recovering? The day of the accident, I had been driving down to see her, and despite the consequences of that decision, life still had meaning for me because I got to spend more moments with her. My dad was at the house, dropping her things off with my sister. My mom was outside walking and talking to her sister in Arkansas, so it was just me and Heather alone. The only things left were the bed and couch. Since they were the biggest, we had left them for last.

Heather tried kissing me again, but I just sat there quietly thinking of all the decisions in my life that had led to this point. Before, I had seen her as the most beautiful person in the world. She had been the light of my life. But now, she showed me just how fleeting her beauty had been. When she took off her makeup, what was left if there was no beauty or compassion within? All that remained was a shadow of the person I once fell in love with. I realized we had both changed. She didn't seem like before and had grown distant with each passing day. My physical appearance and perspective were drastically different than when we first met, but nothing had changed with regard to how I felt about her. That stayed constant. It stayed true. My hope was that would be enough.

I told her it was time for a decision. In my heart of hearts, I believed if we could make it through this storm together, there was nothing we couldn't accomplish. No matter what, we would always overcome because we had been through worse. I had said this to my family, Heather, and her family many times before. This was a make-it-or-break-it moment. She had to decide whether she wanted a future together or if I wasn't going to be in it. It was a simple yes or no answer for me, and I told her so. I said, "This," motioning to myself and all around me, "is not forever. The love I feel for you is, but I'm not holding you hostage. You can decide if you want this or not. The ball's always been in your court." We had moved to the living room and were sitting on the carpet. I grabbed her hand and said, "Te amo ... but ... do you love me?" As soon as I said it, the next moments of silence felt like an eternity. It was the ultimate question, and I needed her to answer. She could have continued not helping, and I would've been fine with it if she had just said yes. Her love was enough for me.

For me, Spanish words have always had a deeper meaning and always meant more. People nowadays use the word love so habitually that it feels like its meaning has depreciated. This could just be a notion I have, but when I truly love something, I use the Spanish translation of love, "amor." I truly love my family, which is why I've always said it to them in Spanish. I want them to know they stand out from everything else and that they are the most precious things in my life. That's why I told Heather, "Te amo." I wanted to make sure she understood I wasn't saying it lightly. I didn't love just anything or everything; I loved her.

She understood the type of love I was referring to because she was quiet for several minutes before responding. As tears formed in her eyes, I prepared myself for what was coming. Like the fear of seeing lightning and not knowing when the thunder would hit, I was scared and anxious about what she would say. "Do you want this, or not?" I asked again. Only then did she speak, and as she did, I felt like two trucks hit me all over again. The only difference with this pain is I was conscious and can remember it to this day.

"I think it's best if I go," Heather said amidst tears. I couldn't believe it, but I didn't try to change her mind. How could I? Pleading for her to stay would've been useless. She had made this decision a long time ago but was just now verbalizing it.

"You're lucky you actually have a choice," I said. "What choice do I have? You think I wanted this?" I asked, motioning to myself. "I can't run away from this shit like you can." Throughout the next hour, I felt like I was underwater, suffocating, trying to hold on to what was left of me. Everything Heather had done started coming back to me. It made me angry to see how love truly is blind, and it didn't help that I had suffered a brain injury. "Why wait until now?" I asked. "You could've left a long time ago. You could have gone before I spent money on a new apartment *for us*, paid for your college application, gave you everything you asked for. What was the deciding factor? The fact you won't have a nice apartment with all the amenities to show off to your friends?" I was angry at Heather, life, the world, God, everything that had culminated into that very moment.

She said she appreciated the time we spent together. She thanked me for the memories and for teaching her so much about music, insurance, taxes, credit, life, etc. "I don't regret the time I spent with you," she said. That blew the door open on what I had been holding back the entire conversation.

"I've always prided myself on living life to the fullest and with no regrets," I told her. "You changed that. You'll forever be my only regret."

I could've avoided the worst pain and suffering of my life if I had never met her. I would not have driven down to see her that January, and my life would still be intact. It's the smallest decisions in life that sometimes make the biggest impact.

"I didn't tell you to drive down to see me that day," she said. "Plus, you can't regret everything that's happened because you have a strong connection with your family now." I'm not sure if she was trying to make me angrier, but she succeeded.

"You think you and this accident are the reason my family and I have a strong connection? You're out of your fucking mind. We would die for each other, but that's not something you'll ever understand; you don't love anyone but yourself. This pain my family's been put through is something I can't take back, but I would if I could. So yeah, I regret you ever walking into my life." I thought I was done with what I needed to say, but I needed to get it all out. "You leave this place with more knowledge in every aspect of life and with more than what you came with," I said. "I learned nothing from you, got nothing from you, so what do I leave this relationship with? Nothing." The money I spent on her was something I could recover in time, but the time itself was the biggest loss. Time spent was something I couldn't get back, and I felt stupid for having wasted almost three years with the wrong person. At this point, I was pacing back and forth, trying to keep my emotions under control the best I could, given the circumstances.

My parents and Carolina came back to the apartment. It was such a drastic change in the atmosphere as they stepped through the door. They were happy that almost everything was moved to the new house. Their smiles faded when they saw Heather and me crying. They asked us what was wrong. Heather didn't speak, so I told them everything and that she had decided she didn't want this anymore. I squeezed my mom's hand and hugged her. I needed to feel some warmth, an embrace of some sort that showed me love still existed. My mom was shaking because no one really knew how I would react when Heather decided to leave.

Everyone had dreaded this moment, wishing and praying it never came, yet here we were. My mom worried most about my state of mind. The following morning, I had to be in court for the criminal trial of Alexander Lopez Vasquez. It would be my first time seeing him face to face, and the whole week leading up to it had been filled with a mixture of emotions. I would spend days daydreaming of causing him the most unbearable pain just like he'd done to me. The anger I felt toward him had been subdued to small embers as I continued recovering, but now that Heather wanted to leave, it was an all-consuming fire once again. The last part of my life that had remained intact was now breaking away.

How much pain can a heart and body endure? I was about to find out. If anger was energy, that night I could have lit up the city of Vegas for days. I told Heather to call her dad so he could come and get her stuff. She called Tito, and then I called him to explain what had happened. "I've never shied away from letting you guys or your daughter know that I love her," I told him. "I wanted to start a life with her, but she wants a more social life with friends and wants to party. I can't give her that right now... so she has decided to move on. I'm sorry things have to end this way, but I have a deep respect and appreciation for you and for everything you've done for me. I received more love and care from you than I ever did from her."

He said he was sorry to hear things didn't pan out because he thought very highly of me and my family. "Heather is still young and very immature.

Once she's back home, we have a lot of talking to do with her," he said, "and who knows? Maybe it wasn't meant to be right now, but in a few years, you guys could rekindle everything again." I know he was trying to be nice, but in my head, I wanted nothing to do with Heather in the future. After I got off the phone with him, I sat down next to my dad. He just put his arm around me and whispered, "Everything is going to be okay."

Carolina had been silent the entire time but now spoke: "I spent all day packing her stuff and putting it in boxes. Her stuff is all at the house now. She didn't even help, and now we have to go bring all her stuff back?" Heather shook her head and said her dad would stop by and get it in the morning. If you think I was mad, my sister was just as angry.

In Carolina's eyes, Heather was the worst. She couldn't believe she hadn't helped and that she decided to end our relationship the day before I had to be at the trial and see the guy that did all this to me. It was past midnight, and we sat on the apartment floor, waiting for Heather's parents to arrive. All the while, I was on Facebook and Instagram, deleting pictures of us together. I couldn't change the past, but I didn't want to be seeing it daily, so I erased everything. The anger just kept boiling, and I wanted the earth to swallow me. My mom tried speaking to Heather to see what made her decide to leave. "You have the right to make any decision. Just make sure it's your decision and not one which your mom or your friends have put in your head. In the end, you're the one making this choice," she told her. When her parents arrived, I walked out with her to meet them. My parents and Carolina were close behind. It was the most surreal feeling. I handed Heather her bag and asked if she had everything she needed. I felt like a dad leaving a child at a bus stop, making sure they have their lunch. I gave her mom a hug and thanked Tito again for everything. "You let me know whenever you want to stop by to get her stuff, and I'll have it ready for you," I told him. Everyone said goodbye, and Heather avoided my eyes. At the very end, I gave her a hug and just said goodbye. I didn't say anything else, nor did I wish her the best because I wouldn't have meant it. In my mind, she didn't deserve a second thought from me. I walked back to the apartment with my family. Once inside, I broke down.

My mom held me in her arms, and I just cried. I hadn't cried like that in a while. They were tears of anger, pain, and despair. How much more did I have to endure? Just when I was starting to see the light at the end of the tunnel, I was thrown deeper into darkness. It's crazy to think how one moment changes your life. Had I left work a little earlier or a little later on January 12, my life would be totally different. If only I had stopped to get gas sooner. If only I had never met Heather. *If only.* That's what my life was. Just hypothetical questions of what could have been had I made just one small but different decision. I asked my mom to walk with me because I couldn't be in the apartment. Those walls held memories, and I needed to get away from them. We walked for a while around the complex. It was a quiet night with a cool breeze, but in my head, there was nothing but noises and screams. I kept looking up toward the sky and asking why—repeatedly. There was no reason why any of this should've happened, or should still be happening to me and my family. *What more do you want from me? What more can you take?* Those were my questions to God.

I was completely broken at that point. My thoughts raced. I thought of everything I had accomplished before my accident and wondered if it was all meaningless. I was searching for an answer, something to give me peace of mind, but all I had were more questions. We finished our walk and drove to our new house. As I walked in, I walked past Heather's stuff in boxes. I stopped and just stared. Part of me wanted to go put all her stuff in the closet and assume this was all a bad dream, but the other side of me wanted to watch it all burn. I did nothing and just walked upstairs to the room that was supposed to be ours. My dad brought an air mattress, and he sat down and told me to be thankful Heather left now and not later. "This new home doesn't have memories of her," he told me. "This is a new beginning for you. I think you've gone through enough pain for her already. She doesn't deserve your tears." As much as I needed to hear that, I couldn't help but cry even more. I knew he was right, but it still didn't stop the tears. Like every pain in my life up until that point, I just had to let it run its course and hope I was strong enough to endure. My mom came in and told me, "If you need to cry, go ahead and let it all out today because tomorrow is a new day, and it's time to get your life back." I cried myself to sleep in her arms.

In the morning, I still felt the pain as I walked past Heather's stuff again, but it was less. I took a long look in the mirror and told myself I was stronger than I gave myself credit for and I would push on with more fervor and tenacity than before. As I started getting dressed for the trial, my mom asked me if I still wanted to go. "You know you don't *have* to go if you don't feel like you can handle it," she said as she tied my shoes. "We can just call them and say you won't be attending." I shook my head and told her, "I need to do this."

"I got this, I promise. I'm not gonna do anything stupid," I reassured her. My dad believed me and told my mom it would be beneficial for all of us to see the guy and maybe get some closure. Once I finished getting ready, I texted Tito and told him Heather could keep the iPhone I purchased for her. I told him I would pay it off completely that same day and they could use it for another phone plan. He was aware I had to be at court, so I told him I would disconnect Heather's line once I got back from trial. Part of me wanted to disconnect it that very morning and have her running around with no phone signal, but I chose to do the right thing. I did it once I was back like I told Tito. He told me there was no problem in doing it after the trial and thanked me again. After everything I had been through, I still wanted to believe doing the right thing mattered. Sure, it was hard to believe when I saw how life was treating me, but still I longed for it to be true. In time, I'd have to learn to accept the breakup with Heather and forgive her. Just like everything that had happened in my life thus far, I'd have to accept and come to terms with it. In the end, I'd be able to remember everything without reliving the pain.

CHAPTER 17

The Man Responsible for My Pain

MY FAMILY AND I ALL KNEW THAT ACCEPTING THE things you can't change had always been the biggest challenge. I asked my dad to pack my camera to record the trial. I knew if he was recording, I wouldn't do anything stupid, and I needed that reassurance because I still didn't fully know how I'd react. In addition, it would be my first time seeing the drunk driver who hit me, and I wanted to be able to look back on those moments. I wanted to tell my story. Whatever happened, I was determined to use my pain to do something positive and help others.

The entire ride to the courthouse, I tried to imagine how the proceeding would go and the possible outcomes. I wanted Alexander to look me in my eyes, see my pain, and just give me a fucking answer. Why? He didn't know me nor the hell he made me go through, but he was about to find out. As Maya Angelou once said, "I can be changed by what happens to me. But I refuse to be reduced by it." My life had been drastically changed but here I was still standing, refusing to go down without a fight. I realized I didn't need anything from him. The only closure I needed was him seeing me still standing and pushing forward. Almost everything in my life had broken since he came into my life. But my fighting spirit was made of something stronger than bone, and I needed him to see that. Usually, no recording of these proceedings is allowed unless you have consent from the judge. Several weeks prior to the trial, I called the county clerk's office and asked for permission. The lady told me I'd have to submit a written letter requesting permission to record on January 27, 2020, when Alexander Lopez Vazquez would be taking a plea.

I called and sent my letter several times before I finally got a reply allowing me to record the proceeding. My brain injury was healing well, and despite my impairments, all I wanted to do was help others and motivate them to keep going. I knew if I could do it, there was no reason anyone couldn't. We got to the courthouse and my parents kept telling me everything would be okay, but I could tell in their voice that even they weren't sure. They had us go through a metal detector and told my dad to leave the camera in the car. I told the cop I had been given permission by the judge. She told me to wait while she talked to the public defender assigned to Alexander. Several minutes passed, and the lawyer finally came to greet me. He said he had spoken with Alexander regarding my request to record the proceeding and asked me if I would like to speak directly with Alexander in one of the conference rooms before the trial commenced. I turned to look at my parents, but it was the first time they didn't know what to say.

Cesar A. Perez

Dear Judge Helton,

I am writing to you regarding the Alexander Lopez-Vasquez case. I am the victim of said case and I'm still trying to fully recover from all the damages I sustained (physically, emotionally, and mentally). You will be glad to know that I have put forth all my strength and effort into my recovery. It is truly a miracle I am alive and walking but none of this would have been possible without my family that has stuck by me 24/7 since that awful night in 2018.

My medical records allow a small glimpse at my damages and how incredibly difficult these past two years have been; not just for me but my entire family and close friends. That being said I want to do something that will help other people. I have been documenting my recovery and healing process as a way to help other people. While I was an inpatient at Shepherd hospital, I met some extraordinary individuals that had also been in tragic events. Some of them were in better shape than I was at the moment, but we were able to relate to each other and understand our struggles.

Thanks to my parents never leaving my side I was able to find the strength to not give up and keep pushing forward. I focused every day on going one step further with my therapy and just trying to do things better than the day before. Other patients and nurses saw my determination and it helped to motivate them. The same was for me. I would sometimes see other patients' optimism and I would use that as motivation to not get down or feel sorry for myself. I made a promise to my mom one night (on a dry erase board because my mouth was wired shut) that I would not give up and that people would look at my journey and get inspiration/motivation from it.

Fast-forward a little over two years and my recovery has been nothing short of extraordinary. The worst part of this entire journey is the fact that my family and I had to go through it. It will definitely take several years for the pain to ease. I know my family is very blessed that I somehow survived (although I did code on the paramedics several times) but there are families that go through something similar and don't survive or are injured permanently. That's why I am trying to create a documentary/video of my story. I want people (potentially patients going through something similar) to see my story and derive motivation to keep going. It's true what they say, "you never know how strong you are until being strong is your only option."

Healing isn't just physical. After a traumatic event like mine you have so much healing to do emotionally and mentally. There's a moment (part of the healing process) in the recovery where all you feel is anger. You are angry at that person that took everything from you just because they didn't care about their own life and were being irresponsible driving under the influence. I believe this is the hardest part of the recovery process, coming to term with what has happened. I am glad to say I have removed all the anger and hate from my life and have

Cesar's letter to the judge asking for permission to record the trial

come to terms with everything that happened that night. It is unfair that this would happen to me, someone that's always tried to help others and the community but nonetheless these are the cards I've been dealt and I'm trying to make the most with it.

Now I know Alexander Lopez-Vasquez is taking a plea on January 27, 2020. My request is for permission to record this with my camera. My reasoning behind this request is that people (patients) will see how getting rid of the anger/hate has helped me recover quicker by focusing that energy into my body. I am assuming that as the victim I might be asked to speak on January 27, and I think that it would be good for people to see the power of acceptance. Acceptance doesn't mean forgetting what happened, but rather it means being able to remember without pain and anger.

None of this should have ever happened. There is no excuse for what happened to me or for what Alexander Lopez-Vasquez did to my family and I. That being said I'm not filled with anger or hate like I was months ago and I'm proud of the man I've become. I can't change what has happened, but I can make the most of this second opportunity at life that God has given me and that's what I will do. It's been a long journey but I'm not feeling sorry for myself. I'm taking full responsibility of getting myself back to where I was professionally, emotionally, mentally, and physically. I did it once so I know I can do it again. In doing so, I hope my story helps many other people, patients, and families that are going through difficult times to focus on the positive and let go of the anger and hate.

P.S. I would have hand-written this but it's still quite hard to write a lot with my right hand due to the nerve damage I sustained the night of the accident but please know I would have if I was able.

Sincerely,
Cesar Perez

Maybe I should've thought about what to do in case of this scenario, but it never occurred to me I'd be given the opportunity to talk to the person that had caused me so much pain. I hesitated but ultimately caved and told him I'd do it, so long as I could record the interaction. He would have to consult with Alexander first, but he didn't think it would be a problem and proceeded to show us to a conference room. As my parents and I waited, I could hear both their heartbeats beating rapidly too. My mom sat next to me while my dad recorded.

I'll never forget the moment I saw him walk in, orange jumpsuit, my height, curly hair tied up in a bun, and a lost look in his eyes. I don't know where I found the courage or clarity to speak. The most surprising thing was that I managed to keep my anger at bay. He sat down right across from me and looked down until his lawyer started talking, trying to introduce us. I just stared at him the first few minutes. How could this person be the cause of all my pain and suffering? He was a stranger to me and yet had changed my life completely. It was a weird feeling. I'm sure even the public defender could feel the tension in the room. He said he and Alexander had read the letter I wrote to the judge and that Alexander was willing to speak with me. "Alex is from El Salvador originally," the lawyer said. "He went on to end up eventually serving in the Air Force." I know he was trying to give me a summary of the guy's life, but I wanted to just skip over it and get down to the reason we were all gathered. Perhaps he mentioned he was from the same country in hopes that we could somehow relate to each other, but it did the complete opposite. In no way could I relate to him. Yeah, we were born in El Salvador, but we were on opposite spectrums. This guy was a criminal. I was just a guy desperately holding on to the remaining parts of my life he had broken. As the lawyer kept talking, he pushed me further and further away from wanting to understand Alex.

He told me Alex had served in Afghanistan and that was what led to his drinking problem. If that was supposed to make me empathize with him, it didn't. I have great respect for our military and armed forces, but in no way did this outweigh what he had done to me. Thoughts kept going in and out of my head about what I would say when it was my turn to talk. Troops fight to defend and protect their citizens. So, what is the point of fighting if you come home and practically kill one of the people you've sworn to protect? I had been a United States citizen for several years at that point, and I couldn't understand how this story was supposed to make me see Alex in a different light. I felt more anger toward him for desecrating the memory of real-life heroes who wore the uniform with pride and protected their citizens. All my life, I tried being an outstanding citizen, not just because this country had adopted me but also to remodel the perception people had of Salvadorans. All anyone knew about El Salvador was gang violence and MS13. The US president at the time didn't help my cause. He had called El Salvador, among other countries, a shithole. Though we did have bad people in our country, not all of us were bad. My family and I had made sure to stand out from amongst that crowd. We wanted to show people good things do come from El Salvador, and everyone has a choice to make.

Everyone has a choice to make. Those words resonated in my head as it was my turn to talk. I looked at Alex and told him, "I don't know your struggles. Again, I had never met you. But the hardest thing, for some reason...the thing that hit me really hard was the fact that we're from the same place." I couldn't continue after that. All my energy was focused on making sure I didn't cry, but it was impossible. I paused for several minutes to try and find the words again. "I just don't want this to happen to anybody else. I don't think anyone should have to go through this, man, I really don't." As the tears started to form again, I decided to end by saying, "You didn't just ruin my life and my family's, but (pointing to him)...I hate to see someone from my country behind bars. It's something I never wanted to see." I choked at the very end with the tears I was holding back.

Dialogue came to a halt, but my mom didn't let the moment slide in silence. Best believe she had a lot to say. If there was anyone going through more pain than me, it was her. "He had all the injuries you can imagine. This is my son," she said as she pulled out pictures of me. "How can you give that back? How? You can't." There was more anger in her voice than mine. I know she wanted the guy to feel the same pain I had, multiplied ten times. My eyes caught glimpses of the pictures as the lawyer and Alexander looked at them. Yeah, that wasn't me anymore. No sentencing would ever be enough or make up for what he had done to me. Though the trial was meant to bring some form of justice, it didn't feel like it. The only justice I wanted was to beat him to a pulp. But how could I with my arm not functioning properly?

They stared at the pictures a little longer, looking down and back up at me. I would have given anything to make him feel the pain I had experienced. Someone had to pay for this, and I wanted it paid in blood. I was alive but I didn't feel like I was living. That had been stripped from me long ago. All I was doing was surviving, and it wasn't for me but for my family. They had sacrificed so much to keep me alive, which is why I had not given up yet. There was no lack of wanting to give up, especially after Heather left, but I had to keep holding on for my mom.

It must've been the pain in my mother's voice and the anguish in her eyes that got through to Alexander. He was quiet for several minutes but then spoke, "I have two daughters, and if this happened to them . . . because of someone like me I . . . I would hate them just like you. I would want them to suffer for what they did . . . to someone I love." My mom and I were quiet, just listening to what he had to say. He said it in Spanish because he wanted my mom to understand. Even though I was the victim of his wrongdoing, my mom was suffering seeing her only son struggle with everyday life. So, when he said those things, he spoke directly to her. My mom has that effect. She brings out any redeemable part in a human being, even someone like Alexander. The purpose of our meeting was to give my family some closure and humanize Alexander in our eyes, or at least that's what his lawyer hoped. This was done in hopes that the judge would be more lenient in his sentencing. I knew what the goal was. I had prepared myself for this moment for months.

"You need to take responsibility for your actions," I said. "Whether it be two years or twelve, accept it because you made this decision. Be a man and accept the consequences of your actions, no matter what they are." I said all of that with such conviction because I believed it. There was no reason to stop now. Even if I was just doing it for my family, I would give it my all.

Alexander nodded and threw the script out the window. "I want there to be justice for you guys. Whatever happens to me . . . it's my fault. I caused it myself. You're right . . . I accept whatever comes." The lawyer had no idea what was being exchanged, but he let us all talk, and for that I am grateful. We finished the conversation and got ready to leave toward the courtroom when Alexander stopped me and said, "Look, I know you want to tell your story and help other people going through tough situations. I don't know what is waiting for me, but should you ever need anything, I am willing to help in any way." His hands were handcuffed together, but he gave me a handshake motion in the air. I didn't respond because I didn't feel I had to. He was trying to start making amends, but I knew after that day, I would never see him again. I saw him once and that was it. There was no need for our dialogue to continue. He had come into my life out of nowhere, and he was leaving it just the same. We proceeded to the courtroom, and I prepared myself for whatever verdict would be reached. Nothing they would say could bring me justice, but at least I faced my demons that day and spoke with the person who had brought so much misery to my life.

Had I forgiven him? I don't think it was that simple. He had ruined my life, and forgiveness wouldn't come easily, especially from me. He said he was sorry, but that didn't erase what he had done. Was I even capable of forgiving him, or would I forever live with that resentment? I was asking this as I walked into the courtroom and then I remembered a quote. I once heard Celia Cruz say, "Forgiving is not forgetting. Forgiving is remembering without pain." That was the moment I realized I had not yet forgiven him. The pain was still very real every moment I remembered. Time would have to do its thing and take care of the pain. For the moment, I was content just starting the closing process of this chapter in my life.

The trial was held in Dublin, Georgia. As soon as we stepped into the courtroom, I noticed we were the only Latinos in the room until Alexander was brought in. My parents and I sat in the front row because I wanted to make sure my dad had a clear view to record. From the corner of my eye, I noticed two women sitting two rows behind us. The reason they caught my eye was because they were Latinas. That's when my head put two and two together. They must be related to Alexander, or at least know him.

I turned around to see them better. Only the older woman looked directly in my eyes. Despite her stern face, I perceived pain in her glossy eyes as she looked at me. I realized I had just made eye contact with Alexander's mother. The pain wasn't for me but rather seeing her son in an orange jumpsuit. He had caused my family and me the most unimaginable pain, and now it was my turn to repay the debt. I would get called to the stand for questioning, and I was ready. All I had to do was tell the truth because it was worse than anything I could ever make up. Never did I imagine I would be involved in a trial, let alone the victim of a case. As I made my way to the stand, my legs felt weak. It was the strangest feeling looking out across the courtroom at everyone. I managed to sit down just in time before my legs gave out. The lawyer asked me to raise my right hand and promise to tell the truth and nothing but the truth. I laughed because that's all I wanted to do, just lift my right arm. I smiled and nodded toward my right hand, which I elevated as far as I could. "That's fine, as best you can," he said. He then proceeded to ask me about the events that unfolded in January 2018 and how it had affected me.

He asked me what injuries I sustained because of the accident. "How much time do you guys have?" I asked him. I could've spent hours telling the court how my life had been turned upside down. We talked about all the medical procedures I had undergone and the ones I had yet to experience. My lawyer spoke about how the injuries affected every aspect of who I was. The musical talent I was known for had been heavily compromised because of the injuries to my face and arm. My athleticism and the health of my body, something I had always prided myself on, had been dramatically reduced. The rising star I had been in the film industry fizzled out that day in January. My losses were huge. I wasn't thinking in terms of money. They were bigger than that. I lost my identity, who I was. As I spoke, I made sure to emphasize that this should've never happened. It was all because of an irresponsible individual who didn't care who he affected the day he got into that truck inebriated. I said my last words and looked at Alexander's mom. I wanted to see in her eyes some of the pain my mom had felt in the last years. There was some semblance of sadness in her eyes, but when I looked at my mom, it paled in comparison to the agony in hers. I came down from the stand and sat next to my mother. We waited anxiously for the verdict.

She held my hand tightly. I don't fully remember the terminology used in the ruling. All I understood was that Alexander would serve eight to ten years. He had served two already, which meant if he was sentenced to serve eight, he would only serve six more. My parents and I found the ruling blasphemous, but what could we do? I had lost two years of my life already, and this guy would only serve six more years? I found it ridiculous and thought our justice system was broken. There was no real justice, at least not in my eyes. As I stepped out of the courtroom with my mom, the two ladies sitting behind us came toward me. They introduced themselves, just as I had guessed, as Alexander's mom and sister. His mom apologized for what her boy had done. She said he was a good person; he just made bad decisions sometimes. I wasn't having it. Nothing humanized him for me. "Look, I get it. We all have choices to make," I told her as I turned to face her. "Look at me. You know how depressing it is to be a prisoner in your own body, unable to move freely? To have everything taken from you? Your son ruined my life. I could've chosen to drown my pain in alcohol too and never face the music... but... I didn't. That was my choice. He had a choice to make that day too." I knew as a mother she was hurting, but I felt no pity for her. We all had choices to make in life. Her son and I were from the same place, but we turned out completely different. The difference was in our upbringings. My mother always made sure I was the best possible version of myself. We went through struggles growing up, but she taught me and my sisters to be a light in the darkness, and that's what we tried to do. Alexander could've been me if I had not had the values my parents instilled in me. That's why I could not empathize with his mom. I believed she had a lot to do with what her son had become. He was wicked in my eyes, a criminal, but she held some blame too.

She told me about his daughters, but I had stopped listening. The conversation was going nowhere. She could never change my vision of her son, and she would never understand the pain I'd been through. We parted ways on the steps of that courthouse. As we walked away, I grabbed my mom's shoulder and hugged her. We had done it and done it together, just like all the difficult moments in our lives.

Back when I left Shepherd Center, they told my parents they could find me a psychiatrist if I needed one. But I never needed anything because my mom was my doctor, nurse, therapist, and psychiatrist. She pulled me out of the dark moments when suicidal thoughts crept in. If ever I was upset, she knew it immediately and would never let me ignore it. We would talk about what was bothering me. It was that devotion and love from my family that gave my life meaning, even when it seemed meaningless to me. That's why I felt so light and free when we left the courthouse. There was no one else I would have wanted by my side that day. At the end of the day, they were the only ones who had witnessed all my pain. "How are you feeling?" my dad asked me as I got in the car. I was honest and told him I felt good, and even though nothing had changed, at least I got to say my piece. This entire time, my life had felt like an interrupted conversation. I had been making a statement with my life when this random individual abruptly cut me off. Today felt like I finally got a chance to finish that statement.

The drive back to Atlanta was filled with conversation about what we had experienced at the courthouse. I dealt with one ghost that had been haunting me for two years, but now there was another I'd have to address . . . Heather. This one was trickier in the sense that it was the most recent crisis to befall me. It wasn't easy seeing Alexander, but I had managed because all I felt toward him was hate. But Heather was a different animal. I had loved her to the fullest, so the pain was worse. I had given her everything, and in the end, I was just left picking up the pieces. Yeah, this pain would be harder to withstand and get over, and it was all new to me.

When we made it back to Atlanta, I asked my parents to stop by a Verizon store so I could cancel Heather's line. Since I was the account owner and paying all the bills, the Verizon agent said it would be no problem canceling the line but that it would still be active until the next billing cycle, so Heather had enough time to keep her old number if she wanted. I stopped him right there. I told him I wanted to disconnect it immediately. Whatever happened would happen. I had given Heather and her family enough time to change her line, and if they hadn't done so, it was no longer my problem. We had come and gone from the trial, and this was the last thing I needed to do that day.

I explained to the agent that my girlfriend and I had broken up and I had been paying for everything. He just laughed. He said he completely understood where I was coming from and that I could rest assured the phone would be disconnected immediately. I couldn't help but grin. If her parents hadn't gotten her a new line by then, it meant she would lose her old number and the area code she was so fond of. Again, it wouldn't be my problem anymore. I had stayed on top of everything when she was with me, making sure she had everything she needed, but now, I felt a sense of relief. It was one less thing weighing me down. We went home, and after about an hour, Bertha called my mom. I was surprised she called at first, but then I remembered Heather's phone and it started making sense. I heard my mom speak at the end with an assertive and serious tone, something she usually never did.

When she finished speaking, she told me Bertha had asked why I disconnected Heather's phone. "They had plenty of time," my mother said. "They said they were going to do it today, but Heather had stayed with some friends after school. Only when she needed someone to pick her up did she realize she had no signal, so she was running around lost." At that moment I burst out laughing. I pictured Heather running around like a lost little penguin, all because she had no idea what responsibility was. We didn't expect to ever hear from them again, and for my family it was a relief. For me, it was still a mixture of emotions. I felt like a weight had been lifted, but I can't say I wouldn't have answered if Heather had called that day. My heart was faced with the conundrum of trying to find peace in a future without her but also aching for what used to be. My mom asked me to delete their contacts off her phone. She was eager to close that chapter and move on to the next one. But I couldn't do it. Beside their names, I just added in parentheses, "Don't answer."

Only days later did I realize it was meaningless to keep Heather's contact info in my phone since she had a new number, but I still couldn't erase it. Aside from my family, she had been the only constant after my accident. Erasing her from my life would mean starting over. I was tired of starting over; I was tired of losing so much. Making Heather lose the area code she was fond of was never my goal but more like an accidental outcome of her irresponsibility. Still, I took it like the tiniest of victories.

My attention turned to my appointments. Who would take me to them if Carolina was at work? We had relied on Uber and Tito for transportation, but I wouldn't be able to afford Uber for all the appointments coming up. There were too many. I was relieved Shepherd had cleared me to drive before Heather left since that was my only option. My mom had gotten in the car with me only a few times before the accident, so there was no way I thought she would get in a car with me now. But despite her fears and trauma, she agreed it was the only choice and only asked me to avoid the highways. I was done asking for help and feeling dependent on others. I needed to do this. It was one more step in the direction of taking back my life. It had been two years since I last sat in a driver's seat (excluding when I took the test), and yet it felt like I had only stopped driving for a few weeks. Everything came back naturally, and the amazing part was that I did not have the trauma or memory of my accident. It was a small miracle we were all grateful for. As I adjusted the steering wheel though, it brushed against the scar on my leg, and I realized the wheel was what had broken my femur.

When I drove the car for the first time to my appointment, part of me wanted to just keep on driving with my mom. *Let's just leave*, I thought, *forget everything and just run away*. If only it were that easy, leaving all the memories behind and pain that came along with them. I felt peaceful on the road and reacted calmly to all the traffic hazards. My mom, however, constantly held on to the door handle. Her fears never left, but she tried to control them so I wouldn't feel frightened or scared driving with her. The easy choice would've been for my mom to stay home and let me go on my own, but try telling that to a mother who had seen her only son nearly die. She was not going to let me go by myself. Each day, we left fifteen minutes earlier than we should have, to avoid the highways and still get to my appointments on time. We somehow made it work and didn't miss any appointments. Though accidents as severe as the one I had been involved in were not the norm, my entire family agreed I shouldn't drive a compact car. Carolina told me I could drive her car, a RAV4, while she drove the Yaris (a tiny blue car). I had driven the RAV4 in college, and it quickly took me back to those moments—much simpler and happier times. Finally, I had a car to drive. It was liberating, like the shackles holding me in this prison of misery were starting to break.

CHAPTER 18

Stitching Up Wounds

N MARCH, I FINALLY GOT SOME OF THE CLOSURE I needed on Heather. I was certainly getting better at acceptance, even if it took some hard lessons to get there. Heather walked out of my life in February of 2020, in search of a more social lifestyle with friends. Ironically, soon after, the world began to shut down. I would turn on the news and hear about the threat of a rapidly spreading virus, but nobody seemed particularly worried. Just like most everyone else, I didn't think too much about it. In early March, I went with my sister to a retreat held in New York. The retreat focused on reestablishing a connection with your body. My mom was concerned about us going, but everything had been paid for in advance. And despite news of the virus, my sister and I decided to go because she felt it would be a great opportunity for me. We wore masks on the plane. Everyone traveling was wearing one at the airport, but the virus had not exploded into a full-blown pandemic yet.

Carolina was always searching for things that would help me reconnect with my arm and regain full mobility. She tried everything and bought me several things to try and stimulate sensation in my hand and see if some receptors came back online. I was hesitant at first to try something different, but if it somehow helped, I would give it a try. In the end, if nothing improved, at least my arm wouldn't be any worse than it already was. Truth be told, I didn't go to the retreat expecting a miraculous change in my arm, but rather I decided to go and meet people who had been through tough situations and learn from them. I wanted to know how they dealt with pain and grief. That was something in which I didn't have much experience. There would also be several brain professionals at the retreat, and I wanted to meet with them. At the event, I tried all the mental and physical exercises. I truly opened myself to the possibility that maybe, just maybe, something positive could happen in my arm. Nothing did, but at least I tried. The next day, after lunch, I told my sister I would go run around the lake and exercise. I wanted to be alone with my thoughts.

I ran and then sat down on the bench by the lake's edge. When I looked down, I could see my reflection and then ripples appeared. The pain and tears had somehow found me all the way in New York. I figured I couldn't run away from it forever. For the first time since Heather had left, I talked about it...not to anyone but to myself, the only person who could understand what I was feeling. I had a long conversation with myself that, in the end, brought me what I wanted, what I had hoped to accomplish on this trip...some closure. I poured my heart out, talking to the old me and asking forgiveness for not being able to take care of him, for unknowingly putting him through so much pain. I felt a part of the old Cesar was still somewhere inside me, and that's who I was speaking to when I said, "I'm sorry, man. You deserve so much more than this." After I wiped my eyes, I felt better. *Maybe*, I thought, *I needed to make amends with myself first before being able to truly move forward.*

My trip to New York was fruitful in that it gave me the opportunity to spend some time alone with myself and truly reflect on all the events up to that point. I had been broken down in every possible way. When Heather left, it felt like I was starting over again from the day I left the hospital in 2018. Two trucks to the face I could handle, but a broken heart, how does one cope with that? The pain was agonizing, and furthermore, I was angry at myself. I was angry for having placed myself in the vulnerable position of wanting to share my life with someone else. Heartbreak was just the last missing piece I needed to pick up off the floor to try and put myself together again. I found what I needed in New York that day. I came back determined to keep pushing forward, never forgetting the past, but accepting it and taking the responsibility of getting myself back to where I was.

I flew back, invigorated, and Carolina by my side. The day we flew back to Atlanta was March 8, 2020. Three days later, the World Health Organization (WHO) declared COVID-19 a pandemic. I thanked my sister for going to New York with me. Fortunately, we were able to go before the coronavirus was declared a pandemic. Cases continued to rise, and watching the news became our nightly ritual at home. As cases rose, so did deaths, and it was clear that the virus was no joke. Masks and social distancing were what the medical professionals recommended. As cities started to implement crowd restrictions and businesses began closing their doors, I couldn't help but think of Heather. She had left wanting to go out and party with her friends. She told me she wanted a more active social life like before my accident. Just one month later, her social life had been cut short since social distancing became the new norm. As I thought about the irony, I couldn't help but smile. She went back to live with her parents full time, which is the one thing she never wanted, but in the middle of a pandemic, it was the smartest choice. Many people I knew started complaining about not being able to live a "normal" life because of all the restrictions brought on by the pandemic. The people complaining were obviously people who had not suffered the consequences of seeing a loved one battling COVID-19. My heart ached for all the grandmas, grandpas, mothers, and fathers who were battling the virus or had lost the fight altogether. I didn't complain. Why would I? Nothing in my life had truly changed. I had been socially distancing since 2018, before it was in style. My daily routine didn't change. I continued working and trying to achieve the best version of myself possible. To me, the pandemic meant I could hide my face with a mask, and in those moments I felt normal. I would wear my mask everywhere, even outside where it was okay to take it off.

I wasn't scared of catching the virus so much as I didn't want to unknowingly contract it and pass it on to someone else. My body could handle anything—it had proven it—so I was never worried about myself. My parents were a different story, however. They were healthy, but older, so it became my number one priority to make sure they were safe. For them and Carolina, the priority was me and making sure nothing got in the way of my surgeries. That year held all the big surgeries I needed to feel more like myself. Everyone had witnessed my long, hard journey to recovery, so the last thing they wanted was to prolong it. Since coming back from New York, I had been methodical about working out and doing my therapy. Despite the monotony of my days, I remained persistent, always reminding myself to trust the process. I knew the world would come to know my story by the time everything was said and done.

I was optimistic for 2020 because my facial reconstruction was supposed to happen that summer. It was a tentative date, but I was excited to be getting closer. My orthodontist said my teeth would be surgically ready by the summer. The plan was to cut my jaw again and structure it back, as best as possible, to how it used to be. I knew this surgery would be no joke, but I was eager to get it done. During the procedure they would also try to fix my cheek bones that jutted out substantially. This part of the surgery would be done in conjunction with Dr. Amin, whose training included strong emphasis on trauma.

As we got closer to summer, the pandemic blew out of proportion. Every day when I turned on the news, a new record of cases and deaths were reported. One by one, hospitals started reaching maximum capacity. As the disease spiraled out of control, my dreams of getting my facial reconstruction went with it. My surgery was categorized as an elective surgery. The hospital then called to inform me that all elective surgeries had been postponed until further notice. I couldn't believe it. I was so close to the finish line, and it had been moved farther away yet again. People were dying by the hundreds, and the lucky ones who were still holding on were on ventilators. I knew what it felt like to gasp for air, fearing each breath could be your last, so I understood my hospital bed could be better used to save someone's life. I didn't complain. I picked myself up, after getting the call, and went to work out. It was just another setback, and I had come too far to give up. I was going to finish this no matter how long it took.

Two years had come and gone since my accident. Some days felt like an eternity, but for the most part, time had flown by. I was breathing, eating, and running almost completely normally again. It was a night-and-day difference from where I had been two years prior. Days, weeks, years... I had waited this long, so what was a few more months? Many of my friends and therapists asked me how I stayed so positive all the time, always seeing the good instead of the bad. My response was simple, honest, and always the same: "I have to." There was no other way around it. There is no alternate reality in which I would've recovered better or faster if I had not chosen to see the good in all the troubling moments. Once I realized this was the best approach, it became easier to accept because I had been so close to losing everything. I had a newfound appreciation for all the small things, the things we take for granted. Many times, before my accident, if I couldn't find a parking space close to the store, I would get frustrated. Now, when we had to park far away, I enjoyed the extra walk and thought of it as therapy. Each step I took just reminded me how close I had been to not being able to stand again. How could I complain? So I couldn't eat what I wanted. At least I could eat. So tomorrow I had another surgery. At least I had the opportunity to fix what was damaged. So I didn't look the same, but at least I was alive. That was enough. It had to be.

The next few weeks are a blur in the sense that each day was almost an exact replica of the previous one. I would wake up early and go for a three-mile walk then come home and do my therapy. I did all this before breakfast, and then I spent the rest of the day working on my portfolio, doing my French lesson, reading, and working on my music. On days it wasn't raining, I would ask Carolina to go to the park with me and kick the ball around. She was always more than willing to go and play like we used to. We were passing the ball around one day, and I turned to go get it and immediately fell to the ground. I had recently finished physical therapy for my PCL, so I panicked, thinking I injured it again. I finally realized I was holding my right leg, so my PCL was fine, but I still couldn't stand on my own. My sister thought I was messing around and only realized I was serious when I asked her to help me up. I couldn't straighten my leg, so I hopped to the car on my left leg while Carolina held me up with her shoulder. We were both amazed at how I had just injured myself. My knee felt locked and looked swollen. Our field time was cut short that day as we quickly made it home so I could call Dr. Kimmerly and get an appointment to see him soon. As I made the call, I was nervous they wouldn't be able to see me because of the pandemic. This wasn't a life-threatening injury, so they might make me wait. Luckily, the doctor agreed to see me that same week because I couldn't extend my leg.

I remember being so happy the day I said goodbye to my crutches once my PCL healed, but here I was again using them as I made my way to Dr. Kimmerly's clinic. He saw me and with a smile asked, "What'd you do now?"

I laughed and told him how I fell to the ground from just turning. "It's not even a cool story," I said. "I could lie and say I did a bicycle kick, but I was literally just walking when I turned. I don't get it." He told me not to worry and did a few diagnostics on my leg before sending me off for an X-ray.

"You have what we call a bucket handle meniscus tear," he told me as he indicated on the X-ray. "This is common and can happen in a twisting motion, and your body has been through a lot, plus that meniscus was torn when you tore your ACL years ago, right?" It had been torn years ago but not fully, and from what I knew, the torn parts had been scraped away. He told me he highly recommended surgery because, although my leg felt fine now, it could happen again.

"Given the pandemic," I asked, "would I be able to get it done soon?" He told me he could get me in if I chose to have surgery. That was all I needed to hear. I told him I would do it. My facial reconstruction was still on hold, and who knew for how long? So I figured I could get this done before then. Physical therapy would play an important role once again. I started giggling because I had just been discharged from Peachtree Orthopedics not too long ago, and they never expected to see me back so soon.

Surgery day came around, and by that point, I had lost count of how many times I had been put under. Anesthesia was just as normal to me as drinking water. My mom worried more than anyone about my recovery. I was used to the pain of physical therapy, and I craved it. Deep down, I knew the pain was part of the process to becoming what I wanted to be, which was just healthy like before. The struggle was always having to use crutches since my right arm, though better, was still not fully functional. No matter what procedure I underwent, my parents always waited in the car until I was discharged. The surgical incisions on my knee were very small. I kept my leg elevated while I still had the knee bandaged, and once again, the couch became my bed.

The hardest aspect of my recovery with this procedure was staying still and letting the surgical area heal. I was so used to working out and pushing my body to its limit that it was torture not being able to do it anymore. I mostly spent my days on the couch, but I asked my parents to bring some equipment to exercise my arms. Every surgery felt like I took three steps back and had to relearn how to do everything. Not this time. I wouldn't allow that to happen. I made sure to let my leg heal, but whatever I could do to keep progressing in my recovery, I did.

Dr. Kimmerly told me it was time to start therapy, and I called my friends at Peachtree Orthopedics to schedule my sessions. When I came in for the first evaluation, all the therapists saw me walk in with crutches and a brace, but on my right leg this time. I knew they were confused, and I understood why. It was not too long ago they had seen me jump and run. I had walked out of there fine. Sean came toward me and said, "When I saw the name Pérez on my schedule, I was like, 'No way it's him.' What did you do this time?" We both laughed about it while I explained what had happened. "I have the surgical notes here, and although it's not going to be as long a recovery as your PCL procedure, we want to make sure your meniscus heals properly so it does not happen again," he said.

Yet again, I was back at square one. My left leg was thankfully strong enough to support most of my body weight. Everything I had done with my left leg, I would now have to do with my right. *Bring it on*, I thought. It was nothing I hadn't done before. It felt like I was in a loop, recycling events that had already happened, and I wanted out. If Sean told me to do thirty squats, I did thirty-five. If he told me to stay in a certain position for forty-five seconds, I did it for a minute. It hurt, no doubt about it, but my goal was bigger than the pain. There were many times I could've easily skipped a set or done fewer reps without anyone knowing, but I would have known. Just like David Goggins, I was honest with myself and kept myself accountable. I could either stay where I was or keep moving forward. Only hard work could help me with the latter, so I didn't shy away from it. I ran toward it.

While I was going to therapy and the pandemic was raging out of control, I started applying to positions at COX. I figured it was time to start making those moves. My heart would race every time I saw an open position in which I would fit perfectly. I applied for those positions knowing very well I still had the big facial surgery pending but with no exact date. Some of the positions I applied for were put on hold indefinitely because of the pandemic. I understood the reasoning and was relieved I wouldn't have to go back to work full time yet. Going back to COX was a goal, a promise I had made to myself. I'm sure I could've applied elsewhere and received an offer in a short time, but I wanted to get back to where I was when my world collapsed. I wanted that to be the exclamation point at the end of my story. What a way to end a journey if I somehow managed to get myself back to where I was through determination and hard work. There was something I always said: "I got myself there once; I know I can do it again." Thankfully I still had my insurance and wasn't on COBRA yet, but I just didn't know how long that would last. I couldn't put all my hope on chance, so I kept applying and learning new things to boost my portfolio. In the meantime, I kept doing freelance work for MyBookie and any other recommended clients. I knew my work was good because I was passionate about it, but I still needed a full-time position with benefits should my luck run out.

Everything was pretty much closed, and everyone was being urged to stay home. For my family and me, it seemed like any other day of the previous year. I kept up with my daily routine of working out and doing my therapy. Thoughts of Heather would come into my head every now and then. The gyms were closed, so I couldn't take out my frustration there. I decided it was time to start putting my feelings down on paper once again. My body was healing well, but my heart needed some guidance. I had only pushed away and blocked the memories of Heather. It wasn't the best way to cope with it because eventually, the ghosts would rise again. My arm was better, so I decided to start writing everything down. Every word was filled with the sincerest emotion, and the only audience was my guitar, which felt the pain of every word. I wrote several songs, but none felt as real as the one I titled "Here Comes the Rain."

★　★　★

You say you love the rain

But hate it when it pours

You ask me for some roses

But can't stand the thorns.

You say you love the sea

Just not when it gets rough

Well suddenly I'm scared of how you love

I'm scared you say you love me

When skies begin to gray

Because you've always lived in the sun

But here comes the rain.

★　★　★

I found the inspiration for those lyrics after reading a quote from Bob Marley. He said, "You say you love rain, but you use an umbrella to walk under it. You say you love the sun, but you seek shelter when it is shining. You say you love wind, but when it comes you close your windows. So that's why I'm scared when you say you love me." It's so true in how most people perceive love nowadays. They say they love something but only when certain things please them. They are unable to take the good with the bad. Even gray skies are part of what makes beautiful scenery. That's how I felt as Heather walked out of my life and I was left standing alone in the rain. It's easy to love something when there is no fear of pain. If you say you love roses, you must appreciate the thorns because although they can be painful, they are still a part of that which you love. If you truly love someone, you will be there with them through the good and the bad, no matter how unbearable the storm may be. You can call it what you like, but don't call it love if it's only there when skies are clear. That's not love but rather self-interest. The purpose of writing these songs was again to create something beautiful from all the bad that had happened. You can break someone entirely with just a few words. It takes way more effort to try and create something. I chose the latter because I have always enjoyed a challenge. This wasn't going to define me. It would be the other way around.

I kept applying for open positions at COX, hoping they would make me an offer but also fearing the "what if they did?" I had two interviews around July that I felt pretty good about. My work was never my concern, but rather I was always hesitant in saying I had a big surgery coming up which would put me out for two weeks minimum. Because of the pandemic, I still didn't have a definite surgery date, but when I did, there was no way I would post-pone it any longer. I knew this might hurt my chances in an interview, but I wanted to be up front about everything. Nothing would stand in the way of my surgeries and recovery. I was battling to retake control of my life, and these were things that had to get done. For some positions, I never heard back, and for others, I received an email stating they had chosen to go with a different candidate. They wished me the best for my remaining surgeries and recovery. The interviews had been virtual, and I knew my portfolio was good, so I suspected it was because I looked different, had braces, had long hair, couldn't fully move my right arm, etc. The list was long. There were so many reasons why someone else would be a better candidate, I thought. Depression hit me hard for the next few days. I just needed a break, a win of some sort that could set me on the path to success again.

My mom said she was glad I was not offered a position because no one in my family wanted me to go back to work yet. I had taken my discipline to a whole new level since Heather left. My hard work was paying off. Even my friends who visited noticed my body and muscles were getting more defined. I had a long way to go, but I knew I was heading in the right direction. The days weren't long enough to complete everything on my checklist. It was the best way to keep my mind from going crazy or falling further into depression. If I was busy, my thoughts wouldn't turn to the past or what could have been. I had a routine going for me that was proving fruitful. No one wanted me to break that routine because they could see how much I was improving. It was summer already and Heather had been gone for about six months. I had already put on ten pounds of muscle. I understood where my mom was coming from. If I had been offered a position, my entire routine would have to change, and it would undoubtedly affect my recovery. It just wasn't the right time.

I had to look at the positive side of things. Fortunately, I still had my health insurance, and I wasn't on COBRA. Thanks to Christopher Smith, I was able to generate some income working with MyBookie. I was getting better each day, and my surgeries would hopefully happen soon. Things could definitely be worse. This was a year in which millions lost their jobs and were trying to make ends meet. I was somehow making it work and still generating an income amidst the biggest economic crisis since The Great Depression. All I asked was for patience and strength to keep moving forward. The call from Emory finally came, to schedule me for the first procedure of my facial reconstruction on September 16, 2020. I had been calling often to get updates because they had told me they could tentatively do the procedure in April. We were now in early August. I had met with Dr. Drew several times to discuss the steps to get my face symmetrical again and restructure my jaw. She said she wanted to split the facial reconstruction into two procedures because it required a lot of surgical time. The first part would be to realign and fix my lower jaw. She wanted to get that portion in place and let it heal before tackling the rest of the reconstruction. I trusted her and told her I was ready for whatever she had to do.

The pain I would feel was irrelevant for the moment. I just had to get through the month as quickly as possible, so I doubled down on my work and kept myself busy. In August, I also had appointments with Dr. Peljovich regarding my arm. I had been working out and doing my therapy constantly, but I still couldn't externally rotate my arm or feed myself. The muscles that had been innervated with the nerve transfers were filling up nicely, but I wanted to know what other options were available for me to regain external rotation. Almost two years had passed since my nerve transfers, so I feared maybe they didn't take well. Dr. Peljovich told me the year prior I just needed to give it time and not to worry because there was a "plan B" should my external rotators not activate. Well, it was time to start talking about "plan B."

We spoke for a while because he wanted me to understand everything the procedure would involve and wanted to give me realistic expectations. The plan consisted of disconnecting my latissimus dorsi and reconnecting it on the exterior part of the humerus to help with external rotation.

There wouldn't be any nerve transfers this time, so recovery wouldn't take as long as the first surgery. I just wanted to be able to feed myself again and asked him when I would be able to raise my hand over my head. Dr. Peljovich took a second to answer. He told me there was unfortunately not much more they could do to give me that movement back. I nodded and asked him about my shoulder extension and if I'd ever be able to reach back. Again, he shook his head and told me he wished he could give me everything back and prevent all of this from ever happening, but unfortunately, there was only so much he could do. My arm wasn't paralyzed at least, and I could bend my elbow again. I kept telling myself that and tried focusing on what I still had instead of what I had lost. It was tough hearing I'd have to get used to not having certain movements. Out of all the injuries I received the day of my accident, this one was the least apparent and yet would be with me forever. Nothing else was permanent, but when I looked at pictures of my car again, I couldn't help but think something had to stick and leave its mark. That was my brachial plexus injury. My legs were back and more muscular than before. Yeah, there were scars, but I didn't mind those because I could still do everything, and even scars could be reduced with plastic surgery. My arm, however, would never regain full mobility. It was a hard pill to swallow.

Before leaving his clinic, I asked Dr. Peljovich if I could get another electromyogram (EMG) to see if some of the nerve transfers didn't take and were causing me not to externally rotate. He put the order in for me. I was on board to proceed with the tendon transfer if it would help my external rotation. "I'll email some case studies so you can get more information on this type of procedure and what to expect," he told me. "Ultimately, it's your decision, so you let me know what you decide after reading some of the studies. The good thing is we can do it whenever. There's no time window we have to get it done by, as with nerves." That last part made me feel relieved since part one of my facial reconstruction surgery would happen in September. I had put forth all my energy, time, and effort into strengthening my right arm, but I could not postpone my facial surgery any longer. There would be no problem holding off until 2021 on the tendon transfer since doing it sooner would not increase the surgery's success. Despite hearing I would never have full mobility in my arm, I left his clinic feeling positive about the next procedure.

I got a call a few days later to schedule me for my EMG. If you've never had one done, count yourself lucky. It involves sticking fine needles into your arm to evaluate the electrical activity of your muscles when contracted and when at rest. The needles aren't too terrible. It's only painful when they test a nerve that's functioning and sending electricity to the muscle. The doctor then sends an intense electric shock to test the response of said nerve(s). Most of the nerves originated from the brachial plexus, and he would proceed to shock me in that area, but he had to dig deep. It hurt so much. After digging in between my clavicle and first rib, he would send the shock, and I would hold my breath until it was done. Once the test was over, I grabbed my jacket and thanked him as I exited the room. I checked out of the clinic, and walking to my car, I started giggling because it had been my idea in the first place to ask for another EMG. Some of the nerves had healed and therefore had made the experience much less pleasant.

My surgery at Emory was happening in a few weeks, but before that, I had to get tested for coronavirus. They emailed me the results the following day, and as I expected, it was negative. We had accomplished our goal of not catching COVID-19 and postponing my surgery any longer. My procedure was scheduled to begin early in the morning on September 16, 2020. Dr. Drew said I didn't have to cut my hair for this first portion, but it'd be best to cut it before the next one. I didn't sleep that night because I was excited to get it all done. My mom didn't rest either but for different reasons.

She had always told me I didn't have to go through with this surgery if I didn't want to because I still looked handsome to her. The last thing my mother wanted to see was her son bleeding and in another hospital bed again. I understood where she was coming from, but I was ready, and the pain didn't scare me.

CHAPTER 19

Forever and Always

THEY SAY LIFE IS NOT MEASURED BY THE BREATHS
we take, but by the moments that take our breath away. After everything I had been through, I didn't think anything could surprise me. I
was wrong. Just like me, my family was trying to turn the negatives into
positives in the midst of this storm. Their goal was always to help me continue to see the beauty in life and remind me that there was no reason to
quit. They were about to give me one more fluffy reason to continue, but
I would have to undergo surgery first. None of my family wanted me to
have more surgery because they loved me how I was, but they understood
I would do everything necessary to get back what was taken from me. If
this surgery allowed me to look more like myself, it would be worth it, no
matter the pain.

My parents and Carolina went with me to the hospital on the day of surgery. Because of COVID-19 restrictions, I was the only one allowed to enter the building. My mom brought the little sloth, Diego, which had accompanied me in every surgery. I had forgotten about him because I had hidden or gotten rid of everything sloth-related that would remind me of Heather. My mom handed him to me. This would be one of our last surgeries together, and what a crazy ride it'd been. Before heading to the hospital, I tried to reassure my mom everything would be okay. "I know I won't ever look the same, but even if it only helps 2 percent, I'm at least moving in the right direction. They wouldn't be doing this surgery if it were not going to help me." That last sentence made her feel more at ease, and my dad nodded in agreement. My mom called out the window that they would wait in the parking lot until I woke up. There they stayed.

As I checked in for my procedure, I kept going over what I could expect after surgery. No matter the type of surgery, I always researched other people's experiences and what steps to take for a fast recovery. My face would be super swollen, and I was prepared. I wouldn't be able to eat solid food for a while, and my mom and I were prepared. We had spoken about it, and I told her what foods I needed blended to make sure I met my caloric and nutritional goals. The pain was something I couldn't prepare for, but I knew my body could handle it. The nurses talked to me about my case, and they were all surprised at how well I was doing, given all the injuries I had sustained. I would have a splint on my top teeth when I awoke. This surgery just involved my lower jaw, so the splint would serve the purpose of aligning my bite, despite the top jaw still being misaligned. I gave the nurses a thumbs-up before speaking to the anesthesiologist and falling asleep.

There was a mirror next to the sink when I woke, but I had to get up if I wanted to look at myself. The nurse plugged in my charger and handed me my phone. I waited until she left. I wanted to be alone when I saw myself. My initial response was to laugh when I saw my reflection. I noticed I couldn't because my muscles were still asleep and there was a splint on my top teeth. I looked like the fattest chipmunk. Everyone who knows me knows I love fat things. I personally have never been fat, but I've always thought chubby things are the cutest.

When I called my mom, I told her she would like the new Cesar because he looked like he had been fed well. The splint in my mouth gave me a lisp, so I'm not sure how much of our conversation she understood, and to be honest, I was still kind of loopy. Thankfully I didn't feel much pain, but I figured it was from the anesthesia. I decided to walk a little inside my room. I had been working out a lot, and this surgery wasn't about to set me back again. My weight was almost where I wanted, so I figured if I wasn't going to be working out, I could at least walk and do some form of cardio. The nurses even told me it was good to get up and walk around because it would help the inflammation go down quicker.

I got a chance to speak with Dr. Drew, and she explained everything she did during the procedure. The surgery took all day, but she was pleased with how everything turned out. The swelling would last several months since they injected the area with a solution to help bone growth. I wanted to give her the biggest hug. Despite the way I looked at that moment, I fully trusted her, and hearing that she was pleased with how the surgery went made me optimistic about my recovery. She smiled as she left the room, and although I couldn't fully smile, I was smiling too. This was one more step in getting my life back, my confidence, and my image. None of this would've been possible without the amazing care I received from the medical professionals I was fortunate to know. Dr. Drew didn't have to take my case when my mom and I first came to her. She could've easily said it was too complicated or referred me elsewhere, but she took me in. I was now her patient but more so, her friend. We were going down this road together, and I am thankful for her giving me the chance to be myself again. I was discharged from the hospital, and my parents took me home. "One down," I told my mom as I hugged her. She smiled. They were just glad to have me back.

I began my liquid diet again. I had some work to do for MyBookie, so I went to my office afterward. As I worked on my computer, I heard the front door open and Carolina's voice. "Let me see the fatty," she said as she started up the stairs. She stopped short of my door, and I heard her and my mom whispering. Minutes later, Carolina opened my office door and hugged me. "Glad you are back, man," she told me. "How are you feeling? Oh, also, I got you something." She then pulled her arm from behind her back and gave me a book. It wasn't just any book. The front cover was a picture of Diego (the sloth), and the title said *Forever and Always*.

Carolina opened the book and started reading it to me. On every page, there was a picture of Diego posing or doing something. "When did you have time to do all this?" I asked her, surprised as she showed me the pictures.

"I've been preparing this all year and actually wanted to give it to you before this surgery, but we had to wait," she said. The very last sentence in the book said, "but actually...he is your dog." I laughed at first, but then it hit me.

The book Carolina made for Cesar as a gift after his surgery

Carolina presenting Cesar with the book she made of Diego

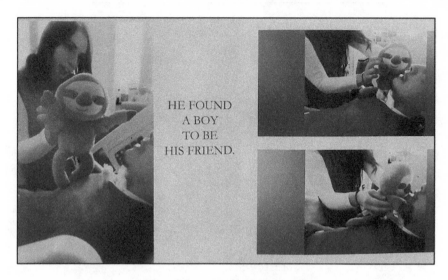

HE FOUND
A BOY
TO BE
HIS FRIEND.

One of the pages inside the book

HE IS YOUR DOG.

DIEGO FERDINAND
PEREZ

The last page in the book

"Wait. I have a dog?" I asked. Carolina turned to the last page and there was a picture of my new puppy. Beneath the picture, it said "Diego Ferdinand Perez." It was the cutest puppy I had ever seen. I was still a little incredulous that she had gotten me a dog because I didn't see the puppy, but then they brought him. He was so beautiful and soft.

"This is Diego," she said. "We thought this Diego (the sloth) had accompanied you long enough on all your surgeries, but you're coming out of all this a new man, so we got you a partner to build new memories with. He's yours now. You guys can grow together." I felt a wave of warmth go through my body, and I was just grateful for the family I'd been given. Now there was a new member of the family, and he couldn't have come at a better time. We had given away our two dogs after my accident because everyone was in Atlanta with me. I felt it was my fault, and I know it broke Carolina's heart to get rid of them. She told my mom she would never get another dog because she was tired of losing things. I thought she meant it, but seeing her with my new puppy in her arms, I knew we were starting to close that chapter. We were all beginning to heal.

I was letting go of the last remnant reminding me of Heather. She had given me that sloth, and he had been there with me when she hadn't. There were still a few surgeries left, but now I'd have a real Diego to come home to, someone I could always count on to bring me joy. My mom packed up the other Diego (the sloth) and put him away. She put him away like a book that's been read, going back on the shelf, its purpose served. Despite the upcoming surgeries, I was done with that book and never picked it up again.

My face was still swollen by the end of October, but it didn't bother me as much as the splint on my teeth. I could not speak correctly, and I had a lisp. The splint would collect saliva and made me drool at times. It wasn't something I could prevent, but I kept telling myself it would be worth it in the end. I just had to be patient. Patience had served me well the last two years, but now we were nearing the finish line, and my eagerness to be done was almost too much. Thankfully, Dr. Drew had me scheduled for the second portion of my surgery on November 10. She told me this one would be more intense than the first, but I was ready. I decided to cut my hair that weekend since Dr. Drew mentioned it would make things easier for her and Dr. Amin. Whatever would help me help them, I was ready to do. I told my hairdresser I wanted to donate my hair, so she tied it in a ponytail and cut it. That's when I noticed it still wasn't long enough to donate. Somewhere, I had read that hair must be a minimum of six inches in length to donate. Mine was barely five. There was nothing I could do because I couldn't keep growing it out. I was not going to give up on my promise, however. "I'll grow it out again after this one," I told my mom. "I made a promise."

The procedure took nearly ten hours, and when I awoke, I had drains in my head to expel blood from the incisions. I tried to look at myself on my phone, but I could barely open my eyes since they were filled with blood. The doctors went in through the outside corners of my eye to fix the ocular bones and replace plates. The incision on my head stretched from ear to ear, and the drain they placed was running across below my scalp. I felt around my mouth with my tongue and noticed the splint had been removed. There was that to be happy about. I felt miserable, however. I had not eaten prior to surgery, and I definitely couldn't eat now. My body was used to consuming a great deal of food and always being active. Now I didn't even have the energy to go to the restroom. Being alone in the hospital for almost a week made it worse. My mother had always been there, ready for anything I may need. It was just me this time.

This surgery floored me. It was a combination of things, really. I couldn't move much because of the drains dangling from my head. Oh, how great it would have been to have my mom there. The pandemic had halted the world, so I was fortunate to even be getting my surgery. I decided this was the moment to prove my independence and prove to myself I could do anything. The nurses told me to try and walk a little if I could. Knowing that walking helps prevent blood clots and would help reduce inflammation, I attempted to walk every day, at least to the restroom. The process was difficult because I couldn't let the drains dangle from my skull. My left hand had to do all the work, and I just hoped I didn't fall and yank the drains. Little by little, I got used to getting up and taking a few steps. One night, the nurse came in and asked me if I had had a bowel movement or if I had urinated. Neither had occurred, but I was more concerned about the urine because fluid was all I had consumed, and my bladder was full. She told me we could give it a few more hours, but if I hadn't urinated into the container by the time she returned, she would have to insert a catheter to relieve my bladder. There was no way in hell I was going to let them place a catheter in me. I'd had them before, but the difference was I was fully awake and conscious this time.

Time was ticking, and I almost started crying, thinking how it would feel to have something go through my urethra. The nurse came in and looked at the container, then at me. "No luck?" she asked. I just shook my head and stared at the ceiling. The nurse was sweet and told me it was common for some parts to take a while and restore their function after a huge procedure like the one I had. "It might sting at first as it's going in," she said as she started disinfecting everything. I clenched my jaw as soon as she said that, even though I wasn't supposed to do that, given my surgery. All I remember was a stinging sensation as she pushed what felt like a needle through my urethra. The initial portion was the worst part, but afterward, I felt relieved as my bladder emptied. I said thank you and just hoped I wouldn't need a catheter again. The days were dragging. My body was getting weaker by the minute, and I could feel it. I kept daydreaming of sushi, chicken, and burgers, none of which I would be able to have for a while. It was making me feel desperate, and I wanted to leave the hospital. They brought me food every day, and halfway through my stay, I decided it was time to give it a try before my body gave up on me.

I started with yogurt and then scrambled eggs the next day. It was annoying how messy I would get trying to eat. Dr. Drew came to check on me. She smiled as she came in. "You're one strong guy. We worked on you a lot," she said, "but I didn't come across anything we weren't anticipating, so that was good. I'm pleased with how everything was done." That was all I needed to hear. I knew recovery would take a long time, but I was used to waiting. It didn't scare me. One of the resident doctors came in later to check on my drains. They emptied them every few hours if they contained too much blood, but this time the doctor wanted to inspect the incision on my scalp. He told me everything was looking good, until he got to my right side. There was a little bulge on my scalp, and he said it appeared to be a hematoma. They were common after surgeries as intense as mine, but he would have to cut the area open to relieve it. I closed my eyes as the doctor cut.... I wanted to go home NOW. Out of all the surgeries I'd had, what made this one difficult was not having my family there due to the pandemic.

Each day, I asked the nurse if I would be going home. The answer always depended on how I felt throughout the day and whatever the doctor said. I wanted to cry but didn't even have the energy to do that. Finally, one afternoon, the nurse came in and told me I would be going home the next morning. *Just one more night, man,* I told myself. *We just have to make it through one more night.* I barely slept, eager for the morning to come. In the middle of the night, I woke up and decided to walk to the only window in my room. It was peaceful seeing the night sky sprinkled with road lights. I'd lost track of all my surgeries, but I was nearing the end of it all. Seated on the couch by the window, I just stared out and drank an Ensure to get some energy for the morning. Some time passed, and the nurse finally came to my room. She asked me how I was feeling as she finished some notes on the computer. "I feel so happy to be going home," I answered. "I'm ready. You guys have been great and have taken great care of me, but I need my mom's homemade soup. You know moms have the cure." I tried laughing at my own joke, but only my eyes indicated I was trying to laugh. It was a surprise I could even speak. The splint was gone, so it was easier to talk, as opposed to the first surgery.

I got dressed as fast as possible. By the time the nurse came back with a wheelchair, I was ready. This was the moment I had been waiting for. My parents were already in place with the car, ready to take me home. It had been the longest week for us all. They had so many questions for me, but I told them I would answer after I ate because I felt faint. My dad rushed us home, and there waiting for me was a broccoli cheddar soup they had bought from Panera. They knew it was one of the only soups I liked, and I scarfed it down. The change was almost immediate. My energy drastically improved, and even the pain subsided. While I finished the soup, I proceeded to tell them how I felt and what to expect for the upcoming days. "The swelling is only going to get worse," I said, "but it is to be expected." My mom stood to inspect my head and look at the incisions on my scalp. She was shocked at how long the cut was. I hadn't seen it, so I asked her to take a picture for me. When she showed me the photo, I too was surprised, and not at the length but the fact that there were a few bald spots. My hair was short, and aside from growing it out in hopes of donating it, I had always liked keeping it that way. Now, I wouldn't be able to keep it short because the scar would always be noticeable with several bald spots. They only got worse as the incision healed, and my hair started falling out from certain areas along the cut.

The following appointment I had with Dr. Drew, she told me it was all expected. Certain hair follicles could have been affected during the incision, but it was something we had spoken about prior to surgery. I figured if I let my hair grow out, I could hide the scar and make it seem like it never happened. They had used staples to close the incision on my scalp, and they had to be removed. It was a long incision, and it hurt like hell. Like I was on a rollercoaster, I just held my breath every time the resident doctor pulled one out. Somehow, I managed to make it through all of them, and he inspected the area where the hematoma had been. "You're healing well," he told me. "We will just keep monitoring the right side and the incision on your scalp."

I thanked him and Dr. Drew before asking them questions about my eyes. My left eye was still red, and the eyelid was more open than before. My right eye had improved drastically, and I could easily close it now, but my left eye was more slanted downward than before. They told me it was all part of the inflammation preventing my features from going back to their resting position, and we just had to give it time. I knew how long the swelling from the first facial reconstruction took to go down, so I understood it was once again a waiting game. My post-op appointment with Dr. Amin at Grady hospital went well, and she reiterated the same thing. In the end, if I wasn't pleased with something, there were options available, but it was too soon to even think about that. She spoke to me about other procedures I may need, but that would be entering the plastic surgery realm. Rhinoplasty was one of the things she recommended if I wanted to get the bridge on my nose back to how it was. She said I could start talking to surgeons once the swelling subsided. At least the biggest surgery was done...I hoped.

I knew there were smaller procedures I could have in order to look more like myself, but there wasn't much time to think about it. Dr. Peljovich and I had agreed I'd have my arm surgery as soon as I was cleared to undergo anesthesia again. Time was moving quickly. It was the end of 2020, and I told my mom I would be having surgery in February. Honestly, I had envisioned being done with my recovery and procedures by the three-year mark, but that seemed less likely now. Year three would be wrapping up in a month, and although I was light years away from where I'd started, it would likely take another year to fully put this nightmare behind me. It was the first Christmas I spent without Heather, and I felt fine emotionally. There was no sadness or distress. Everything that made Christmas special for me was still there. My family was with me, and I had a new companion in Diego.

Cesar and Diego

There was so much to be grateful for and even more to look forward to. The arm surgery would be the last surgery that was medically necessary in my opinion. Everything else would be to address scars and restore my past features. The coronavirus was still a big concern for everyone, but thankfully a vaccine was on the horizon, and hopefully with it, the end of the pandemic.

We ended the year the same way we had started it . . . together. Everyone who saw me said I recovered more in that year than the previous two, and that was greatly due to determination and not having Heather around to detract from my time and dedication. I felt it too. In 2020, I made sure to stick to my regimen and just trust the process. I always kept myself busy in order to keep my mind from going to dark places. It was a survival strategy that had served me well. Though the hurt no longer remained when I thought of Heather, I still had many walls/barriers that would take time to come down before I let someone else into my life again. I figured I would address it once I was done with the external healing. Maybe by that point, time would have done its thing. Sure, I was going into the new year more swollen than before, but it wouldn't last forever. I was ready to finish writing the ending to this horrible chapter in my life.

Before going to bed that night, I went outside to take a deep breath and ponder everything I had accomplished thus far. There had been a miniscule chance of me surviving that accident, and that was all I needed, just a chance, a breath of hope that not everything was lost. I had beaten the odds, and I was just getting started. My journey wasn't over, and I was focused on what I wanted to accomplish the following year. I didn't feel sorry for myself. I knew I had the ability to change my future. My mom hadn't raised a weak child, and the last lap around this track of misery that had been my life the past three years would be the hardest to finish.

It would be the hardest in the sense that I was close to being done and closing this chapter for good. Most of us tend to slow down or cut some slack when we're near the finish line. We take it for granted. *It's so close*, we think. *We'll get there* . . . But true athletes know you never slow down when you see the finish line. If anything, you go faster. A study published in the journal *Motivation and Emotion* discusses how focusing on a focal point in the distance can make the distance seem shorter, and in doing so, the runner feels less exertion. My goal was simple and still the same one since I had left the hospital: retaking everything that was taken from me. That was my focal point in the distance. I knew if I kept my eyes on that goal, time would go by quicker and heal the things I couldn't.

The year 2021 would be my last year of recovery, and I wasn't slowing down. I was tired of waiting, and I wanted to be done with all this. The only way to do that was to keep running the race. No one else was in that race but me. It was me against myself, and I pushed myself harder than anyone ever had. There was no other way I could've made it out. I took a deep breath and thanked God for giving me the strength to pick myself up and keep moving forward.

CHAPTER 20

What Matters,
I Still Have

'M SURE EVERYONE WAS HAPPY SAYING GOODBYE TO
a year that brought so much despair. I was just happy to be done with the
big surgeries. The arm surgery scheduled for February would not be small,
but it paled in comparison to the facial reconstruction. Dr. Drew was happy
with the work she had done and told me the bones were healing nicely
the next time I saw her. I asked her if it was okay to proceed with my arm
surgery in February. She checked how wide I could open my mouth to ensure
I could be intubated for surgery and told me I was cleared. I could go ahead
and have my arm surgery and thankfully start the healing process before
summer, when I would attend several weddings.

My lawyer called me in early January to inform me that the defendant's
lawyers wanted to meet for mediation of my case at the end of the month.
They had previously scheduled it on the day of my facial reconstruction, but

there was no way I was going to postpone my surgery again. I didn't care about money. Sure, I needed it, but money had never been my goal. My life back is all I ever wanted, and no amount of money could ever accomplish that. Three years had gone by, and my case still wasn't headed to trial or settled, so I figured I could wait a little longer and just have my facial surgery instead. Now that I had healed and could talk, I figured it was time to get the mediation over with.

I met with Jeremy and everyone representing the trucking company at the end of January. Although I could drive, my parents asked to take me. They had been with me since the beginning and witnessed all my suffering, so they wanted to be there should I return from mediation with nothing to show for. Honestly, they were more anxious than I was. "No matter what happens or what they say, I've come this far. I'm not stopping now," I told them as they dropped me off. "We've always made the best with what we've got. You guys taught me that. If they give me nothing, what have I lost? Nothing. I'm alive, and we will make it out. I promise." My mom hugged me and said to stay calm no matter what. My emotions were finally back to normal, and I figured nothing would trigger me.

I took the elevator and mentally prepared myself for what was coming. If you've ever dealt with salespeople, you know that they are the nicest people in the world while they try to sell you on something. That's how I felt meeting everyone, like they were being nice just trying to sell me their idea of how the events had occurred so my case could be settled with minimum expense on their end. Everyone said how amazing my recovery had been after seeing pictures of my vehicle and how sorry they were for everything I had to go through. I just nodded because I knew they were just trying to come across as more humane. No one could ever understand what I went through, so I just let their comments slide. I sat at the corner of the conference table as Jeremy presented our argument with a PowerPoint presentation. We went to another conference room once he finished, and the other guys presented their argument. I thought my emotions were finally in check, but hearing them talk about the accident and seeing the pictures again brought back a flood of emotions I had wrestled with over the past three years.

I was quiet even after the presentation ended and only spoke when they asked me questions. My brain was occupied with trying to figure out what to do if my case wasn't settled that day. *Nothing could ever make up for what happened*, I thought. I kept telling myself this to ease my nerves and avoid feeling let down. After a lot of offers and counteroffers, Jeremy told me it was my decision if I wanted to settle. I took a long pause to think things over and then told the mediator we could settle it that day. I signed the paperwork, and everyone came back to my room to shake my hand and wish me the best in my continued recovery.

Before leaving the room, I wanted to make sure they understood one thing. "This was never about money for me," I said. "I've always worked hard for everything and never asked for a handout. That's why I'm not scared of what the future holds. Nothing scares me anymore, and I'm moving on from this." I left the building feeling empowered and with my conviction intact. I would make it out of all this.

I got to the car and told my parents my case was finally settled. It was mere pennies compared to the damage, trauma, and pain I had suffered, but at least it was over. They asked me if I was feeling depressed about the outcome, but I told them I felt relieved. I had spent months feeling anxious and stressing out about my case, wondering when it would be over. It was finally done. Nothing much had changed, really. No money could help me put my life together. My family and I had done that alone. That's why I didn't feel sad or angry. I was still picking up the pieces of my life. We drove back to the house no different than we had come. Relief was the only thing I felt I had gained. Now I could leave everything in the past and focus on the few surgeries I had left. In the end, the doctors were the only ones giving me what I wanted, which was a chance to take back my life. If only time would move faster.

My focus was now on my arm. Who would have thought nerves were so small and yet their function so vital? I had made my peace with the fact that I would have permanent damage on my right arm, but I wanted to do everything possible to restore its function. February 9 rolled around, and I was ready for surgery. "One more," I told my parents as they once again waited in the car until the procedure was complete. The nurses went through the same dialogue I had heard so many times. "Can you tell us your name, birthday, and what procedure you are having?" they would ask me every fifteen minutes. It was something I was used to. The anesthesiologist stopped by to meet with me. He was the guy I had been looking forward to meeting since he would be providing the good stuff *wink wink*. I wasn't nervous. The pain I would feel waking up from surgery, if any, could not be any worse than what I had experienced already. That kept me calm as once again my world went dark and they began to operate.

I remembered to call my parents when I woke and let them know I was good. One of the nurses brought a wheelchair, and it was time to go home. We drove home and it was back to the couch for me. I had to keep my arm in a certain position and not let it fully extend or elevate while the muscle healed. They prescribed me Percocet for the pain, but I only took it that night. My pain tolerance was through the roof, and this was a walk in the park in comparison to everything prior. A few days went by, and I realized pain wouldn't be an issue, but the itching from the bandages would be. They had shaved my armpit because Dr. Peljovich wanted to use the same incision from the first surgery to avoid more scarring. My armpit was on fire by the third day. Due to sweating, the hairs growing back, and the stickiness of the bandages, the itching was unbearable.

It got to the point where I could no longer block it out. I started reaching toward my back and into my armpit to scratch around the incision. Parts of my arm were still numb, so I didn't think I was scratching hard. My post-op appointment with Dr. Peljovich was conducted virtually, and he told me I could finally remove the bandages. Only when my mom took them off could she see the scratches on my back. Thankfully the incision was healing well, and I had not touched it, but my back and below my armpit looked like I had been whipped several times. Even now, I can still see faded scars from some of the scratches. Dr. Peljovich cleared me to shower, and that made me feel brand new. Not only would I be clean now, but I hoped the warm water and soap would help with the itching that seemed to get worse at night.

I was scheduled to start therapy at Shepherd in early March. This would be the first time being back in the building since the pandemic began. As I walked inside, I felt empowered by the fact that I had made it out of there, but for the most part, I was just grateful. The halls that had once seen my parents push me in a wheelchair had so many stories to tell. I was grateful a place like this existed, where people were given the opportunity to live again. With my arm in a sling, I decided to take the stairs to the third floor. There was no reason for me to use the elevator when there were people in wheelchairs waiting to go up. I vowed never to take the elevator again, and I felt a little more like the old me, always pushing myself, never taking the easy way.

Upon reaching the third floor, I went to the gym where I was meeting my OT. I had not seen Sherri in over a year, so I was curious if she would notice any changes, not just in my mobility but also my appearance. My face was still swollen, but luckily, we were all wearing masks. As I walked in with my sling, she was as happy to see me as I was to see her. We couldn't believe how fast a year had gone by and how COVID-19 had derailed everything. This was an evaluation session to see how the incision was healing and formulate a strategy for my future sessions since I would be coming twice a week.

The incisions were healing well, and the scar seemed flat, which at least meant I wouldn't have a keloid scar or much scar tissue. My session didn't last long, but before I left, I just had to ask, "So when do you think I'll be able to run?" Sherri burst out laughing. She told me I needed to take it easy and not run while I was still wearing the sling. Dr. Peljovich was the one who would decide when it was safe to leave the sling behind, but even after that, I'd be on limited movement for a few weeks while the muscle healed. I laughed along with her because I don't think patients typically came to therapy asking when they could run or exercise more. This was just my personality and the person I had always been, so my goals never shifted. I always wanted to do more. Sherri and all the other therapists knew I would do anything and everything I needed to get my life back. They didn't have to worry about me pushing myself or doing my therapy at home. On the contrary, I was so eager to do more, so they often had to discourage me from doing any movements that could hinder the surgical site from healing. Thankfully, I trusted them and I now had more patience too. So far, all my medical professionals and therapists had been right in everything they said. It was a waiting game once more.

That was really all my life had been for three years—a waiting game. It damn near drove me crazy, but through it all, I learned to appreciate everything on a deeper level. Now, when I saw people walk, run, raise their arms, or just breathe, I couldn't help but wonder if they were grateful for being able to do so. They were everyday things we as humans do naturally, and many of us take them for granted. I know I used to. My body was in top form before, so walking and running were something I didn't even give a second thought. I was able to do thirty-five pull-ups in one continuous set at the height of my physical capacity. Now, I couldn't raise my arm to touch my nose. How envious I was of people stretching their arms, raising their hand, or just pointing at something. The mundane things everyone did were things I craved and longed for. My desire to do everything I did before kept driving me forward. When I felt like giving up or thought it was no big deal to miss a therapy session, my desire held me accountable. Out of the countless therapy sessions I received over the previous three years, I can honestly say I only ever missed one, and it was due to traffic. I pride myself on having that determination, but again, it stemmed from me wanting to get my life back. Everything else was secondary.

CHAPTER 21

Become Unbreakable

T HE END OF MARCH CAME, AND WITH IT, MY BIRTHDAY. In my mind I felt like I was turning twenty-five, but really, I was turning twenty-eight. I felt like the last three years had been stolen from me because this was not how I would've lived them out. Regardless, time doesn't lie, and on March 30, I woke up and went straight to the bathroom mirror. Looking at my reflection, I shook my head and thought, *Twenty-eight, huh?*

When I settled with the trucking company, I thought to myself, *I would have paid them tenfold for none of this to have ever happened.* It was still true. But rather than being upset that the last three years had been nothing but pain, I thought about all the people who had perished because of the pandemic. These were fathers, mothers, sons, and daughters that would give anything to be here today. I couldn't be upset. Grateful was all I was. My life had been drastically altered in unimaginable ways, but I was still here. I was alive, so what more could I ask? As I came downstairs, my mom hugged me tight. "Thank you for fighting to stay here with us for a little longer," she said. "Happy birthday, son."

It's true I fought tooth and nail to stick around. Death would've been much quicker and painless, but I've never taken the easy way out. The unbreakable spirit and determination I emerged with didn't come easily, naturally, or quickly. My scars represent the biggest battle I've ever faced, and they keep me grounded in the reality that every moment is precious since it could be your last. I'm still not done with surgeries, but the worst part is over. The next few procedures shouldn't be too invasive, and recovery won't take months. I'm optimistic about the future, no longer afraid of it.

I no longer fear the uncertainty of what comes next. I live in the moment and make sure everything I'm doing is helping me reach my goals or helping someone in need. My mentality never changed, but my perception did, and I see things clearly now. They say in your darkest moments is when you see a clearer picture. This is true. You see who your real family and friends are. It puts all your actions into perspective and lets you know what must change for you to make it out. When I began writing my story, my goal was always to help others navigate safely across troubled waters. I wanted to be a light that could guide them out of the darkness. I didn't know my good intentions would benefit and heal me as well. It served as a catharsis for my broken soul. Every day, as I kept writing, I felt more pieces coming together to form the puzzle that is now my life. The tears stopped flowing after a while, and I could recount everything without pain or anger. I accepted everything and have managed to move on.

We all go through painful or traumatic events, varying in severity, that transform us. My two trucks to the face could be your recent unemployment, your eviction, your new illness, etc. Notice how I didn't mention death. That is because death doesn't come in different shades. It is complete darkness, and there is no way around it. However, everything else gives us the chance to make the rest of our days a little less gray, even if we don't see completely clear blue skies. Every breath you take is an opportunity to make the most of that moment. There is a quote in Spanish that says, "No hay mal que dure cien años," which basically means that even the longest night must end. No matter what pain or suffering befalls you, it too shall pass. We just have to be strong enough to endure.

Lord knows I sometimes felt I couldn't continue. Those times will come, but true success is measured by how you respond to those moments. My story was always about hope, love, and resilience. Despite my going through a stage where I had a negative view of hope, in all honesty, it's what helped me endure the toughest moments. When I was recovering from surgery and the pain in my head was unbearable, I kept thinking of tomorrow. *Tomorrow it will be better.* It helped me stay calm and push through the times when giving up felt like a good choice. This isn't to say all I did was lie in bed, hoping for a better tomorrow. No, I did everything I could to bring some relief. It was the combination of hope and determination that got me through it. So I'm not saying that if you want change, just hope for it. Instead, you must actively seek change but let hope get you through the days.

For the majority of 2020, I placed love on the shelf. As it collected dust, I stopped to think where I would be without love. I always hoped my story would end in a way that showcased true love conquers everything. Though it may not have ended how I initially hoped, it ended much better and with the best indication that true love does conquer all. The love I refer to is not a romantic one; instead, it's the unbreakable bond between a mother and her child, a father and his son, a sister and her brother. Because of them, I know what true love is and know it exists. They were my rock and the foundation from which I have built myself up again. No words can express the gratitude I feel at having been blessed with the best support system anyone could've asked for. I know they would go to the ends of the world for me, and they know I'd do the same for them.

I'm reminded of a poem I used to read to my mom when I was little. It's in Spanish and expressed through the dialogue between a mother and son. I still remember it to this day. The last phrase is "¿Y si al fin no encuentras mi felicidad? Será que en el mundo para ti no está. Entonces mi niño cargaré tu cruz para que a lo menos, no la lleves tú." The entire poem is not long, but what it lacks in length it makes up for in truth. It starts with the son asking the mom where she is going, and she simply states she is searching for his happiness. The next few lines consist of questions the boy asks, and the mother is the answer to all of them. If he gets tired of walking, she will be his legs. If he gets cold along the journey, her arms will keep him warm. There is nothing the mother won't sacrifice to make sure he is okay. The last three lines consist of the boy asking what happens if she doesn't find his happiness at the end? She simply replies it means happiness is not in this world for him, but she will bear his cross so at least he doesn't have to.

When I used to read the poem in front of my mom, I would read it and not fully comprehend the magnitude of truth within the words. Today, I see what the poem represents. My mother would go to the ends of the world to find my happiness, and if in the end, she could not, she would at least bear that cross with me. The point is, I would never be alone. No matter the struggles, the pain, and the suffering, my mother was always there, ready to pick me up and keep pushing forward. It was the same way with my dad and sisters. We were all in this together, and no one was getting left behind. That's why I don't think I would've made it out of the dark hole my life had become had it not been for love.

To be honest, I wanted to leave Heather out of my story. When I began writing my journey, I wanted to draw no attention to that aspect of my life, but it was impossible. How could I demonstrate how broken I was if my heart was still intact? How could I ever help someone move forward if I didn't explain that I had experienced it too? How could I serve as inspiration if people didn't know how far I'd fallen? No, I had to share that part of my life I wanted to forget.

Who knows what path my life would've taken had none of this ever happened? Perhaps in another reality, Heather and I would've continued dating, but ultimately, I would've ended up without her. She was never going to stick around when skies began to gray. Though it hurt to my core, it was best I discovered this before I put more on the line and asked her to marry me. All the "what ifs" I've vowed to leave in the past. At weddings, the final question is "Do you take this man/woman to be your lawfully wedded husband/wife, to have and to hold from this day forward, for better, for worse, for richer, for poorer, in sickness and in health, until death do you part?" Every wedding I've been to, both the bride and groom say yes. The truth is, it's easy to agree and love someone when all things are going well, which is why the question asks about being there in the bad times too. Life isn't always blue skies, but that's why you have someone to weather the storm with you.

Before my accident, Heather told me several times she wanted us to get married. Again, this was at a time when there was nothing I couldn't do, and my career was steadily taking off. It was my plan to propose to her in 2018, but neither of us imagined what would happen to me at the start of that year. As I lay in the hospital, all I could think about was my future with her, the one I had promised. My motivation was her, and though it may have been misplaced as I noticed her motives, I was hellbent on making it out of there for her... for us. That's why despite her staying for the wrong reasons, my brain at the time just recognized her and that was enough. If I gained nothing from our relationship, she at least unknowingly provided me with the motivation to get better, and for that I'm grateful.

After taking time to fully heal, I hold no anger or hate toward Heather. It is the reason why I can write all of this down without shedding a tear. I can look at pictures of us from before and not feel anger. At the time those pictures were taken, I was happy, and I cherish that happiness, not her. I chose not to use her real name because I'm not trying to bring attention to the person she is. This is my memoir of the past three years in my life and everything that's happened. Everything started with her, but thankfully my story has a different ending. Like a ravage wind, she came and went into my life, leaving everything a mess, but I'm still standing. If this traumatic experience showed me anything, it was who would be there for me when I needed them most. It's gratifying to know true friendship and love, though rare, still exist. I have worked my ass off, not for anyone anymore, but for me. With Heather out of the picture, what was I going to do? She had been my motivation for the longest time. I wanted to be the same guy she first met. Then I realized, I still was the same guy. Nothing that mattered had changed for the worse inside me, and everything on the exterior could be fixed. *I'm doing this for me now*, I thought. With no distractions and no one eating away at my funds, I quickly saw the huge impact my focal change made. I started feeling more like myself and letting go of the anger that had been eating me up inside. As I progressed, a small sense of hope began to build that perhaps there was a possibility of finding happiness once again.

There was always something different about my story that I hoped would resonate with people. The simplest way I can explain it is by looking at the Disney movie *Frozen*. It received the biggest box office response for an animated movie before the sequel came out. In my opinion, what made the movie different from every other animated movie was how the conflict was resolved. It was not solved with true love's kiss but rather a different kind of love. It was the love between family, the bond between sisters. Just the same, my struggles were not resolved with true love's kiss but rather with love and strength that came from my family. This of course was not the only element that helped me overcome, but it was definitely an important factor. That's why I couldn't leave Heather out of my story. The only reason I was in this predicament was because I had been driving down to see her. She was the reason I drove down I-16 that day . . . forever my only regret. The hardest part of watching her leave was thinking that the only part of my life (before the accident) that had remained intact was breaking off. Only later did I realize I was wrong in viewing it like that. At the dinner table, if I looked to the right, there was my mom. To the left was my dad, and in front of me sat Carolina. There was still something intact I could hold on to that gave me strength. It was them.

I learned numerous lessons along my journey, many of which I have already shared. Here are some of the other discoveries I made and may have had to learn the hard way. I share them here in hopes that they help you or others:

Strength is not just physical. I had so much physical strength before, and yet I consider myself stronger now. The old me had his struggles here and there but nothing in comparison to what happened to me later in life. I used to worry about stupid shit. How I would have traded my current problems for those old issues as I left the hospital in March! After I cried my heart out for everything I'd lost, I promised I would never feel sorry for myself. I wanted no one's pity either. In the years before my accident, I had served as inspiration for many people pursuing professional or fitness goals. My career was on the rise, and my fitness level was never compromised. I told many people who reached out to me through social media, asking for tips in reaching their goals that it was all about being consistent and putting in the work. "Trust the process," I'd always say. The truth is I'd never had much of a hurdle to overcome when it came to my fitness goals. I was never fat, I had good genetics and a good metabolism, and I had a good work ethic. Therefore, I couldn't really relate to someone with obstacles along the path toward their goal. That all changed on January 12. Every obstacle you could think of was now in my way, and not toward my goals but just to where I had been the day before. My goals were now miles and miles away since I had been taken back to the very beginning. If life had a reset button, somehow I had pressed it.

Never be afraid to start over. I didn't want to be one of the people who doesn't practice what they preach. If this was about being persistent and putting in the work, that's what I would do. All my energy went into pushing myself past the pain every movement caused. I had experienced the worst physical pain already, and though I had no memory of it, I knew my body did, so I trusted it could handle it. When I tell you I have never worked so hard in my life, I mean it. I doubled down on my work ethic after Heather left, and I made sure to get everything done that would help me get where I wanted to be. My patience grew each day as I realized persistence and time work collectively to reach my goals. I couldn't rush it, nor could I just sit back and wait. Every day, I worked out. It might not have been the intense workouts I had done before, but what I could do, I did. Each morning or night when I felt like I couldn't do it, I told myself, "If you don't do it today, you'll be one more day farther from where you want to be." That always woke my ass up, and I'd proceed to do my routine. I hated feeling like a prisoner in my own body, so I made sure I did everything to lessen the number of days I had to feel that way. I wanted things to be different but realized only I could change my life.

"Sacrifice who you are for what you will become." I've seen variations of this quote by Eric Thomas in several literary works, and it always resonates with me. Whatever goal we want to reach, we will have to sacrifice something to obtain it. People may think I found a masochistic delight in feeling more pain. My mentality was a bit extreme, I'll admit, but it was my only option. Nothing is free in this world. If you want a better grade in school, you must set aside extra time to study. This might mean giving up your Friday nights with friends and hitting the books instead. If you want to lose weight, you may have to sacrifice your favorite foods for a while. You want to be the best athlete on your team? You'll have to sacrifice more time to train. You must put forth effort to maximize your return. Where most people fail is in being inconsistent and impatient. You won't be the best athlete in one day. It takes time, but at least you've taken the first step. You might find yourself annoyed at spending your free time studying, training, or working more. This is natural human behavior; we don't enjoy being out of our comfort zone. We tend to run away from anything that causes stress or pain. In doing so, we never truly grow or learn how to maneuver in difficult situations. Only when you realize that the singular way to achieve your goals is by weathering the pain and struggles can you actually reach them.

At the point in my life when I came to this realization, I frankly had nothing to lose. Everything had been taken from me. The only way to go was up, unless I decided to feel sorry for myself and stay where I was. I tried to channel all of my anger into constructive energy and build myself up again from the pieces that remained. When I was in therapy, I welcomed the pain. No longer would I run away from it. If I did, it meant staying where I was and never seeing the beauty of where I wanted to be. If my body expected ten reps, I told my mind we would do fifteen. Upon hitting rep ten, I would then keep going because aside from my body, the real muscle I was keen on training was my mind. My brain housed all my fears and insecurities. My body could handle the work, but my mind always thought too much. I tried training my brain in solitude. I told myself the pain was temporary and visualized myself on the other side of the mountain. Visualization is key in helping things come to fruition. Before achieving anything, I made sure I visualized it, savoring the moment of getting it done. That's what helped me get up every morning at 6:30 and work out. Every morning, I managed to cross my exercises off my to-do list before breakfast. I felt accomplished every time I did, despite no one outside my family really knowing about it. But that was also the beauty of it. Long gone were the days in which I wanted to impress anyone. I was doing this for me because I owed it to myself. Working in silence helped me realize I was my own competitor. Never did I take my foot off the gas. I pushed myself harder every day more than any coach ever had. My mission was simple: get to where I was.

I did it once. I can do it again. I kept whispering this mantra to myself, knowing this time around I had more obstacles to overcome. It didn't matter; I kept going. I was so used to pain by 2020 that a new way of coping with it developed. My mind had welcomed pain every day for the past two years, and every time, I endured. Pain started losing its edge. I began to chuckle when I felt pain. It was an involuntary reaction, but pain no longer caused me suffering. I welcomed it, knowing it would eventually subside and let me see a new horizon. It wasn't something I could control. Even my therapist would laugh every time she would touch a tender spot and dig deep to release the tension. Immediately, I would go into a fit of giggles. It was painful, don't get me wrong, but I knew there was a purpose to the pain, and I held my ground while she dug into my muscles. Every time the giggles would increase, she would ask me if I needed a break or if it was too much pain because she understood it was me trying to cope with it. With my eyes closed, I always shook my head no. I was ready for whatever I had to endure. My eyes were set on my goal, and I knew damn well the road would not be easy, but it'd be worth it in the end.

Everything will pass. Though it is hard to see in your darkest moments, the point I am trying to make is that all you must do is hold on for one more day and endure. Nothing lasts forever; this is true. Neither the happy moments nor the painful ones, so make sure you enjoy the moments that make you smile. Acknowledge moments that bring you pain, for they are real, but never let them define your happiness

"Change your thinking, change your life." I distanced myself from the exterior world for about three years and not because I am an introvert. I've always enjoyed being around people. I'm one of the most extroverted people you'll ever meet, but I started thinking from a new perspective. Everything I did from that point forward, I wanted to make sure it would have a positive impact on my life and get me closer to my goal. This is the type of thinking that could change your life. It's not a selfish way of thinking; please do not confuse it as such. This only applies to anything you do that does not include the people you love. God knows when it comes to my family or my friends, I'd do anything for them, regardless of how it would benefit me.

Stop caring about what others think of you. My goals were mine, and I felt I owed it to myself to get me back to where I was. Social media can bend our perspectives since much of what you see there is fake or staged. At first, when I was just getting out of the hospital, I noticed all these influencers flaunting their well-toned bodies and great lives. I was envious and angry that they were enjoying what I no longer could. That's what made me stop using my social media as much, once I noticed the negative impact it was having on my perspective. It wasn't driving my goals; it was making me waste time watching others live the life I'd once had. I decided to structure my time each day and make sure I wasted none. Social distancing was difficult at first, but my real friends understood my goals and method.

They would come see me at my place whenever they could, and for that I am forever grateful. They knew I was hellbent on getting my life back and always encouraged it. Every now and again, I'd get messages from people who claimed to be my "friends" but were really just acquaintances. My circumstances let me see the true side of everybody, who would be there for me in the bad times and who would just talk the talk. It was an eye-opening experience I hope none of you ever have to go through. If they can't be there at your worst, they most certainly don't deserve you at your best, and that goes for everything.

Acknowledge what you have, and keep going. In my solitude, I took time to really analyze what happiness meant to me and understand who I was. As 2020 rolled around with its COVID-19 pandemic, I was so used to social distancing that it made no difference in my life. Literally, I went about my day like I would have any other day. I tried focusing on what I had instead of what I had lost. That may sound cliché, like viewing the glass half full, but really, it's the only way to avoid sinking into depression. I slowly started to realize that if I had breath in my lungs, I still had the ability to live a beautiful life, regardless of my trauma and scars.

Realize what happened is in the past and that acceptance is key. What matters is what happens from this moment forward. Don't fear difficulties that may present themselves down the road. Those will come, but they don't define your happiness. You decide how you respond to adversity. One of my favorite quotes comes from James Baldwin: "Not everything that is faced can be changed, but nothing can be changed until it's faced." Understand you can't ever get back the moment that's passed. It's what you do from that moment forward that you should focus on. I've been nothing but honest with you, and accepting that I couldn't change the past was the hardest hurdle to overcome. Only when you reach that level of acceptance can you finally find some peace.

In the darkest part of my life, I found my own light. Now as I carry my torch, I hope I can light the path and help you find yours. The way I came to my driving force was by realizing everything was up to me. Although everything that happened to me was unfair, it still happened, and I couldn't change it. I could lie down and waste the second chance I'd been given, or I could put forth the effort into living a fulfilling life once again. Once I saw I could walk, my next goal was to run, and then to sprint. I constantly pushed the envelope to see what I could withstand. There was nothing else to lose and everything to gain... my life.

I have a new appreciation for life now, one which stems from almost losing it. I can look at everything and see the big picture of this beautiful painting that has been my life. It was never meant to be a perfect painting embellished with realism. Like splatter-paint art, I have found beauty in the chaos. My canvas is a masterful piece of abstract art, and as I stand back and view it, I see it is only half complete. I roll up my sleeve and pick up the brush with my right hand. It doesn't matter if it's not perfect. It's mine. When the day comes in which the sun no longer rises for me, I'll be okay because I know I gave it my all. It will be beautiful when I'm through. As I try to paint with my right arm, I still can't fully control it and it splatters a bit. But I just smile. If you look at the painting, you don't even notice the unexpected paint drops. I smile because much in the same way, I know life, though unexpected, can still be beautiful.

No matter what happens from this moment forward, just know you can make it out of any place you're in. You're not alone. Just don't give in, and don't give up. Life is filled with tough moments, but these tribulations will only make you stronger because you *will* endure. We are all capable of anything we set our minds to, so never feel small when confronted with an obstacle. Keep chasing that goal, that dream, that light. When you emerge from the darkness, you will see a new horizon that'll prove to you it was worth the fight. Pick up your broken parts and bind them together with patience, resilience, and love. Every one of us can become unbreakable.

—Cesar Pérez

Acknowledgments

THERE WERE MANY TIMES I DOUBTED MY FAITH, rejected it even, but God was with me every step of the way. I'm still here, I'm still alive, and I'm persevering. That's why first and foremost, I want to thank God for giving me that strength and seeing me through it all. He helped me hold on to this world a little longer.

I think I could write an entire additional book that lists the people I would like to thank for giving me a second chance at life. I'd like to first extend my gratitude to each person who saved me on January 12, 2018, and made my family whole again. Thank you to the Navicent EMS crew and Soperton Fire Department for never giving up on me. Josh Cammack, Lee Henry, Justin McNure, Blaine Oxford, Lieutenant Michael Milton, and everyone who was there that day trying to help. I know it took an entire community to rescue me, and words will never suffice, but I truly thank you. To the Air Evac team that airlifted me to the next hospital, thank you.

I'd like to extend my gratitude to the establishments that saw me and kept me around a little longer. Thank you to Fairview Park hospital for stabilizing me and Navicent Health hospital for putting me back together. The medical staff was nothing short of amazing. Dr. Daniel Chan, thank you for giving me the chance to walk again. Dr. Igor Decastro, thank you for monitoring my brain hemorrhaging and injury. Dr. Paul Syribeys, thank you for reconstructing my face at a time when it was a broken mess. I wouldn't be where I am without the care you all gave me. You chose your profession to help those in need. Although we had never met before, you gave me another chance to live, and for that, I thank you.

I'd also like to thank Mothers Against Drunk Drivers for helping me navigate through this dark tunnel and letting me know there was financial assistance available. My family and I were thrown into this situation and had no idea what to expect. Thank you for your guidance and making me feel like I wasn't alone.

Shepherd Center, you opened your doors to my family and me. You were the oasis in our world of misery. Thank you for being a place of second chances and a place where hope is rekindled. To all my doctors who saw me there (Dr. Brock Bowman, Dr. Keith Dockery, Dr. Allan Peljovich, Dr. ChiChi Berhane), thank you for never giving up on me and always treating me with love and care. You always told me the truth, and for that I'm thankful as well. To all my wonderful therapists who are all now family (Carol Ardanowski, Jenna Dreyer, Katelyn Warren, Deborah Vega, Madison Hedges, Jana Candia, Sherry Turner, Shelby King, Thomas Miller), thank you for spending time with me to ensure I had the best chance at taking back my life. Because of you, I can sing, play, laugh, eat, and make music again. Nurses are angels on earth, and the ones I was blessed to call mine (Ali Lucas, Brandon Hatfield, Nick Ozimek, Julie Shepherd) made me feel that life was still worth living. I don't know where I'd be without the care they gave me, and I know there were more nurses involved in my care whose names I can't recall, but from the bottom of my heart, thank you.

I left Shepherd not fully understanding I was still in the first stages of my recovery, and I must thank everyone who continued caring for me after I was discharged. Thank you to Sean Coate, Stephen Breckenridge, and Steven Broadway. My legs still needed strengthening, and because of you all, I can run and play soccer again. That was always my goal, to get back to where I had been, and you guys helped me get there. When my father was injured and our world started to crumble, there was one nurse who made us feel tomorrow would be a brighter day, and for that I just want to say thank you to Hannah Hall. Some paths cross once in a lifetime, but the impact of that moment lasts forever. Thank you for treating us with love and respect and being there for my family.

Though the dental work I had was painful at times, I must thank Dr. Yanina Figueroa for all my root canals and for making me feel optimistic about my future. Thank you for referring me to Dr. Yelena Chuzhin who took me in as my primary dentist. Emory was my peace in the middle of the storm. Living in Atlanta, I saw the Emory name everywhere, and I knew what a renowned institution it was, but I never thought it would play such a pivotal role in my life. It provided me and my family with light in our darkest moments. I can't thank Dr. Stephanie Drew and Dr. Dina Amin enough for what they did for me. My mother and I came to Dr. Drew with an aching heart and a wish to find someone who could address the issues with my facial bones. Several providers had already turned us away. They told us the only place we could get answers was at Emory with Dr. Stephanie Drew. To this day, I consider Dr. Drew and Dr. Amin my heroes and friends. Thank you for giving me my confidence back and helping me smile once again.

My smile has been a process. I tried not to smile in public for the past three years. Georgia School of Orthodontics (GSO) worked with Dr. Drew to straighten my teeth and give me the optimal chance to get my smile back. Though I had never had braces, and everyone kept telling me they were painful, all the doctors who treated me at GSO (Dr. Savage, Dr. Cruise, Dr. Harrell) were kind and understanding of everything I had been through.

My teeth were a mess when I came to them, but they opened their doors and treated me. Thank you for your care and always making time to see me.

None of this would've been possible if I had not still had my health benefits through COX. When my boss and coworkers found out about my accident, they stuck by my side and tried to help in any way they could. Thank you, COX, for never giving up on me and for putting your employees first. The reason I'm here today is because of the care I received from the best medical professionals. This would not have been doable if I had not had my benefits through you, so thank you for never giving up on me and for giving me the chance to fully recover. To all my coworkers (Christopher Smith, Michael Carvell, Brandon Adams, Brandon Walker, Tyler Dragon, Michael Scialabba, Nate Gettleman, Corey Knapp, Hannah Chalker, Kasey Richardson, Pierce Huff), thank you for asking about me and coming to see me at a time when I didn't want to see myself. It meant the world to me, so thank you. I want to give a special thanks to Kim Guthrie for helping find a place where I felt my work mattered and where I could continue to grow. Though our paths crossed only a few times, I hope you know I'm grateful for them. It allowed me to find my place at COX. Lastly, I want to thank Carl Davis and Sharon Roller for always looking out for me and helping me navigate through the hardest time of my life. Because of you, Carl, I felt not everything was lost, so thank you.

At a time when my world felt like the cruelest place, there were people who helped me believe again and let me know life was still worth fighting for. To everyone who donated to my GoFundMe page, thank you. Some of you decided to donate anonymously, and though I may never know who you are, just know you've made a difference in my life. There were a great deal of people who showed their support for me. No matter the quantity of the donation, every bit of it helped. Words can't express the gratitude my family and I felt for the outpouring of support. I'm amazed, seeing how many people this Salvadoran immigrant moved and touched. Thank you to Chick-fil-A on Abercorn for being concerned with my family's well being and making sure my mom ate, despite never leaving my side. Thank you Jazmin Porras and Alejandro Cardenas for visiting and checking in on my parents to make sure they made it through. To all my gym friends at SoFit in Pooler, thank you for holding the fundraising event—Bring Cesar Home. Thanks to your support, I made it out of the hospital and can hit the gym again.

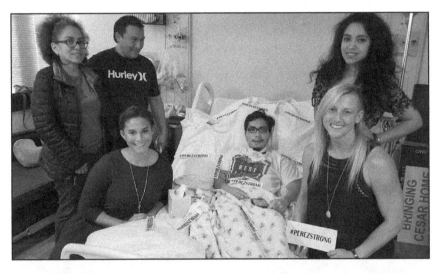

Aisha Samuels and Stacy Weimer bringing the Perez family the money raised from the "Bringing Cesar Home" fundraiser hosted by SoFit Pooler

This next group of people is a long list, but it's everyone who came to visit me at the hospital or once I was discharged because they lived far away. These people didn't care about clout; they weren't doing it for the likes. They came to see me because one way or another, I had made an impact on their lives, and they loved me. That last part sums it all up. Love is what drove them to come and see me. Mo Alaqran, Charles and Bonnie Elvington,

Leo and Taylor DeJesus, Kyle Whitmire, Chris Evans, Sean Hsu, Kenny Risner, Clinique Redding, Jazmin Moreland, Nick Flott, Nita Ravuth, Chelsea Covington, Leslie Wall, Tory Pereira, Stacy Weimer, Elaina Lanson, Yana Jones, Peter and Steven Chrysosfderidis, Bryan Castillo, Maranda Usry, Vannara Sadie, Aisha Samuels, Ebra Khashoggi, Dani Casablancas, Giovanni Ruiz-Raker, Geena Kim, Joshua Roper, Julia Vasi, Chris Kerrigan, Chanyoon Park, Gilbert Lewis, and Jay Bhatt, thank you from the bottom of my heart. These are the people I can remember. I know there were others who visited me, and I wish I could remember them all, but unfortunately, some spaces in my memory are just dark. Regardless, it meant so much seeing all of you. Thank you as well to Mrs. Naomi Fay for keeping me in her thoughts and sending me care packages. You called me superman and this man of steel never gave up the fight. Thank you for never giving up on me. Everyone on this list made me feel like I was still the same, even though my world had just been shaken to its core. In moments like these, you know who will truly be there for you. Just know I'll always be there as well.

Tory Pereira visiting Cesar at Shepherd Center

Leslie Wall visiting Cesar after a therapy session to read him a letter from an old friend

Next, I want to thank the people who have made some of the biggest impacts on my life. Chad Darnell, thank you for taking a chance on this Latino and seeing my potential. You casted me for several productions and helped me develop my passion. Thank you for being my casting director, but more importantly my friend. Because of you, I signed with Atlanta Models & Talent (AMT). Thank you, Sarah Carpenter, and everyone at AMT for showing your support and doing everything you could to help. I couldn't ask for better representation and friends. My passion was always bringing a story to life, and I had the opportunity to work with some amazing actors and directors to do this. Thank you, Daniel Radcliffe, Eugenio Siller, and Clint Eastwood for making me feel like I belonged and for your friendship.

Nava, you trusted me to work with you on different films despite my injuries and severe brain injury. Thank you for never giving up on me and believing in me still. The same goes for Christopher Smith. You never doubted me and continued to view me like the same person you first met years ago. All of you helped me continue to fight. For that, thank you. At a time when my financial woes seemed overwhelming, Christopher came to me with an opportunity. MyBookie and you both allowed me to keep my demons at bay as I focused on the work. You could have asked anyone, but you came to me, and I'll always remember that. To all the people I worked with at MyBookie (Brian Bowen, Raphael Esparza, Blake Mitchell, Jay Price, Joe Kovacs, Eric Yates, Ben Shicker), thank you.

This memoir is unapologetically honest, and because it is, I feel I must also thank Tito. You know who you are, though I did not use your real name. I will always remember you fondly and with gratitude for being there for me. Thank you for taking me to my appointments, and though our paths may never cross again, just know I'm grateful for the moments you were in my life. To my bass teacher and adopted grandfather, Mr. Ray Williams, thank you for always believing I would make it out. Despite my arm being paralyzed, and then not fully functional, you kept teaching me new things. You kept in touch and Skyped me every week to see how your bass student was doing. Thank you for your love, your knowledge, and your friendship.

When my accident happened, I had never been involved in a trial nor had any idea how to file a lawsuit. Jeremy McKenzie helped me understand and fought for me to the end. We both knew nothing could compensate for what I had experienced. I just wanted my medical bills paid for and to know I could make it out of this hole someone else placed me in. Thanks again for fighting for me.

Not many people have a family as close-knit as mine, and it's something I'll forever be grateful for. It's always been a blessing, and I really don't think I would be where I am without their sacrifice and love. To my sisters, Alicia and Carolina Pérez, I love you both equally and can't thank you enough for everything you did and still do for me. It's always been us three, the three amigos forever juntos. I couldn't have asked for better siblings, and just know I'm proud of you both—all the decisions you've made, the way you've carried yourselves, and for always loving our family. Just like you fought for me, I will fight for you both wherever and whenever. You're both a light in the darkest of days. I should know because that's what you were for me. Gracias.

Thank you as well to my aunt Merary, uncle Ricardo, and cousin Kenneth Baños, thank you for spending your vacation days next to my mom and me. You guys could have been anywhere in the world, but when the heart called, you listened and decided next to me is where you wanted to be. From the bottom of my heart, thank you.

Thank you also to my dad's side of the family who came to see me several times. Though I may not have been able to interact much, I carry those memories with me. Thank you, Dora Fernandez and Gilda Romero. I know my dad breathed a little easier when you were there. There's nothing more powerful than love, and the love between family is one of the strongest forms there is. It's what invigorated me and helped me continue to get better. I want to thank Karen and Fred Gassaway for always asking about me and loving my family unconditionally. In a world where it's hard to find people with the same values and principles, we managed to connect and become family. Thank you for all your love and support.

My accident reached people throughout the world, and I know I had prayer warriors on almost every continent. I can stand tall and say your prayers were heard. Thank you for taking time out of your day to say a little prayer for me.

When I started my recovery out of the hospital, my mother always told me my journey would inspire others. The truth is, I needed inspiration at first, and I got it from all the patients I saw at Shepherd Center who, like me, were going through the toughest battle of their lives. They all kept pushing forward and didn't give up, which in turn motivated me and gave me no reason to give up. Thomas, Jesus, and Victor, thank you for showing me life goes on and there is still happiness out there, somewhere. We were there for different reasons, but we were brothers in the same pain of seeing our lives changed. When I was angry at the world, seeing you guys smile despite our circumstances made me think life could still be beautiful. Thank you.

When I was writing about my journey, I wondered how I would get it out to the world. I am so grateful for Scribe and Houndstooth Publishing. My vision would've never come to light, if not for them. They helped me accomplish my goal of writing a book. I wanted the world to know my story and help others wrestle with the demons haunting them. Thank you for letting me live my dream.

Finally, I want to thank my parents. If unconditional love had a physical form, it would be you. You have taught me what true love is, and I know I would be lost without you. The world may never know the sacrifices you both made for your children, but you couldn't care less. You didn't do it for recognition; you did it out of love. Anyone can have children, but it takes a special set of people to build a family. The world may know you as Nuria and Rolan Pérez, but to me you are my guardian angels, my best friends, my water in the desert. Because of you, I have a chance to live again, and that's what I will do. I hope to someday be half the man you are, Dad, and to someday love like you, Mom. From the bottom of my heart and soul, thank you for never leaving my side. I hope to continue making you proud. Gracias por todo. Los amo.

Cesar and his mom walking on the beach for the first time after the accident

Cesar and his dad walking on the beach for the first time after the accident

CPSIA information can be obtained
at www.ICGtesting.com
Printed in the USA
LVHW100740260722
724318LV00006B/10/J